Pious and promiscuous

PIOUS AND PROMISCUOUS

Life, love and family
in Presbyterian Ulster

LEANNE CALVERT

Acadamh Ríoga na hÉireann
Royal Irish Academy

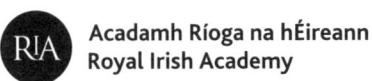

Pious and promiscuous: Life, love and family in Presbyterian Ulster

First published 2025
Royal Irish Academy, 19 Dawson Street, Dublin 2
ria.ie

© Leanne Calvert

ISBN 978-1-802050-39-4 (PB)
ISBN 978-1-802050-40-0 (pdf)
ISBN 978-1-802050-41-7 (epub)

All rights reserved. The material in this publication is protected by copyright law. Except as may be permitted by law, no part of the material may be reproduced (including by storage in a retrieval system) or transmitted in any form or by any means; adapted; rented or lent without the written permission of the copyright owners or a licence permitting restricted copying in Ireland issued by the Irish Copyright Licensing Agency CLG, 63 Patrick Street, Dún Laoghaire, Co. Dublin, A96 WF25.

This publication is an initiative of the R.J. Hunter Scheme.
The R.J. Hunter Scheme was established by the Royal Irish Academy in 2014 using funding generously made available by his daughter, Ms Laura Houghton Hunter, through the Community Foundation for Northern Ireland.

Copyeditor: Helena King
Book design: Fidelma Slattery
Index: Eileen O'Neill
Printed in Poland by L&C Printing Group

General Product Safety Regulation (GPSR): For any safety queries, please contact us at productsafety@ria.ie

Royal Irish Academy is a member of Publishing Ireland, the Irish book publishers' association

To offset environmental impacts during the production of our books and journals we will plant 45 trees with Easy Treesie in 2025.

5 4 3 2 1

My grandparents – Sally and Norman Calvert and Ellie and Frankie Walker – unfortunately did not see this book finished. I think they would be proud. I dedicate it to them all.

INTRODUCTION

IX

CHAPTER ONE

'He said [it] was safe & afterwards he would marry her':
Pregnancy and paternity disputes

1

CHAPTER TWO

'Every little matter is now in order for the
expected stranger': Infancy and early childcare

27

CHAPTER THREE

'I am 16 years of age & I perceive myself
growing now wiser & better': Growing up

49

CHAPTER FOUR

'I felt as if you had suddenly thrown your arms
around my neck and kiss'd me!': Courtship

71

CHAPTER FIVE

'Your mother makes me write that she would grudge & grieve to hear of your marriage with any of these base whores': Getting married

93

CHAPTER SIX

'She declar'd she study'd to carry as a dutifull wife': Married life

115

CHAPTER SEVEN

'And now I'm left alone of worldly company': Widowhood

136

CONCLUSION

155

A note on the Bibliography 163
Endnotes 167
Bibliography 205
Acknowledgements 227
Index 231

INTRODUCTION

Pious and promiscuous: The Presbyterians of Ulster

In April 1713 an unmarried woman named Sarah Campbell appeared before the Kirk Session (church court) of Carnmoney Presbyterian church in County Antrim and confessed that she had 'brought forth a child in Basterdy'.[1] Sarah claimed that the father of her child was John Wilson, a married man with whom she had previously committed adultery in 1710.[2] The couple already shared one child; a product of the earlier adulterous affair. That child had since been raised by John and his wife, Mary Gultry, in Carnmoney, while Sarah had been working in Belfast as a wet nurse (a woman employed to breastfeed and look after a child born to someone else).[3] Sometime in March 1712, Sarah returned to Carnmoney after learning that her child had fallen into a fire.[4] Shortly thereafter she and John Wilson allegedly resumed their affair. Although

Sarah had been 'absolutely disbar[re]d' by the Kirk Session from visiting the Wilson household unchaperoned, she claimed that she and John had continued to meet in secret.[5] It was during one of these clandestine meetings that Sarah said she had become pregnant for the second time.

John 'positively deny[e]d' the allegations against him and claimed that he 'never attempted to commit wickedness' with Sarah since that first 'unhap[p]y time' he had 'com[m]itted adultery'.[6] Sarah, however, did not back down and presented the Session with evidence to prove her case. She told the Session that she and John were 'guilty of that act two different times', and how they had even been caught in flagrante by John's wife.[7] Sarah's brother had also seen the pair together on at least one occasion.[8] Testimonies from those present at Sarah's second birth strengthened her case further. Agnes Craford – the local midwife – and Sarah's sister-in-law both told the Session that during labour she had named John Wilson as the father.[9] Sarah also claimed that she had 'proof' of their guilt. She said that she could produce 'two pieces of money' that John had given to her for the purposes of procuring 'herbs and other things' to terminate the pregnancy.[10]

The case rumbled on for several years: Sarah stuck fast to her story, as did John to his denials. In April 1715 – approximately two years after giving birth to her second child – Sarah was finally 'absolved' of the 'scandal'.[11] She stood before the congregation and professed sorrow for her 'relapse in adultery' with John Wilson.[12] Her co-offender and alleged father of her two children did not. As late as 1723 John declared that he was innocent of the charge, repeating his claim that Sarah had 'wronged him'.[13] It is not clear if he ever acknowledged paternity.

Encompassing as it does a series of (alleged) illicit affairs, at least two extra-marital pregnancies, an unfaithful marriage, and a complex childcare arrangement, the story of Sarah Campbell and John Wilson stands testament to the colourful and oftentimes *very messy* realities of family life in Ulster centuries ago. Their story is just one of many thousands that are captured in what I call the 'Presbyterian archive' – historical evidence produced by and about members of Ulster's Presbyterian community. Anxious parents, love-sick and lovelorn courting couples, unfaithful husbands and unhappy wives, troublesome young people, and grieving spouses punctuate the family stories of Presbyterians in Ulster. This book brings to life for the first time the stories of Presbyterian women and men who lived, loved and laboured in Ulster during the 'long eighteenth century' (1690–1830), enriching our understanding of family life in that era. It uncovers the personal stories that marked key events in their lives, such as pregnancy and raising children, growing up and earning a living, dating and meeting a partner, married life and widowhood. It also tells the stories of the very many Presbyterian women and men whose family narratives did not fit into this neat model: those, like Sarah Campbell and John Wilson, who had children before or outside of marriage, as well as those who never married or, indeed, never had children at all.

Origins of Presbyterianism in Ireland

Who are the individuals that we meet in this look at family life in Ulster? What records have they left behind? And what can their stories tell us about the Irish family more broadly?

Presbyterianism came to Ireland in the early seventeenth century, brought over by Scottish settlers. Although there had always been movement between the two nations, the migration flow from Scotland rose substantially from the middle of the seventeenth century, reaching its peak in the 1690s.[14] In the ten years to 1700, approximately 50,000 Scots settled in Ulster.[15] Such sustained levels of migration changed the population make-up of the province. Before the 1690s most residents in Ulster were Catholic; they were soon replaced by Scottish Presbyterian settlers.[16] In 1691 the community numbered a modest 100,000, and although the tide of Scots migration had slowed by the opening years of the eighteenth century, the Presbyterian share of the population continued to grow; by 1835 it had risen substantially, to almost 650,000.[17] By the opening decades of the nineteenth century, Presbyterians were the biggest religious community in the province of Ulster.[18]

Outside of that, Presbyterians were not so numerous. Pockets of the community existed in Dublin, such as those who were members of Usher's Quay congregation, but their numbers were small.[19] So, despite their numbers in Ulster, in 1835 only about eight per cent of people on the island of Ireland as a whole were Presbyterian.[20] There were also relatively small groups of 'dissenting' Protestants, including Baptists, Methodists and Quakers.[21] Most people in Ireland, however – between seventy-five and eighty per cent of the population in the early eighteenth century – were Roman Catholic.[22] Nevertheless, numbers did not equate to power and influence. The most powerful religious denomination was the Anglican Church of Ireland. Representing the interests of the minority Protestant élite, the Church of Ireland acted as the arm of the state, and its members accessed political power and enjoyed full civil rights. Those who dissented, such as Presbyterians and Catholics, suffered various forms of discrimination.[23]

Presbyterian ministers and lay members were regarded as a threat to the Anglican establishment and were subject to episodes of 'localised persecution'.[24] Not only were Presbyterian ministers prosecuted for preaching, but legal restrictions were placed on the education of children by Presbyterian schoolmasters.[25] Conflict also erupted between Anglicans and Presbyterians over the performance of religious rituals, such as the celebration of marriage, funeral services and baptism.[26] Discrimination was also manifested against Presbyterians in civil disabilities related to the Sacramental Test – a clause added to the Popery Act in 1704, obliging all individuals who held office under the Crown to receive Holy Communion once a year in the Established Church. Presbyterians were subsequently driven out of their seats in municipal corporations, and from their roles as magistrates and officers in the army.[27] Although Presbyterians were granted freedom of worship in 1719 and a degree of reprieve, the Sacramental Test clause remained on the statute books until 1780, and Presbyterians continued to experience discriminatory treatment until the middle of the nineteenth century. This was perhaps most evident in relation to marriage; it was not until 1844 that marriages performed by Presbyterian ministers were recognised as valid in law.[28]

Presbyterians represented a wide cross-section of Ulster society, but they were mainly to be found among the middling and lower ranks.[29] In terms of 'status and privilege', historians generally agree that Presbyterians sat in the 'middle rung' of Ulster society, between the better-off Anglicans and poorer Roman Catholics.[30] Many of the Presbyterians who appear in this book made a living as merchants, tradesmen, weavers, spinners, farmers, agricultural and domestic labourers and servants. Others earned a living from professional occupations, such as the ministry, medicine, law and business. Yet not all Presbyterians fared so well. Some existed on the fringes of Ulster society and eked out a scant living from poor relief and charitable donations received from their communities. Widows, the elderly, orphans, the sick and vagrants made frequent appearances on Presbyterian poor lists.[31]

Presbyterians were diverse too in terms of theological belief. The cohesiveness of the community was severely disrupted in the eighteenth century by a series of disputes over church order and theology, resulting in the fracturing of the church into 'Old Light' and 'New Light' camps.[32] The importation of more orthodox forms of Presbyterianism from Scotland (groups known as Seceders and Covenanters) from the 1740s onwards likewise increased competition among the community.[33] Presbyterianism in Ulster was therefore far from a single religious system, and there were six different groupings active across the province in the period we are dealing with: the Synod of Ulster, the Presbytery of Antrim, Burgher and Anti-Burgher Seceders, Covenanters and Remonstrants. According to Andrew Holmes, although each of these groups defined themselves as 'Presbyterian', they each embodied different understandings of their faith that reflected their distinctive social, ethnic and historical backgrounds.[34] Irrespective of these differences, however, Presbyterians shared the same church structure and embraced a number of core ideas and values, not least of which was the important role of the laity in church life.[35]

Church discipline

In keeping with its Scottish heritage, the Presbyterian church in Ulster was supervised by three church courts. At the top was the General Synod or Assembly; next was the Presbytery; then the Kirk

Session. While each of these courts was responsible for a particular area of church business, all were involved to some degree in the operation of church discipline. The Presbyterian system of church court discipline was designed to ensure that only the 'worthy' accessed the privileges of church membership. Presbyterians recognised two sacramental expressions of their faith: communion and baptism. These represented 'holy Signs and Seals of the Covenant of Grace' and served as symbolic reminders of an individual's membership of the church and their relationship with God and the community.[36] Communion and baptism served important social functions too. These religious celebrations held a central place in the Presbyterian social calendar and were times of conviviality and merriment.[37]

The religious and social significance of these rituals meant that only those church members deemed to be 'worthy' could participate. Persons intending to partake in communion not only had to demonstrate that they possessed sufficient knowledge of their faith, they also had to be free from church censure. Presbyterian standards underlined the fact that individuals who were 'ignorant, unbaptized, and scandalous' were not to be 'admitted' to communion.[38] Similar rules applied to baptism. For a child to be baptised, at least one parent had to be a member of the church and also had to be 'in good standing' – free from church scandal.[39] The discipline system played an important role in maintaining the purity of church communion and acted to include or exclude individuals from the community.

Most discipline cases were settled in the Kirk Session. This local court was staffed by the minister of the congregation and an elected body of representatives known as elders. In the eighteenth and nineteenth century, all these roles were held by men. Presbyterian communities were divided into geographical districts known as 'quarters', which were then assigned to an elder to supervise.[40] Elders were expected to visit their assigned quarter regularly, to report back to the Kirk Session any 'scandals' that had arisen, and to follow up with potential offenders. Kirk Sessions sometimes targeted specific behaviours at certain times. In March 1700 Burt Kirk Session in County Donegal 'agreed' that 'the several elders in their several quarters should take notice that the sin of drunken[ness] might be stopped' and instructed them to keep special watch for drunken behaviour.[41]

A notable feature of Presbyterian discipline in Ireland is its longevity. Although its exercise of discipline did decline over time, the church continued to exert influence over its adherents well into the nineteenth century; in some areas in fact, into the twentieth century too.[42] The uneven survival of Presbyterian minute books does make it difficult to assess the practice of discipline over time (a point discussed more fully below), but a survey of sources from individual Kirk Sessions that do survive confirms the pattern of the continuance of the discipline system. Take Carnmoney Kirk Session in County Antrim. Between 1700 and 1748 it processed 196 cases of discipline, the majority of which concerned sexual misbehaviour. Between 1786 and 1821 the Session handled a further 257 cases, and again most of these involved sexual offences.[43] In both periods, the total number of discipline cases annually ranged from a low of one to a high of eighteen, with the average number for both periods being six per year – by no means an exceptionally high rate. Similar pictures emerge from the minute books of other congregations. Loughaghery Kirk Session in County Down processed 197 offences between 1801 and 1844. Like Carnmoney, the number of discipline cases here was by no means excessive, with an average rate of four cases per year.[44] Breaches of marriage order and sexual misbehaviours were the two most common offences.

Discipline set and enforced standards of moral behaviour, supporting the agenda of the Presbyterian church to create a godly community. For discipline to work effectively, the lay community had to agree on what constituted proper and improper behaviour. This was very important in an Irish context. Unlike its counterpart in Scotland, the Presbyterian church in Ireland had no legal authority to compel its members to submit to discipline. Presbyterianism was not, of course, the established faith in Ireland at this time, but the lack of legal recourse did not impede the ability of the church to enforce discipline. In fact, some historians have argued that the non-established status of the Presbyterian church in Ireland increased the efficiency of its discipline system.[45] Presbyterian women and men who submitted to church discipline did so of their own volition – either to secure access to church privileges for themselves or their children, or because of a deep commitment to their faith. Adherence to Presbyterian discipline may have been voluntary, but the overwhelming majority of those of that faith in Ireland did submit to church censure.[46]

Living and labouring in long-eighteenth-century Ulster

Key to understanding the social contexts of Ulster Presbyterian family life is an appreciation of the rural character of the province. Few Presbyterian congregations were situated in towns or cities, and most were at least one mile from the nearest town.[47] Belfast had just five Presbyterian congregations in 1800.[48] As J.M. Barkley put it, Presbyterians were 'a community of the country-side rather than of the city and the town'.[49] The rural nature of everyday life in Ulster was captured in the types of disputes that arose between church members.[50] Presbyterian women and men argued over land and crops, they complained to the church about roaming livestock, and they charged one another with stealing animals, farming implements and pieces of linen. Others accused their neighbours of casting curses on their children or using magic to steal butter from their cows.[51]

Ulster farms tended to be much smaller than those in other parts of Ireland. Farmsteads of between ten and twelve acres were common in eighteenth-century Ulster; a fact that was partially attributable to the existence of farmer-weavers.[52] The area known as the 'linen triangle', the heartland of the linen industry, was in Counties Antrim, Armagh and Down, stretching west to Counties Tyrone, Londonderry, Monaghan, Cavan and eastern Donegal, which were also areas of dense Presbyterian settlement.[53] Although the linen trade was not new to Ulster in the eighteenth century, it was during this period that the industry experienced marked growth. Described by W.H. Crawford as 'enterprising and ready to experiment', the Ulster linen industry took advantage of opportunities to expand into markets outside of Ireland.[54] Building on an established market for Irish textiles, exports of linen cloth to

England rose during the eighteenth century. Whereas in the 1720s linen cloth made up about one-quarter of Ireland's total value of exports, by 1788 this figure had risen to two-thirds.[55] The Ulster linen trade also benefited from transatlantic markets with North America. Approximately 4.4 million yards of Irish linen were sent across the Atlantic between 1768 and 1771.[56] The domestic linen industry boomed throughout this period and inhabitants of Ulster, among whom Presbyterians predominated, reaped the benefits.

Linen was produced in the home, and the whole family was involved in its production. A series of engravings published by William Hincks in 1783 depict the involvement of women, men and children in the process.[57] Farmer-weavers would grow their own flax, their wives and children would spin it into linen, and then men (or older children) would weave the cloth to sell at the local market.[58] The money raised from the sale was then used to pay the rent, with any surplus going towards food that could not be produced on the family farm.[59] This was likely the set-up in the household of Alexander McGage, a member of Carnmoney Presbyterian congregation in County Antrim. In November 1719 a gang of youths, aged between twelve and seventeen years old, challenged one another to throw 'clods' at Alexander's 'loome'.[60] The gang missed their target and struck Alexander's child instead. Alexander complained to the Kirk Session about the group's 'rude' and disorderly behaviour.[61] His child died twelve days after the incident; its death, Alexander believed, was caused by the 'hurt' received from the flying missiles.[62]

The burgeoning domestic linen industry, with its reliance on intensive flax farming, also created a demand for agricultural labourers. Women and men found work at 'hiring fairs' that were held twice per year in Ulster towns.[63] Their tasks included bringing in the harvest, tilling the land, making hay or saving turf and clearing and preparing the ground.[64] The typical earnings for female agricultural workers in eighteenth-century Ireland could be as low as two or three pence per day, but those who worked on Ulster flax-farms in the 1770s could expect to receive as much as eight pence per day – a rate that reflected the prosperity of the linen industry.[65] Many other Presbyterians made their living as domestic servants. Over the course of the eighteenth century, middle- and small-farming households increasingly began to employ young women as maids; Mary O'Dowd has noted that 'all but the poorest households' in Ireland hired domestic servants.[66] Female domestic servants were hired for a wide range of tasks, both inside and outside of the house. Some worked as childminders or maids, others washed and mended clothes, baked and prepared meals, carried out laundry work, and swept and dusted the floors.[67] Many servants lived in the same household as their masters; a living arrangement that was ripe with potential for conflict. Kirk Sessions not only dealt with disobedient and disorderly servants, they mediated in paternity disputes between masters and servants too. Sexual relationships between masters and servants, both consensual and non-consensual, were not uncommon.

Ulster and its Presbyterian inhabitants did not, however, enjoy continuous prosperity throughout the period we are dealing with. The linen trade experienced recession at various points in the early eighteenth century, most notably in 1718 and again in 1729. Rising rents combined with a series of poor harvests and food shortages meant that life was tough for many. A considerable number subsequently made the decision to leave the province and journeyed across the Atlantic in search of better prospects.[68] Ulster experienced further economic problems at the end of the eighteenth century. Although it had temporarily recovered, the domestic linen industry suffered major depression in the early 1770s. So much so, that as many as one-third of Ulster's weavers found themselves out of work.[69] The introduction of cotton manufacture into the Belfast region in the 1770s depressed the linen industry further, pushing down the price of linen goods and the wages of its workers. Economic hardship was compounded by more poor harvests, rising rents, evictions and rural unrest. A combination of all these factors led to yet more emigration from Ulster to North America, peaking in the 1760s and 1770s.[70]

The fortunes of those who remained waxed and waned over the following decades. While the years between 1780 and the end of the Napoleonic wars in 1815 were not 'ones of unbroken prosperity', historians have described this period as a 'golden age' for Ulster handloom weavers and farmers.[71] Although the introduction of cotton caused upset in the rural linen industry, it did bring some short-term benefits. Wages of cotton weavers were generally higher than those available to linen weavers, and many who lived close to Belfast subsequently made the switch between industries. This helped to sustain demand for linen weavers outside of Belfast.[72] The Napoleonic wars also increased demand for agricultural products. Farmers, especially those who had long leases, were able to reap the returns.[73]

Things then changed. The period from 1815 to the Great Famine were 'difficult ones' for Ulster's rural economy and the Presbyterian families who depended on it for a living.[74] A major cause of this change was the introduction of mechanised spinning and the establishment of factory spinning mills in Belfast in the 1820s. These technological innovations decreased demand for handloom weavers and spinners, who were unable to compete with the faster- and cheaper-produced mill-spun yarn. Many subsequently left Ulster to work in British textiles mills or again went further afield to North America.[75] But the ground was set for the emergence of Belfast as a major economic hub. Workers flooded into the city from rural areas, finding employment in the linen mills and shipyards.[76] As Alice Johnson has detailed, the population of Belfast exploded at a time when most Irish towns and cities were experiencing population decline. With a world-leading linen, and later shipbuilding, industry, Belfast experienced 'phenomenal' population growth and prosperity during the nineteenth century.[77] Yet, despite these developments, it is important to note that the 'spiritual and numerical heartland' of Presbyterianism remained in the Ulster countryside.[78] As Andrew Holmes has argued, 'the sense of place in a small community, of rootedness in the Ulster soil' continued to shape the Ulster Presbyterian experience.[79]

The Presbyterian archive

The 'Presbyterian archive' is the resource used to tell the stories of Presbyterian family life outlined in this book. Two main types of sources make up this archive. The first are records produced by the Presbyterian church in Ireland, including poor lists, congregation censuses, Sunday School reports, birth and baptism registers and marriage registers; discipline cases that were handled by the Presbyterian church courts make up the bulk of these records. The second are family records and personal papers.

Church discipline records

At meetings of the Presbyterian church courts, a clerk was appointed to keep a record of proceedings. The resulting minute books provide an unrivalled insight into the intimate realities of family life in Ulster. I draw on twenty-three Kirk Session minute books, covering the period from approximately 1690 to 1830. The congregations whose activities the books record were overwhelmingly situated in small, rural communities located across seven of Ulster's nine counties: Antrim, Cavan, Donegal, Down, Londonderry, Monaghan and Tyrone. I also explore the records of the upper church courts, including those of the Presbytery and Synod, extending the geographical reach of the book across the entire province of Ulster. The sources surveyed are also generally representative of the different theological varieties of Presbyterianism that existed in Ulster at the time. There were subtle differences in the types of offence that were considered by each of the various theological groups.[80] More orthodox communities, such as the Seceders, tended to discipline church members for a broader range of offences than did many Synod of Ulster congregations. Misbehaviours such as drunkenness, dancing, breaches of the Sabbath and profane swearing were more commonly heard before Seceding Kirk Sessions.[81] Covenanting Presbyterians were also 'unique' in their level of commitment to the discipline of civil matters, including members who signed parliamentary petitions, served on juries and voted in elections.[82] Other, more theologically moderate congregations prosecuted fewer and fewer discipline cases over time. Andrew Holmes observed a 'noticeable decline' in the numbers of discipline cases recorded by Ballycarry Kirk Session in County Antrim; a trend that was shared by other 'non-subscribing' congregations.[83]

The cases that came before the Presbyterian church courts fell into three broadly defined categories. These included breaches of marriage order, such as marrying bigamously or having a marriage solemnised by someone other than a Presbyterian minister; and social and religious offences such as drunkenness, slander and working on the Sabbath day. The third category of offence was 'sexual' misbehaviours. Across the board, sexual offences made up a large proportion of discipline business considered by the various Presbyterian church courts in Ulster.[84] A wide range of offences fell under this heading, including sex outside or before marriage (referred to as fornication and pre-marital fornication), sex with someone who was not your spouse (adultery), and 'scandalous carriage'. This was a term used to describe intimate acts that stopped short of full sexual intercourse, like kissing and petting, but also any conduct that raised suspicions that sexual activity had taken place.

Kirk Sessions made effective use of the local gossip network to bring the bad behaviour of church members to light. Most cases came to the attention of the Kirk Session through a 'public or notorious report' known as a *'fama clamosa'*.[85] Presbyterian women and men used their eyes, ears and tongues to watch, listen to and then report the misbehaviour of their neighbours to the church courts. In July 1711 Henry Work was 'brought before' Burt Kirk Session after he was spied with Elinar Craswell 'behind a bush' in a corn field owned by John Desart during afternoon sermon.[86] James Ading told the Session that he saw Henry enter the field, look behind him at Elinar and then give her 'a signe to follow him'. The pair then went behind the bush and stayed there together until the community left the meeting house after the sermon.[87] James immediately pointed out the pair to his wife, who he sent to the meeting house 'to get witnesses'. James also enlisted the help of a servant boy to watch the couple 'from [the] turf bog below' the field. When he noticed the pair going their separate ways, James leapt into action. He 'apprehended' Elinar as she 'came down through ye corn' and took her straight to Mr Ferguson, the minister.[88]

The sounds of sexual activity also roused the suspicions of church members. In May 1766 Bangor Presbytery met to consider rumours that were circulating about the Reverend Hugh Smyth. The source of the report was Mrs Elizabeth McGaw, who managed an inn in Belfast. Elizabeth told the Presbytery that a woman came to her inn and said that she wanted a room because she was meeting a merchant to sell him some yarn.[89] Although Elizabeth did not know the woman's name, a neighbour had told her that the woman's husband was a weaver who lived in Hercules Lane in Belfast, named 'Rainy'.[90] When the man arrived, dressed in 'Boots & Black Clothes', he and the unnamed woman went upstairs to the room.[91] Elizabeth was sure that the man was 'no yarn merchant, but a minister', because of his distinctive clothing. Elizabeth told the Presbytery that she heard the couple walking towards the bed in the upstairs room. But it was when she heard a noise that sounded like the 'Jigging of a bed' that she went to investigate.[92] The door was pulled closed, so Elizabeth aided her view by peering through the keyhole. She saw the pair 'in Bed together in an unseemly way'. Pressed by the Presbytery for more details, Elizabeth said that 'she saw them in a fair way of being guilty of adultery' and that the 'womans clothes were not seemly on'.[93] Not content with watching through the keyhole, Elizabeth then opened the door. She went in and out of the room twice more, before the couple got out of the bed and sat by the fireside. Before he left, the man – who Elizabeth later identified as Hugh Smyth – 'Begged' her not to 'expose him'.[94] As it turned out, the man was not Hugh Smyth but a Moravian preacher known locally as 'Ray', whose usual attire was 'Black Cloath[e]s & a Grey Wig'.[95]

When dealing with potential offenders, the Presbyterian church courts in Ireland broadly followed guidance published by the Church of Scotland in 1707 called the *Form of Process*.[96] In 1825 the Irish Presbyterian church published a revised version of this guidance in a section of its constitution, known as the *Code*. The church courts approached different offences in different ways. Misbehaviours that included 'prophane swearing, sabbath-breaking, drunkenness, quarrelling [and] undutifulness to parents' could be handled privately by the eldership or the minister.[97] Offenders who demonstrated 'sorrow' for these sins and who 'promise[d] amendment for the future' could be 'admonished' for their behaviour by the minister or 'judicially rebuked' by the Session.[98] Those who repeated their offence, or who appeared unrepentant, could be suspended from the church ordinances of communion and infant baptism.[99] Kirk Sessions proceeded differently in cases that were considered more serious, such as 'fornication, slander, [and] habitual drunkenness'.[100] These 'gross' offences were to be immediately investigated by the Kirk Session, and those found guilty were suspended from church privileges.[101]

The method of punishment in all these cases was at the discretion of the Kirk Session. The Presbyterian church courts exercised a large degree of latitude in how they exercised discipline. As the *Code* made expressly clear, while 'every scandal implie[d] offence … every offence [was] not necessarily scandalous'.[102] Sessions were advised to weigh up the pros and cons of proceeding in cases of scandal. Because the main purpose of discipline was to reclaim and reform the sinner, Sessions made every effort to bring erring members back into the church community.[103] This even-handedness likewise extended to their preferred method of punishment, which was directed to be appropriate to the offence itself. According to the *Code*, guilty persons were to be 'admonished, rebuked, or cut off from church privileges' in line with the 'nature and magnitude' of their offence.[104] In practice, this meant that some offences were handled with private rebukes before the Session, while others that were considered more serious were resolved with a public confession of sorrow before the congregation. Most offenders who were directed to stand publicly did so on two occasions, after which they were restored to church membership.[105]

Cases that were complex or serious could be referred by the Kirk Session to the Presbytery (the middle church court). Petitions for divorce and offences like adultery and incest were among those usually referred. When Burt Kirk Session discovered in 1702 that Andrew Bogs had committed 'incest' with his sister-in-law, Mary Ewings, he was referred to Londonderry Presbytery for advice. The Presbytery ordered that Andrew be sent back to Burt, where he was to confess his sin before the Session and then again before the congregation. Andrew made a total of five appearances before the congregation.[106] In December 1702 the Session decided that Andrew could be 'absolved' of his sin, 'having givine satisfying Evidences of his grief & sorrow'.[107] Thirteen years later Jean Glendinning underwent a similar punishment, having confessed her sin of 'Incest and Adultery with her brother in law Thomas

Walker'.[108] Jean was finally absolved in April 1715 after making four public appearances before the congregation and demonstrating 'Evidences of humiliation'.[109] In addition to hearing serious offences against lay members, the Presbytery was the forum where cases involving misbehaving ministers were considered.

As an archival source, however, Presbyterian church court minutes do come with some caveats. First, minute books do not survive for every Presbyterian congregation in Ireland. Fewer than twenty Kirk Session minute books dating to the period before 1800 have survived.[110] Many of those that do survive are in relatively poor condition, and some have been closed to public consultation as a result.[111] It is possible that records have been lost over time, but it should be noted that not all Kirk Sessions consistently kept records, and some may not have practised discipline at all.[112] As Andrew Holmes has pointed out, the 'degree of discipline experienced in any given area' depended on 'practical' matters, such as whether a Kirk Session existed and if there were a 'sufficient number' of elders available and willing to do the job.[113] Second, the degree of detail recorded by individual Kirk Sessions varies considerably. Cases that were complicated or required the calling of witnesses tend to record the greatest detail, including places, names, occupations, relationships and the circumstances leading to the alleged offence. Many cases lack this level of detail, with the record noting only the name of the person involved, their alleged offence and the discipline meted out. Finally, it should be noted that Presbyterian court records capture those individuals who maintained some type of relationship with the church. Some Presbyterians were devout in their adherence to church principles, but there were others who used the courts only for the purposes of accessing privileges like baptism. Others still had 'no formal link' to the church, but they might have thought of themselves as Presbyterian for ethnic or cultural reasons.[114]

These points aside, Presbyterian church court minutes provide a tantalising insight into the family lives of women and men in Ulster. What makes these sources so special is that they allow us to access, at least partly, the worlds of individuals from the 'lower orders' of Irish society, who were less likely to keep written records of their lives. Nuggets of information are contained in the minute books on household living arrangements, the agricultural calendar, fair days and festivals, occupations, childcare practices, rites of passage and relationships. The voices of Presbyterians are discernible too. Statements made by offenders, complainants, witnesses and members of the Kirk Session were transcribed by a clerk into the minute book, partly preserving the words spoken by Presbyterian women and men of centuries ago. The qualifier *partly* is important here; sources such as court records are not 'authentic' representations of what people said in the past, nor are they reflective of what people really thought and felt.[115] Clerks generally paraphrased what was said in the space of the Kirk Session, and the cases are usually transcribed in the third person. Some clerks even added their own notes to the words of offenders, to indicate whether or not they believed what had been said.[116] Individuals who testified before the Kirk Session may also have phrased their words in certain ways in order to elicit the best outcome for themselves, to establish the innocence of a friend or family member, or to placate a parent, their master, or someone else in a position of power.[117] It might be more useful to think of the minute books as 'collaborative' documents rather than as the words of a single individual. As Margo Todd put it in her work on Scottish Presbyterian church court records, 'multiple voices' emerge from the pages of the minute books.[118] Not only do we hear the (albeit mediated) voices of those who appeared before and represented the church courts, we also get a sense of the communities they inhabited. The minute books reveal not only how Presbyterians 'told stories' but also the wider social and cultural values that they drew upon to understand the world around them.[119]

We should also acknowledge that most of those who appeared before the church courts did so because their behaviour was deemed to be disorderly or 'deviant' in some way. Discipline cases therefore tend to focus on the 'problematic' and are not necessarily, on first reading, representative of the 'ordinary'.[120] Just as the records of the church courts were created to record acts of deviancy, so too were the voices captured by the courts shaped by societal views on what was deviant and what was not. While we should be aware of these points, and they should remind us to treat the evidence carefully, they in no way lessen the value of church court minutes as sources;

the details they record reveal much about the 'ordinary' aspects of family life. As Julie Hardwick observed in her work on intimacy in long-eighteenth-century France, court cases illuminate the backstories of relationships through the words of couples, their friends, families and neighbours.[121] The Presbyterian church court records do the same for Ireland – they reveal the hidden aspects of family life, lifting the curtain on the conflicts and tensions that shaped daily life, as well as the moments of joy, sadness, anger, jealousy and everything else in between.

Personal papers and family records

In addition to sources produced by the church, the second source within the 'Presbyterian archive' that this book makes use of are the letters, diaries and personal papers that belonged to five Presbyterian families who had ties to the province of Ulster. These are the Crawfords and Tennents of County Antrim; the Drennans of Belfast and Dublin; the Kennedys of County Tyrone; and the Youngs of County Londonderry. Additional material has been drawn from the diaries of three ministers: the Reverend Robert Magill of County Antrim, the Reverend James Morell of County Monaghan, and the Reverend James Morgan of Belfast. These families belonged to what we would describe as the 'middling ranks' of Irish society. Neither very poor nor very wealthy, these families led reasonably comfortable lives. They and the members of their social circles made a living as merchants, medical men and ministers.[122] The records they left behind enable us to hear about their lives and experiences in their own words. Families wrote to one another about important life events. They shared news of pregnancies and the births of babies, they discussed the welfare and schooling of young children, they traded gossip about potential marriage matches, and they notified one another about the illnesses and deaths of loved ones. Family members might even write about these life events in their diaries, offering an insight into family life at the level of the individual.

Like the discipline records produced by the Presbyterian church courts, however, there are also some caveats to be aware of when it comes to letters and diaries. Although they contain useful information, letters offer only a partial picture of family life. From the outset, we must acknowledge that archives of family letters are by their very nature incomplete collections. As Shannon Devlin has pointed out, letters that survive in archives 'represent only a fraction of those that were sent or received by an individual'.[123] Letters could be lost in transit and never reach their intended recipient, or they might even be destroyed by their reader (and sometimes at the request of their sender).[124] Historians who work with letters are often left reading only one side of the conversation.[125] While 'luck' plays its part, many collections that survive do so because of the archiving efforts of families. The Crawford letters, for example, 'cover practically the whole' of the Reverend Alexander Crawford's adult family life, from the year before his marriage to Anna Gardner in 1823 until his death in 1856.[126] Later generations of the Crawford family attributed their survival to the efforts of the Gardner family, an 'appreciative … group of readers' who 'cherished every word' that they received from Anna and Alexander.[127] So valued were these letters, that they were 'carried hand to hand' and passed to family members for reading. It is perhaps lucky that they survive at all; according to the family archivist, the letters showed 'signs' that they had been 'kept in pockets' and had been handed about so much that some were 'literally falling to pieces'.[128] The fact that letters survive because they were 'treasured' and deemed important enough to keep serves as a reminder that the reverse could also be true. Moreover, some recipients may not have been fortunate enough to keep and sustain a family archive – research on the uneven survival of letters between kept mistresses and the men who maintained them provides ample evidence of this.[129]

As well as being incomplete collections, those letters that do survive are not uncritical sources for family life. Letters were highly coded forms of communication that reflected contemporary cultural practices.[130] Katie Barclay points out that letter writing followed 'rules' that 'govern[ed] its performance'.[131] These 'rules' covered, among other things, the structure and content of letters, their length, the frequency of their writing, the ways that the writer addressed their recipient and how they ended their missive.[132] These rules also varied by and depended on the relationship between the writer and the reader.[133] Letter writers thought consciously about what they wanted to say to their reader; they might choose to disclose or withhold information depending on the identity of the intended recipient. Letter writers also put pen to paper for a specific purpose and they crafted their missive to elicit a particular response from their reader.[134] What people chose to say in their letters may not have been a true reflection of what they really thought or felt.

Likewise, while we might think that diaries are unique sources, in that they tell us about an individual's inner-most private thoughts, they also involve a degree of 'self-fashioning' and construction.[135] The diary of John Tennent, an Ulster apprentice who features in this book, serves as an example. John wrote in his diary about how much he hated his master, a man named Samuel Givin. The pair often came into conflict and John wrote about these occasions in his diary. His descriptions paint a picture of himself as an obstinate opponent, who refused to back down in the face of his master's (perceived) abuses of authority. Yet, John's versions of these incidents may not be a true reflection of the reality. It is very possible that John was more confrontational on the page than he was in real life.[136] Hannah Barker has argued that diaries 'tell us not just about how people behaved (or said they did)', but how they were and how they wished to be.[137] Considered in this way, John's diary may tell us more about how he saw himself as a young adolescent and how he understood his relationship with his master than it provides a true account of his lived reality.[138] Like letter writing, diary writing was a cultural practice that changed over time, and historians have debated the extent to which diaries were always written with 'privacy' in mind.[139] Diary-writers might censor their entries or remove what they considered to be incriminating pages. John Tennent possibly removed pages from his diary relating to what he described as the 'Portrush affair'; an event that resulted in a warrant being issued for his arrest.[140]

In addition to Presbyterian church court minutes and family papers, this book also uses contemporary printed literature, reports and minutes of charitable societies, newspapers, and folklore sources to place Presbyterians within the broader picture of family life in long-eighteenth-century Ireland.

Ulster and its Presbyterians: Pious or promiscuous?

The province of Ulster, home to many Presbyterians, has historically been portrayed as a hotbed of illicit sexual activity. Contemporaries in the eighteenth and nineteenth century regularly commented on the apparently 'loose' sexual morals of Ulster's inhabitants and drew comparisons with the 'chastity and high moral character' of the Irish everywhere else.[141] In the 1830s, compilers of the *Ordnance Survey Memoirs* for County Antrim published a scathing account of the residents of Islandmagee (a parish that happened to have a large Presbyterian population). According to the report, a 'more immoral race' could not be 'found in any other rural district in Antrim'.[142] Inhabitants of Islandmagee were said to bask openly and with 'want of shame' in their immoral behaviour.[143] In addition to their excessive indulgence in 'raw spirits', women and men in the parish reportedly practised little sexual restraint.[144] Whereas 'Conjugal fidelity' was wanting among both husbands and wives – and worryingly more so on the side of the latter according to the report – most women were said by the compiler to be pregnant on their wedding day, their marriages having been 'preceded by an improper intimacy'.[145]

Ulster's reputation for sexual permissiveness was supported to some extent by the demographic evidence. Illegitimacy rates in Ulster were noticeably higher than those recorded in other parts of Ireland. In 1864, the first year in which official statistics became available, less than four per cent of births in Ireland were recorded as illegitimate. This stood in contrast to 6.2 per cent of births in the north-east of Ulster; a figure that was roughly the same as that recorded in England and Wales.[146] Illegitimacy rates in Ulster continued to diverge from Irish patterns into the twentieth century.[147] Ulster not only gained a reputation for illegitimate births, but the province was also associated with high levels of bridal pregnancy. Parish registers for the eighteenth century revealed that a high number of Ulster women were pregnant on their wedding day.[148] What this shows is that in Ulster, marriage usually followed sexual intercourse and not the other way around.

Presbyterians add an interesting dimension to historical studies of Ulster and Irish sexuality because they have simultaneously been presented as sexually promiscuous and as a community that had a strict attitude towards sexual morality. Historian Paul Gray has called this the Presbyterian 'paradox'.[149] Presbyterian church court records certainly give the impression of a community whose sexual (and social) behaviours were subject to strict moral policing. Between 1700 and 1744, Templepatrick Kirk Session in County Antrim dealt with 198 cases of sexual misbehaviour; a figure that represents over seventy per cent of all offences recorded in its minute book. Sex between unmarried and not-yet-married couples dominated proceedings in Templepatrick. In the period covered by its minute book, the Kirk Session considered 118 cases of fornication and 55 cases of pre-marital fornication.[150] A similar picture emerges from the minute book of First Dromara Presbyterian church in County Down. Between 1780 and 1805, its Kirk Session processed 375 cases of discipline. Of these, 230 related to sexual misbehaviour, the majority of which were for fornication and pre-marital fornication.[151] The 'Presbyterian paradox' was not lost on contemporary commentators either. As the *Ordnance Survey Memoirs* observer for the parish of Rashee wryly commented in 1835, while the 'Presbyterians, of the north of Ireland' 'unhesitatingly' claimed for themselves a general character of 'extreme morality', they were 'not the pious race' that they imagined themselves to be.[152] Which label, then, is correct? Were Presbyterians pious, promiscuous, or something in between?

It is certainly true that the Presbyterian church courts spent most of their time dealing with sexual misbehaviour between unmarried and not-yet-married couples.[153] It is also true that they appear to have tolerated pre-marital sex so long as the couple married afterwards. This does not mean that Presbyterians were sexually liberal.[154] While some members of the community did have sex before marriage, many did so as part of the rituals of courtship and marriage. Presbyterians who married after having sex may not have thought they had broken any moral codes, and pregnant brides were considered by the Kirk Session as much less problematic than were unmarried mothers.[155]

Historians have pushed back against the idea that Presbyterians were unusually 'promiscuous' by Irish standards. In fact, it is now accepted that pre-marital sex was common across all religious denominations in seventeenth- and eighteenth-century Ireland.[156] Infanticide rates were also relatively high in Ireland; another fact that shows the existence of extra-marital sex.[157] As Myrtle Hill has noted, it is likely that many couples behaved in similar ways to Presbyterians, 'but their experiences lack the detailed records of the Presbyterian Kirk sessions'.[158]

The conflicting image of Presbyterians as both pious and promiscuous is a helpful way of understanding the social, sexual and family worlds of the community. Alive with contradictions, this image captures the messy diversity of individual experiences. It also shines a light on how the realities of everyday life could both conform to, and deviate from, societal expectations. It is from within this complexity that this book draws its title. The stories it tells reveal the colourful worlds of Presbyterian women and men in long-eighteenth-century Ulster. They allow us to trace the family stories of Ulster's Presbyterians from the cradle to the grave, broadening and deepening our understanding of Irish families in the past. The Presbyterian women and men who appear in this book became parents, both inside and outside of marriage; they grew from children into young adults under the watchful eyes of their communities, who viewed them as both lustful and virtuous; they engaged in sexual and romantic relationships, sometimes with an intention to marry and at other times with none. Some Presbyterian couples formalised their relationships with marriage, a union that ended for some lucky folk in happy, loving marriages and for others in misery. The Presbyterians in this book also experienced grief, loss and social dislocation in widowhood, a life stage that not only occurred much earlier for some than others, but whose effects were experienced very differently too. Diverse in terms of gender, social background, marital status, age, and even theological belief, all were united in their connection to Ulster and its Presbyterian community.

CHAPTER ONE

'He said [it] was safe & afterwards he would marry her': Pregnancy and paternity disputes

In January 1726 Jane Colvill, a member of the Presbyterian congregation of Ballycarry in County Antrim, lay in bed gravely ill. She called her sister, Agnes, to her bedside and with her dying breath confessed that not only was she pregnant, but that she believed she had been poisoned by the father of her unborn child. The man in question was Robert McLery, with whom Jane already shared one child. Jane alleged that Robert had 'given her a powder which he said was safe & would only cause her [to] miscarry' and that he promised he would 'afterwards … marry her'. Before Agnes could call their neighbours into the room to witness the allegation, Jane lost the power of her speech and died. Robert was later called to appear before the Kirk Session to respond to Jane's death-bed revelation. He denied giving Jane any sort of powder and stated that he 'knew nothing of her being w[i]t[h] child'.[1]

Although the Presbyterian church discouraged its members from engaging in sexual intercourse outside of marriage, many women and men failed to heed its warnings. Presbyterian women and men engaged in a colourful spectrum of sexual activity that ranged from non-penetrative behaviours like kissing, touching and caressing, through to full sexual intercourse. Women who became pregnant had two options: they could carry on with their pregnancy or, like Jane Colvill, they could attempt to end it. In their efforts to induce miscarriages, couples resorted to powders, herbs and other types of abortifacients, with varying and, at times, fatal results. Women who did not want to, or were unable to, end their pregnancies were then faced with the problem of establishing the paternity of their children. While some men readily accepted their fatherly responsibilities, many others did not. In an era that predated DNA testing, proving the paternity of a child was difficult. The Presbyterian church courts played an important role in determining the paternity of illegitimate children. Kirk Sessions interrogated mothers for details on the place, time and frequency of their alleged intimate trysts. Women, however, were far from passive participants in this process. Whereas some women – sometimes acting alone and sometimes in collusion with others – wrongfully named men whom they thought could best financially support their children, others placed the blame on 'innocent' men to cover up their extra-marital indiscretions.

Detecting pregnancy

Before the invention of the pregnancy test, how did women like Jane Colvill know they were pregnant? In Ireland across this period, individuals looked to women's bodies for evidence of pregnancy. Medical professionals published pamphlets that aimed to give advice on how to diagnose pregnancy and treat ailments in pregnant women. In addition to attracting the readership of medical practitioners and female midwives, these texts were also read by sections of the literate lay population.[2] One such publication was the *Speculum Matricis Hybernicum*, also known as the *Irish midwives handmaid*, which was published in 1671. Written by James

Wolveridge, an English surgeon who spent time in Ireland in Cork, the pamphlet was intended to act as a guide for English midwives.[3] Section twenty-seven was dedicated to 'the signs of Conception', and it listed signs of pregnancy that would sound familiar to us today. Changes to the size and shape of the breasts and nipples; vomiting and 'weakness of stomach'; pains in the back and belly; and 'heaviness about the loins' were among the symptoms listed. In addition to bodily changes, pregnancy could be identified in alterations to a woman's mood and eating habits. The seventh sign of pregnancy was 'an absurd appetite' and a 'great loathing of meat and drink, with longings after various meats'.[4]

Medical texts of this type were probably not read by all levels of Ulster society during this period. Many of Ulster's inhabitants possessed only rudimentary literacy skills; reading, more so than writing, was taught as a basic skill. Yet this does not mean that women and men from the lower ends of society did not consume reading material of a medical nature. Ulster society had a population of what J.R.R. Adams has termed 'literate but not learned' individuals who were avid readers of popular literature.[5] Their reading material was supplied by the 'chapman' – an itinerant trader who sold cheap books and pamphlets known as chapbooks, among other items.[6] Chapmen in eighteenth-century Ulster sold versions of two medical books that were popular among 'less learned' readers: Nicholas Culpeper's *A directory for midwives* and the *Works of Aristotle, the famous philosopher*.[7] These texts combined materials from other medical publications, resulting in a 'hotchpotch of ideas and information' on pregnancy, fertility, childbirth and sex advice.[8] An edition of Culpeper's *Directory for midwives* was published in Belfast in 1766.[9] Like Wolveridge's text, Culpeper listed signs of pregnancy that included 'Loss of Appetite', 'sour belchings', changes to the nipples and breasts, and 'Griping pains like Cramps' in the belly.[10]

Many of these pregnancy symptoms could, of course, be attributed to other ailments and conditions. Moreover, not all pregnant women experienced the same changes to their bodies. Anna Crawford, the wife of the Reverend Alexander Crawford, minister of First Randalstown Presbyterian Church in County Antrim, used the presence or absence of toothache to determine whether or not she was pregnant.[11] Indeed, Wolveridge himself conceded that it was 'hard to know if a woman hath conceived yea or not' and cautioned his readers against using a missed period as a sure sign of pregnancy.[12] The stoppage of a woman's 'terms' – a phrase used to describe menstruation – was not necessarily a sign of pregnancy.[13] Moreover, periods were known to stop in cases of 'false conception' just as they did in 'true' pregnancy.[14]

Even if women and men in Ulster were not *reading* about pregnancy symptoms, this in no way means that they lacked the ability to *recognise* the signs. Evidence from Irish Presbyterian Kirk Session minute books suggests that women (and the communities that they were part of) were very much clued in to the pregnant body. Despite the difficulties in identifying pregnancy, it was the physical signs of pregnancy that communities noticed and about which they gossiped: growing bellies and swelling breasts attracted the eyes (and tongues) of watchful community members. In May 1701 Isabel Campbel defended herself against historical charges that she had given birth to a child outside of marriage, when a woman named Mary Osburn turned up in Burt, County Donegal, and claimed to be her daughter.[15] Mary was unable to offer any solid evidence for her claims, other than she had been told that Isabel was her mother by her 'foster' parents.[16] Her story did, however, receive some backing from two individuals in Burt. Patrick Orr and his daughter told the Session that Isabel had once been suspected of being 'with child' and that she had 'went out of ye contrey' not long after.[17] When Isabel returned '6 weeks' later, she was allegedly 'seen to milk her breasts in the fire'.[18] Although Isabel had not come back to Burt with a baby, the sight of her milk-filled breasts had clearly roused suspicions and were remembered by Patrick Orr years later. Isabel was not, however, proved to be Mary's mother. Other witnesses, including Mary's own cousin, disputed her claims that she had been raised by foster parents and that Isabel was her biological mother.[19]

Neighbours who suspected that an unmarried woman was pregnant often reported their concerns to the church courts. It was the force of community gossip that led Templepatrick Kirk Session in

County Antrim to initiate an investigation into the reputed pregnancy of an unmarried woman named Agnes Robison in April 1702. A woman named Jean Little had come before the Session to relay some rumours that were circulating about Agnes. According to Jean, 'it was reported by some that Agnes Robison was with child to Gavine Cudbert' and that she had 'miscarried of it' the previous February. Jean added that she had also heard of Agnes being 'familiar' with 'some other' man in addition to Gavine, implying that multiple men could possibly be the father. Another neighbour, Agnes Campbell, said the same thing, adding that Agnes Robison had told her personally about the miscarriage in January and confirmed that the father was Gavine Cudbert.[20]

The Session decided to investigate the case and they soon tracked Agnes down to the area between Lisburn and Hillsborough.[21] In August 1702 Agnes made the trip back to Templepatrick and not only told the Session that had she never been pregnant, but also denied telling anyone that she had been with child.[22] Jean Little, the initial reporter of the scandal, was then called to appear before the Session. Jean stood by her former testimony and said that a man named Archibald Byers and his family would be in a position to back her up.[23] Malcome Craford, the elder who was sent to talk to the Byers family, reported back to the Session in September that Archibald and his wife were willing to swear an oath that 'they know nothing of Agnes Robisons being with child' despite Jean Little saying that they did.[24]

Despite the issues raised about the legitimacy of the gossip surrounding the supposed pregnancy, Templepatrick Kirk Session continued its pursuit of Agnes. In June 1705, three years after the initial charges were raised, Agnes appeared before the Session and asked it to provide her with a 'certificat'.[25] Also known as a testimonial, this document was essentially a certificate of good behaviour that enabled church members to access the social and spiritual benefits of church membership. Individuals who were suspected of bad behaviour could not receive their certificate, which not only made it difficult for them to join new congregations but also prevented them from having their marriages celebrated or their children baptised. The Session denied Agnes's request, noting that she would receive it once she brought 'in evidence to dissanull what she formerly said of her self' (that she had been pregnant and had miscarried).[26] Undeterred, Agnes appeared again before the Session in November and requested her certificate. The Session refused her once more and directed that she either 'confess fornication with Gavine Cudbert' or 'say that she was guilty of a lie' when she told others that 'she was with child'. Agnes refused both options and 'departed without her certificat'.[27]

It is difficult to judge whether Agnes was telling the truth about having never been pregnant. Denied her certificate for such a long period of time, Agnes would have been excluded from the religious community of the church. The pregnancy rumours would have also likely followed her to Lisburn, making her the object of gossip in her new community. But it is possible that Agnes was innocent. In September 1706, more than four years after the Session investigated her, a woman named Mary McCanles testified that Agnes had been the victim of malicious gossip. According to Mary, the witnesses should not have been trusted. Agnes Campbell 'was half witted' and had been bribed by Jean Little with the promise of '2 pence' if she would make a statement against Agnes Robison.[28] It is not immediately clear from the minutes if Mary's evidence served to vindicate Agnes. But in July 1727 a woman named Agnes Robinson came before the Session for fornication. This woman confessed guilt and requested baptism for her child, which was subsequently granted.[29] If this was the same Agnes, the Session would not have admitted her child to baptism while the other pregnancy accusation was still outstanding. The sheer length of time that Agnes's case remained under investigation demonstrates how seriously the church took cases of sexual misbehaviour.

As Agnes Robison's case reveals, Kirk Sessions (and the communities they represented) did not readily accept women's denials; instead, women who were suspected of being pregnant were treated with suspicion. Some Kirk Sessions went to great lengths to establish the truth of pregnancy rumours and employed the services of other women to physically examine women they suspected of being pregnant. This was the tactic used by Templepatrick Kirk Session in June 1702 when it received a report that Jean McClane, a servant maid, was 'with child'.[30] John Henderson, the elder who was dispatched to investigate, consulted with a local midwife named Margaret Weir on how to proceed.[31] The pair agreed that Margaret should examine Jean for signs of pregnancy. Margaret would likely have poked and groped at Jean's breasts, stomach, and perhaps even her genitals, in order to discover signs of pregnancy or childbirth. In Scotland and England during this same period, midwives and other women performed similar bodily inspections.[32] But things did not go to plan in Templepatrick. When John returned to the Session in July, he reported that Jean 'would not permitt' Margaret to 'try whither she was with child or not'.[33] The Kirk Session lacked the power to compel Jean to submit to examination. Unable to proceed, her case dropped out of the minutes. It is likely that Jean remained under surveillance and was watched for signs of developing pregnancy. The lack of any further information on her case may be a sign that the pregnancy was never realised.

Other Kirk Sessions temporarily paused their investigations into sexual misbehaviour, committing to reopen them *if* and *when* evidence of premarital pregnancy emerged. This happened in the case of two servants named James Neil and Jane Murray, who were caught in bed together by their master in Carnmoney, County Antrim, in November 1705.[34] James denied that he and Jane had been intimate and claimed that he had not 'attempted any such thing'. Describing himself as a 'simple harmless fellow', James explained that he had gone to Jane's bed because he wanted to converse with her privately about marriage.[35] James even offered to swear to the same on oath, repeating his assertion that the pair had 'committed noe wickedness'.[36] The Session agreed to rebuke James privately for his offence, but refused to absolve him from guilt. The problem for James was that Jean had since left the area, and the Session therefore had 'no distinct account of her'. Without any evidence of pregnancy, the Session could not be sure that the pair had had sex. Hearing a rumour that she was in 'Kirkdonald' (also called Dundonald), the Session decided to delay dealing with James.[37] It would be another twelve months before James was cleared of suspicion. In December 1706 the Session noted that 'nothing appearing of [Jane] being with child', James could now receive his 'Testimonial'.[38]

Miscarriage and abortifacients

Not all pregnancies in the eighteenth and nineteenth century were welcome. Women's and men's understandings of pregnancy and abortion in this period were, however, quite different from modern understandings. At this time, pregnancies were confirmed only when women felt the foetus move; a development that usually took place from the third or fourth month of pregnancy. Known as the 'quickening', it was at this point that children were believed to gain their soul. Before this stage of pregnancy, women who took powders or potions to induce miscarriage may not have considered their actions as an abortion; instead, they would have understood it as restoring menstruation.[39] Moreover, the terms 'abortion' and 'miscarriage' were also used interchangeably to describe pregnancies that 'went wrong', meaning they did not result in the birth of a live child.[40] The medical writer James Wolveridge, for example, explained that abortion or miscarriage occurred when a woman brought 'forth an untimely birth'.[41] Miscarriage could be brought on by both internal and external factors.[42] The former included weaknesses to the vessels and structures of the womb, ulcers and 'distempers' in the tissue, sickness, or 'things that shake the body too much'.[43] Hot baths, 'Stinking Smells', eating 'salt, coals, dirt', immoderate exercise, 'sudden fury' and 'unsatiable copulation and lust' were listed among its external causes.[44]

Abortion was also subject to different legal restrictions than it is today. Before the eighteenth century, common law did not impose criminal penalties on women who induced miscarriage before they felt their babies move.[45] As noted above, it was not until the 'quickening' that pregnancies were deemed to be viable. Pregnancies that were terminated after the quickening were regarded as misdemeanours and were punishable with a fine or imprisonment.[46] Legal and medical opinion on the issue changed over the course of the next century as the idea that the foetus was alive from the point of conception gained ground.[47] In 1803 the English Parliament passed Lord Ellenborough's Act, which clarified the law relating to abortion in England and Ireland. According to the act, anyone who induced miscarriage in a woman 'quick with Child' using poison 'or other noxious and destructive' substances could receive the death penalty. The act also made it an offence to terminate pregnancies that had not yet quickened. Those found guilty of this offence could be punished with a fine, imprisonment, a spell in the pillory, whipping, or be transported for a maximum term of fourteen years.[48]

The death penalty for inducing miscarriage in a quickened foetus was affirmed in 1829 with the 'Act for consolidating and amending the Statutes in Ireland relating to Offences against the Person'.[49] This act also made inducing miscarriage in a non-quickened foetus a felony. Offenders could be transported for a term of between seven and fourteen years, or imprisoned (with or without hard labour) for a maximum term of three years. If the accused were male, an additional punishment of public whipping could also be passed.[50] The legal distinction between procuring the abortion of a quickened and non-quickened foetus was removed in 1837. In that year an act was passed that made the procurement of miscarriage in 'any Woman' punishable with transportation for a minimum of fifteen years or imprisonment for up to three years.[51] The Offences Against the Person Act (1861) made the procurement of abortion (by either the mother or any who assisted her) punishable by life imprisonment.[52] This act remained in force following the partition of Ireland in 1921.[53]

In their respective studies of women's reproductive lives in the twentieth century, Cara Delay and Leanne McCormick noted that many Irish women ingested oral substances to effect abortion.[54] While historians such as K.H. Connell have suggested that abortion in pre-Famine Ireland was 'rare', there is much evidence that women in eighteenth- and nineteenth-century Ulster engaged in the practice.[55] Like their twentieth-century descendants, Irish women in this earlier period imbibed potions, pills and powders that were made of naturally occurring abortifacients. Plants and herbs commonly known to induce miscarriage included savin or juniper, motherwort, honeysuckle, ergot and quinine.[56]

Knowledge of the medicinal properties of plants was passed down orally and in print form. The first herbal to focus on Irish flora was titled *The Botanalogia Universalis Hibernica* and was printed in Meetinghouse Lane, Cork, in 1735.[57] The pamphlet listed the properties of herbs and plants that were useful for all manner of medical ailments, including reproductive health. Savin was listed among the contents of the pamphlet as a 'Dieuretic and Emmenagogic' that could be found growing wild on the 'Islands of Loughlane in the County of Kerry'.[58] The herbal advised that savin leaves should be mixed with wine and then drank, to expel a 'dead Child' and the afterbirth.[59] Other herbs and plants were noted not for their abortifacient properties, but for their ability to promote menstruation, facilitate labour or prevent miscarriage. Motherwort, for example, was described as a plant with 'square, brown, woody Stalks' and 'large, & broad, deeply Indented' leaves with 'three sharp points' like nettles.[60] It was to be found 'in untilled places' and on 'old Walls, Lanes' in the months of June and July.[61] While motherwort was noted for its uses in preventing inflammation and stopping bleeding, it also had the ability to kickstart labour. The herbal advised that it should be 'pulverized' and 'a dram of it given in Wine' as a 'powerful Remedy to facilitate the Birth'.[62] Likewise, black briony – a climbing plant with 'Fruit ... like small Grapes' that could be found 'about Hedges and Trees' – was described as 'very dangerous for Women with Child'. Its root was known to 'provoke Urine, the Menses' and bring on 'Purges', while the 'Tops of it Eaten in Sallads' would 'Purge Watery humours', making it a plant likely to induce miscarriage.[63] Although the herbal cautioned pregnant women from ingesting these plants, the warning served to inform individuals of their efficacy in ending pregnancy.

Scattered amidst the records of the Presbyterian church courts we find fragmentary references to women using herbs and potions to induce miscarriage. In the early eighteenth century Carnmoney Kirk Session dealt with several cases involving abortifacients. In 1706 herbs with abortive properties were said to have been found in the possession of Elizabeth Morton, an unmarried servant maid, who claimed that the father of her unborn child was her ex-master, William Johnston. When asked by the Session about the pregnancy, William 'utterly deny'd any such thing' and claimed that Mary had made the allegation out of 'malice' and a desire to 'defraud him of some money'.[64] In his efforts to cast doubt on Mary's claims,

William called various witnesses to attest to her (alleged) promiscuous behaviour. Samuel Nivan, for example, told the Session that he had found Elizabeth in 'naked bed' with a man called Samuel McKee 'about 3 or 4 years agoe'.[65] Another witness named Agnes McKimm told the Session that she knew Elizabeth had a 'suspicious carriage', having witnessed her behaving 'immodestly' with 'little boys'.[66]

Further suspicion was cast on Elizabeth's character when other witnesses testified to having either seen or heard that she had abortifacients in her possession. Agnes McKimm repeated a conversation she had with Agnas Russell, the wife of William Johnston, about the provenance of 'some herbs' that resembled 'parsley' that she allegedly found among Elizabeth's things. Looking at the herbs, Agnes McKimm confirmed that they were not parsley, but 'a herb call'd March'.[67] Also known as 'March Violet' or 'Purple Violet', this herb was used in a variety of folk remedies, including cures for inflammation, colds, cancers, and falling-sickness (epilepsy).[68] Its abortive properties lay in its ability to treat 'inflammations' in the 'matrix' (the womb).[69] The name of the herb evidently resonated with Agnas Russell, who, 'knowing the nature of that herb', lifted 'up her hands' and 'begging mercy' told Agnes McKimm 'that she would have no hand in it'.[70] Samuel Thoburn, the husband of Agnes McKimm, also said he had seen Elizabeth 'one day carrying herbs in her apron' and that he 'earnestly desir'd her not to make any ill [with] them'.[71]

As Elizabeth's case indicates, men were not unaware of the medical properties of herbs and their abortifacient qualities. In her study of infanticide in late-nineteenth-century Ireland, Elaine Farrell noted how some men 'attempted to deal with an impending birth' by procuring powders to effect abortion.[72] The same is true for the eighteenth century. In fact, the evidence points to the existence of a shared culture of reproductive knowledge among women and men. It was not uncommon for women to tell the Session that they had been pressured into purchasing herbs by the fathers of their children for the purposes of inducing a miscarriage. In some cases, the pressure came not only from the father of their child, but from his wife too.

In May 1710 a servant named Florence Macky appeared before Burt Kirk Session in County Donegal and complained that she had been raped by her master, William Smith. Florence told the Session that William had lain 'carnally' with her on three occasions and she provided the dates and places the incidents occurred.[73] The first time she knew exactly: 28 April 1710, it having coincided with the fair day at Buncrana. The second time was 'on the last sabbath' in April and the final occasion was in the byre (cowshed) before the rest of the household had gotten up.[74] Asked by the Session why she had not cried out for help, Florence replied that the devil 'had hindered her'.[75] Florence's brother, James, also appeared on her behalf. He told the Session that William Smith had bribed his sister to leave Ireland and not return until she was sure she was not pregnant, offering her money 'to go over the water till she should see what god would do w[i]t[h] her'.[76] William's wife was also implicated in the bribery plot. According to James, she had offered Florence 'a years wages' (a considerable sum) to 'make the thing black' (terminate the pregnancy).[77] William Smith denied the allegations. He told the Session that Florence had made the whole thing up out of revenge after he discovered she had stolen a 'bottle of aquavite' (whiskey).[78] The case rumbled on for over two years: Florence stuck fast to her accusations and William to his denials. In the absence of solid proof, the Session finally decided in August 1712 to bring the case to a close. The minister 'advised that the matter should be laid home' to William's 'own conscience' and the 'sin' left 'at his own door if he was guilty'.[79]

Women who concealed the bodies of newborn children who died were also subject to criminal punishment. In 1707 the Irish parliament introduced an 'Act to prevent the destroying and murdering of bastard children'. The act was a verbatim copy of an earlier English law, ratified in 1624, that made infanticide a capital crime. Targeted specifically at unmarried women, this act assumed that illegitimate babies were the victims of murder unless their mothers could prove that they had been born dead. Unmarried women were regarded as guilty if they concealed their pregnancies, if they gave birth alone and without any assistance, and if their child was later found to be missing or dead.[80] As Elaine Farrell has pointed out, the infanticide statute focused on the concealment of the newborn child and not on the act of murder itself. Women who gave birth alone could therefore be found guilty of infanticide in cases of stillbirth.[81] The law was amended in 1803 to place the burden of proof of murder on the courts. Concealment of an illegitimate child who was later found to be dead was also criminalised. Women found guilty of this offence could be sentenced to prison with hard labour for up to two years. In 1821 the act was extended to the concealed births of babies who were born inside marriage.[82]

Throughout the eighteenth and nineteenth century then, concealment and death of illegitimate children were regarded as criminal offences that carried very serious judicial penalties. In Ulster, four women were sentenced to death for infanticide in the 1740s and 1750s.[83] Although infanticide cases fell properly under the remit of the criminal courts, we find occasional references to concealment and child death in the records of the Presbyterian church courts. In January 1701 the grisly discovery of a child's bones prompted Templepatrick Kirk Session to initiate an investigation into the alleged sexual misbehaviour of Michael Paul and Jean Cudbert, who were both at that time unmarried. A man named John Craig had presented the Session with 'bones' that he claimed belonged to a child who had been fathered by Michael. According to John, Michael had told him that he 'had unhandsome dealing' with Jean, causing her to become pregnant.

When Jean went into premature labour and gave birth 'before the time', Michael had 'buried the child' and then showed John the burial site. John later returned to the spot where the child was buried. He dug up the body and brought it to the Session. Unsure how to proceed, the Session resolved to keep the bones until it got advice from a doctor.[84] The Session likely wanted advice on the size of the bones to indicate the age of the child, as well as whether the remains showed any signs of violence. It probably also wanted to make sure the bones were indeed human.[85] Although the timing of this case predated the ratification of the 1707 Irish Act, the Session would have been aware that the discovery of the bones placed Michael and Jean under suspicion of child murder.

Two months later, Michael confessed to the Session that John Craig's story was true. He distanced himself and Jean from any criminal activity, however, by explaining that Jean had miscarried 'through sickness' when she was 'a quarter on with child' (meaning that she was less than three months pregnant).[86] The reference to the duration of Jean's pregnancy was significant: being less than three months pregnant, it was likely that she had not yet felt the 'quickening' and the pregnancy would not be regarded as viable. Jean came before the Session and confirmed Michael's story about the pregnancy and miscarriage.[87] She denied that she had taken any methods to restore menstruation, telling the Session that 'she had no hand in her miscarriage'. Jean also expressed sorrow for 'sinning against God'; a reference to her having engaged in sexual intercourse outside of marriage.[88] Both were directed to make public acknowledgement of their offence the next Sabbath.[89] The case does not appear to have been referred to judicial authorities and was settled 'in house' by the Session, underscoring the important place of the church courts in the lives of their members.

As suggested by the case of Michael and Jean, when women gave birth in secret or hid evidence of their pregnancy, they placed themselves at risk of judicial investigation and punishment. Such concerns were raised by Ballycarry Kirk Session in November 1738 when it received the confessions of John McMechan and Anne Ferguson for adultery. Both parties were directed to be publicly rebuked three times for their offence. Anne, however, was to stand in public one extra day on account of the 'aggravations of her sin'.[90] This was likely because Anne had not only concealed the pregnancy and told 'lies' about her condition, but she had failed to call 'for assistance when she was delivered'.[91] Although the minutes do not go into any detail as to the circumstances of the birth, we can assume that the child was safely delivered. The concerns of the Session were, however, justified; under the terms of the 1707 Act, if a child was stillborn and the mother gave birth without any assistance, she could be regarded as culpable for its death.

Identifying fathers

Women who were unwilling or unable to end their pregnancies were subsequently faced with the task of establishing the paternity of their children and securing their financial support. In eighteenth-century Ulster this was no easy feat. Ireland did not have a statutory system of poor relief in place until 1838. Also, there were no legal mechanisms in existence before 1864 that enabled mothers to sue fathers directly for child maintenance.[92] Reputed fathers could not be compelled to pay towards the support of children that were born outside of marriage, and the mothers of illegitimate children were forced to rely on the goodwill and charity of their neighbours, friends and family members for assistance. Women who were members of the Presbyterian community, however, were able to turn to their church for help. In the absence of a formal process enshrined in law, the Presbyterian church courts stepped in and acted as mediators in paternity disputes. The church even had guidelines to help its courts make decisions in cases of illegitimate pregnancy. The Irish Presbyterian church closely followed the published guidance on how to handle sexual misbehaviour set by its parent church in Scotland in the 1707 *Form of Process*.[93] From 1825, with the publication of their own constitution, Presbyterians in Ireland also followed the disciplinary process as set out in the *Code*.[94]

When the Kirk Session received a report of suspected extramarital pregnancy, it began an immediate investigation. When an unmarried woman was 'known to be with child', the Kirk Session cited her to appear and 'interrogate[d]' her to name the father.[95] Women who refused to name the father of their child were to be 'held contumacious'; a punishment that cut women off from the church privileges of communion and baptism. It was only when women engaged with church processes and named the father of their children that they could be restored to church membership.[96] In spite of the potential punishment, many women refused to engage. Some expressed their willingness to go through the motions of church discipline but requested to keep the name of the father secret. In July 1710 Jean Purdie told Ballycarry Kirk Session that she was willing 'to give obedience to the session' and undergo 'what so ever they shall impose upon her', but she declined to 'show who is the father of the child'. But this was not accepted, and the Session refused to receive her again as a member.[97]

In their work on paternity disputes in Presbyterian Scotland, historians Leah Leneman and Rosalind Mitchison suggest that many Scottish women claimed to not know the father of their children because the man in question, usually married, had urged them to keep quiet.[98] Similar evidence exists for Ireland. In June 1753 Jean Riddel told Cahans Kirk Session that John Moor was the father of her illegitimate child and that she had 'at his request' promised to 'conceal his being the father of it'.[99] Other women told the church courts that the real father of their child had pressured them into naming someone else. Some, like Mary Main, alleged that they had even been bribed to do so. In January 1704 Mary told Templepatrick Kirk Session that Michael Paul (implicated in the case, discussed above, in which a baby's bones were concealed), had 'bid her [to] father the child' on a man named 'Johnston' and 'not trouble him with it', and in return he would give her 'ten shillings'.[100]

The Presbyterian church offered guidance to the courts on how to proceed in cases in which women claimed not to know the identity of their child's father. If women said they had been raped 'by a person unknown', Kirk Sessions were advised to look into their 'former behaviour' (including their previous sexual history).[101] After seeking advice from the Presbytery on the case, Kirk Sessions were then to urge women who reported rape to 'declare the truth as if … upon oath'.[102] Some women subsequently decided not to report sexual assault and rape because they believed their former indiscretions could stand against them. In July 1755 Jean Riddell was again before Cahans Kirk Session, which she told she had been 'waylaid' by a 'Papist' as she made her way 'on the road thro' the mountains to Castleblany to see a friend'. She was raped by the unnamed man, who 'seized her and forced her into the mountains'. Jean told the Session that she did not think her account would 'be believed because of her former sin of fornication giving people a bad impression of her'.[103] The Session moved to discipline her for fornication.[104]

Other women who had been raped were able to use their 'good' reputations to their advantage. In June 1755 Martha McGregor came before Cahans Kirk Session and named 'her late master' Robert Nesbitt as the father of her child.[105] Martha claimed that the child was the product of rape and relayed to the Session in vivid detail the events surrounding its conception. On Tuesday, 6 August 1754, Robert returned home from Monaghan market 'very late' and 'partly intoxicate with liquor'. He was unable to get into the house on account of the 'door being bolted', so Martha rose from bed to let him in. When Robert entered the kitchen, he asked Martha to make his supper. At this point, Martha said Robert 'began to jest' with her; an action she 'did take but little notice of until all on a sudden he laid violent hands on her and forcibly carried her into the room adjoining the kitchen'. After bolting the door behind them, Robert 'attempted to debauch her' and despite making 'all the resistance in her power by strength of her body & force of argument', he succeeded in 'forcibly lie[ing] with her'.[106] Martha declared to the Session that 'She never knew any man on earth except' Robert and reiterated that she 'never gave her consent to such abominable action directly, nor indirectly'.[107] The midwife who attended Martha's labour confirmed her account of the child's conception. The midwife's testimony was also confirmed by the 'some of the neighbouring women … who were present at [Martha's] delivery' and who were described as 'persons of credit'. These women, the minister said, 'generally believed' the 'contents of [Martha's] oath', partly because she 'always bore an exceeding sober, & chaste character' before her pregnancy.[108] The Session then voted as to whether Martha was to be considered 'censurable as a fornicator OR NOT?' The vote was unanimous in favour of 'NOT censurable'.[109]

After a woman named a man as the father, the Kirk Session requested him to give his account. If he denied paternity, the Session brought both parties together to bring about a confession.[110] While a woman's words were not enough to fix paternity charges, the Session could be convinced if there was evidence from other people that the couple were known to spend time together alone.[111] So when women charged men with paternity, they were expected to back up their accusations with corroborating details. Many did so by providing details of their alleged intimate trysts, telling the Kirk Session the places, dates and number of times that they had engaged in sexual intercourse. In February 1723 Katherine Carson declared to Ballycarry Kirk Session that John McTire, with whom she already shared one child, was the father of her child and 'no other man'. Katherine then provided the Session with the circumstances of conception, explaining that the pair had sex towards 'the latter end of May ... in the barn in the night time' when John had 'brought some meal' for their child.[112]

Some women demonstrated a great deal of anxiety in their efforts to get the date of conception correct. When Jean Lock appeared before Templepatrick Kirk Session in November 1701 and named Andrew McKeown as the father of her child, she initially claimed that they had engaged in sexual intercourse in the house of John McCord 'about the first of May'.[113] Jean reappeared before the Session the following week to clarify the date and time of her encounter with Andrew. Having 'now more seriously consider[ed]' the time, she declared that they had sex 'about 14 days or 3 weeks before may' [sic].[114] Getting the right date was important, because men often disputed paternity on the grounds that the dates did not add up. While some men confessed to having sex with the women who charged them, they claimed that they could not be the father because the time of birth did not align with the date of conception. The emphasis placed on the exact date of intercourse reflected wider beliefs about conception during this period. Whereas today we tend to measure pregnancy from the start of the most recent period, in the eighteenth and nineteenth century people dated pregnancy from the last event of sexual intercourse. While estimates varied, nine months was generally used to determine paternity.[115]

Drawing on this measurement, a common phrase used by men was that the birth 'did not come to their time'. These words were uttered by Andrew McKeown in April 1704 when he told Templepatrick Kirk Session that Jean McCullan's child could not be his, 'it being brought forth ... a month before his time'.[116] Like other women in her position, Jean attempted to prove her charges by providing the dates, times and places of her intimate trysts with Andrew. Jean testified that the 'act' was committed on Ballyclare fair day, when Andrew's mother was 'abroad', his brother was at work and his father was 'about the house'.[117] Evidently, the Session believed that Jean was telling the truth. With the support of the Presbytery, Jean was admitted to swear an oath 'that she never knew any man but Andrew McKeown'.[118] Andrew eventually appeared before the Session in April 1705 and confessed his sorrow for having 'offended God and his people'.[119] He stood publicly before the congregation on two Sabbaths before he was absolved of his sin in May 1706.[120]

Another reason why Kirk Sessions asked women to provide the circumstances surrounding conception was so that others could be called to corroborate the details. Some men disputed paternity charges by claiming they were not in the place at the time alleged. In August 1707 Mary McClaine told Templepatrick Session that Andrew Malcomson was the father of her child. Mary said that the child was conceived '6 weeks before hallowtide' in the house of Patrick Flood, she and Andrew 'wakeing him' in his 'time of sickness'.[121] In his defence Andrew produced two witnesses, a woman named Widow Steel and Margaret Malcomson (his sister). While both women acknowledged that Andrew and Mary did indeed 'wake Patrick Steel', they disputed Mary's timeline of events. The women told the Session that the event happened much sooner than Mary claimed, being '14 dayes or 3 weeks before hallowtide'. Moreover, they swore that they were present in the house at the time and that 'they did not see any indecent behaviour' between Andrew and Mary. Of this they were also sure: not only was the company together in the 'one roome' that made up the house, the candle was 'burning all night'.[122] If Mary and Andrew had engaged in sexual intercourse, the two women claimed they would have seen them.

At times, the investigative efforts of the Kirk Sessions took a laughable turn. In addition to asking for the dates and times of sexual intercourse, some Kirk Sessions questioned women how they could be sure that the man they charged with paternity was the same man with whom they had sexual intercourse. In the darkness of night, for instance, how could women be sure of a man's identity? This line of questioning was used by Templepatrick Kirk Session when Grizell Mathison named Thomas McConnell as the father of her child. Grizell told the Session that not only had she seen Thomas 'r[i]se from his own bed' and come 'to her bed', but that he 'gave his hand to her to marry' before they committed guilt.[123] The Session asked similar questions of Catharin McConnel when she claimed that Robert Bryson was the father of her child. When Catharin alleged that the pair had 'frequent carnal dealing', the Session 'interrogat[e]d' her as to 'what discourse they had at any of these times'. When she answered that 'they had never none', the Session asked her 'how she knew it to be Rob[er]t Bryson more than any other man'. In response, Catherin remarked that 'she knew very wel[l], for she saw him go from her bed in to his own'.[124]

When men denied guilt and women persisted with their charges, the church courts again turned to the wider community for help. The innocence or guilt of men often hinged on what their neighbours knew about the alleged relationship. When Margaret Girvan confessed her guilt of fornication with Samuel McClintock and named him as the father of her child in March 1811, Carnmoney Session requested that she attend the next meeting 'with evidence of his having acknowledged being the father of [the] Bastard she bore'.[125] Margaret Margress appeared the next month and told the Session that Samuel had given her 'spirits' to bring to Margaret Girvan while she recovered from birth.[126] Such a gift implied that Samuel was the father. The Kirk Session subsequently agreed that Margaret could name Samuel as the father of her child.[127] Likewise, in July 1703 Jean Henry's paternity claim against James McIlroy was jeopardised when a witness came forward and claimed to have seen evidence that someone else was the true father. John Affleck told the Session that he was present in a room with James McByrd, Jean Henry and the child she fathered on James McIlroy. John said that he heard Jean tell 'the child go to your father' and he watched as the 'child went to James McBryd'.[128] It was on the strength of this encounter that made John 'suspect' that James McByrd was the true 'father of Jean Henrys child'.[129]

Midwives and other women who had knowledge of childbirth could also be asked to provide evidence in paternity cases. It was commonly believed that women would tell the truth about paternity during childbirth, the pain of labour being enough to extract a true confession. In England and Scotland, midwives were instructed to extract paternity confessions from labouring women and some even refused to come to the aid of women in labour until they named the father. Similar practices were followed in Ireland. Midwives were sometimes invited to appear before Kirk Sessions to relay the words that were said in the birthing room. When Jean Henry told Templepatrick Kirk Session that James McIlroy was the father of her children, the midwife who attended her labour played a crucial role in supporting her case. Jean had given birth to what appears to have been a set of twins, three weeks earlier than expected, causing James to dispute paternity. Jean volunteered to swear an oath that 'she never knew any other man' except James and explained that she had gone into premature labour following an illness.[130] Catharine Malhallon, who attended the birth, appeared on Jean's behalf and told the Session that the 'children [had] not come fully to their right time' and that Jean had sworn during 'her agony' that 'she would give her children no other father than James McIlroy'.[131]

For some women, the refusal of midwives to assist them during childbirth heightened the terror of the ordeal. Such was the experience of Mary Wilson, a member of Carnmoney Presbyterian congregation. In December 1720 Mary named Adam McCreagh, a married man who belonged to Templepatrick congregation, as the father of her child.[132] Adam 'utterly' denied the charge. The Kirk Session tasked Agnes Craford, the local midwife, with finding out the identity of the father.[133] When Mary went into labour, Agnes brought with her 'several neighbours' who could 'bear witness to what was to be said'. Being 'very willing to find out the truth', Agnes asked Mary 'again & again who was [the] father of [the] child'. Mary continued to name Adam as the father. At this point, Agnes changed tactic. Piling on pressure, she told Mary that there was a problem with the delivery, noting that there was 'something extraordinary in her labore' and that 'she might be a grave to her child'. Motioning to the other women in the room, Agnes told them to 'go & leave her'. Believing that Agnes and the women were going to leave her to die, Mary cried out 'bitterly' and asked Agnes,

'What would you hear me to say'. When Agnes again urged Mary to 'tell [the] truth', the woman swore that she had 'no other thing to say but adam mcreagh [sic] is father to my child'. The baby was born fifteen minutes later.[134]

As the eighteenth century wore on, the evidence that was provided by midwives was gradually replaced by the testimonies of doctors and other male medical attendants; a change that reflected the growing 'professionalisation' of maternal medicine. While many women in rural Ulster (and Ireland) continued to rely on the assistance of 'handywomen' – female family members and neighbours who had informal training in midwifery – to support them during childbirth into the twentieth century, there are references in Presbyterian church court minute books to the role of male doctors.[135] A paternity suit that was brought by Elizabeth Nesbit against George Taylor in May 1811 hinged on the testimony of the doctor who was present at the birth. Elizabeth, who had recently married someone else, appeared before Ballybay Kirk Session in County Monaghan, and charged George as the father of her child. She told the Session that George had seduced her with promises of marriage, and that she had never had sex 'with any other man before' the child was born or 'with any man since, but her own husband'. George denied that he had ever promised marriage to Elizabeth and swore that the pair had never had sexual intercourse.[136] The case was then referred to the upper courts for a decision. When the Presbytery of Monaghan met the following month, Elizabeth produced a medical attendant named only as 'Doctor McAdam', who told the court that when he assisted her in childbirth she 'told him that George Taylor was the father'.[137] The Presbytery 'unanimously' agreed that George had 'criminal connections' with Elizabeth before she married her present husband.[138]

As several of these cases show, women supported their paternity claims by swearing that they had not engaged in sexual intercourse with any other man than the one they accused. Men sometimes sought instead to clear themselves of paternity charges by discrediting the character of their accuser. Many men took aim at women's sexual characters and gathered evidence from neighbours, family members and friends to try to undermine their accuser's reputation.

This was the strategy employed by Hugh Young, who in April 1726 was named by Martha Cowan as the father of her child. Martha initially told the Kirk Session that a man named Robert Morton was the father of her child. She claimed, however, that she had been pressured into naming Robert by Jane Young, the sister of Hugh Young, with whom she had worked as a servant.[139] Hugh denied that he had been 'guilty with Martha' and produced two witnesses in his defence. The first was a woman named Margaret McKinstrey, who told the Session that she had seen Martha 'in bed naked' with Robert Morton and that the pair were engaged 'as she thought in the act of uncleanness'. Margaret's testimony was supported by Mary McMurthrie, who claimed that she saw the pair 'in naked bed' and that Robert was lying 'above' Martha's body. Mary, it appears, was also in the room at the time that Martha and Robert had engaged in intercourse. She told the Session that she had overheard Martha telling Robert that he would 'be a fool to have to do with her for Mary [McMurthrie] was not sleeping yet'.[140]

Other men told Kirk Sessions that their accusers were notoriously promiscuous. When Adam McCreagh was charged with fathering Mary Wilson's baby in 1721, he brought with him witnesses who could testify to having seen Mary in the company of other men. Thomas McComb appeared first. He told the Session that he had bumped into Mary and her friend on the road from Carrickfergus. The two girls were in the company of three soldiers, and Mary was holding hands with two of them. Thomas said that when he told Mary to go home, the soldiers challenged him 'what was his bisness' and added other 'profane words' and 'horied cursing[s]'. Thomas even insinuated that Mary was earning money as a sex worker. He told the Session that the soldiers said to him that Mary would be 'well paid' for her services. Janet Johnston also testified that Mary was known to the soldiers at the local barracks. She told the Session how soldiers often called at her house to ask for Mary, and had even offered her 'a crown' to go and fetch the girl. When she refused, Janet claimed that the soldiers attempted to bribe her with half a crown 'to hold her tongue'.[141] It was not only soldiers with whom Mary allegedly kept company. Adam's final witness was a man named James Johnston, who claimed to have spied Mary in an inn near Ballymena with a sailor. James told the Session that he had visited the inn with his friend to share a mug of ale. The pair were shown into a dark room, and when they lit a candle they saw Mary Wilson sitting on a bedside with a sailor. When Mary left, James inquired what the man was doing with Mary. The sailor, he claimed, told him that he had been waiting for Mary for 'foure and twenty ours' and showed them a 'silk belt' that she had given him as a symbol of their courtship.[142] Adam's attempts to discredit Mary were, however, unsuccessful.

Swearing on oath

If men continued to deny the claims made against them and their accusers remained steadfast, the Kirk Session would offer an oath by which the accused could clear themselves of guilt. Known as the 'Oath of Purgation', it was only to be administered as a last resort.[143] Kirk Sessions were to seek the advice of the upper courts before offering church members a form of the Oath. Persons who took the Oath were to swear it before either the Kirk Session or the Presbytery, and then notice that they had done so was announced to the congregation. The person was then to be 'declared free from the alleged scandal'.[144] Once the process was complete, the woman was to be censured for her offence, 'without naming' the man she had initially accused. The Session reserved the right to enforce further censure if the real father was ever discovered.[145]

Kirk Sessions were hesitant to offer men the opportunity to clear themselves by oath because of the potential for perjury. In January 1704 Mary Main named the married Michael Paul as the father of her child.[146] Michael denied the charge and claimed that the pair had never engaged in sexual intercourse.[147] Mary was referred to the Presbytery, who believed her version of events. She was directed to stand before the congregation as an 'adulteresse' and make public acknowledgement of her sin.[148] Despite being urged by the Session 'to search and try his ways before he would offer to persist in the denial of his adulterie', Michael continued to deny the charge.[149] When he requested baptism for one of his children in September 1706, the Session asked him about the pre-existing adultery charge.

Michael denied the charge once again and declared that he was 'as free of scandal with mary main [*sic*] as the child unborn'.[150]

The case dropped out of the minute book, reappearing almost six years later in June 1712. This time, Michael changed his plea. He confessed his adultery with Mary, a charge that he 'had hitherto obstinately denied and desired liberty from time to time, to purge himself by oath'.[151] Asked by the Session why he now came 'freely to confess', Michael responded that he was compelled to appear from 'the conviction and terror of his conscience'. Over the past six years, he had suffered 'from the remarkable judgments of God upon his family'. Whereas he had experienced 'extreame poverty', 'one of his hopefull Children was suddenly struck blind', and 'the other turn'd an idiot'.[152] Believing that he had received a judgement from God, Michael 'beg[ged]' to be admitted to public confession; he subsequently appeared before the congregation on 21 September 1712.[153] As Michael's case reveals, Kirk Sessions could be justified in not admitting men to take their oath.

Once paternity was confirmed, women could try to elicit financial support from the fathers. While the Presbyterian church courts could not make men acknowledge the practical and financial responsibilities of fatherhood, they could put sufficient pressure on them to do so. When the Kirk Session announced the name of a father publicly, the community would expect him to take on responsibility for the child. Men who refused to take on this role, or who were judged as lacking in the ability to fulfil the demands of fatherhood, were subject to public disapproval.[154] In May 1816 Carnmoney Session signalled discontent with Thomas Seaton by 'reprov[ing]' him 'for his bitterness in not paying maintenance' for the child he shared with Jane Davison.[155] In general, however, most men appear to have accepted the ruling of the Kirk Session and expressed a willingness to take on their responsibilities. In 1704, Daniel Rea refused to accept Jannet McAlexander's claim that he was the father of her child until Templepatrick Kirk Session stepped in. The Session held a special meeting at the house of the Reverend James Kirkpatrick to determine the matter. It was only after Jannet was directed by the minister to swear the truth of her claim that Daniel accepted that she was telling the truth. According to the minutes, after hearing Jannet 'with uplifted hand voluntarily swear by the eternall God maker of heaven and earth that' he was the father, Daniel 'promised to do all the duties of a parent to ye child'.[156]

Jane Colvill's family

The tragic story of Jane Colvill that opened this chapter was not an unfamiliar one in eighteenth- and nineteenth-century Ireland. Jane died after ingesting suspected abortifacients that were allegedly given to her by the father of her unborn child, Robert McLery. Stories like Jane's are usually (and wrongfully) pushed to the margins of histories of the Irish family. We do not tend to think about illegitimacy, extra-marital pregnancy and abortion as belonging to the 'normal' pattern of Irish family life. Yet, Jane's family story was far from unusual. Like many women in Ulster during this period, Jane appears to have been intimately involved with her partner, Robert, for a considerable period of time. With one child living and another on the way, Jane had created a family unit outside of the frameworks of marriage. In a similar fashion to other courting couples in eighteenth-century Ulster, it is quite likely that Jane and Robert had first engaged in sexual activity as part of the courtship ritual, and it is possible that they may have eventually progressed to marriage. Both Jane and Robert also appear to have been knowledgeable about how to manage an unwanted pregnancy. Responsibility for reproduction did not rest solely with women, and it was likewise not a subject shrouded in secrecy. Men like Robert knew about abortifacients: what they were, where to find them, and how they should be taken. It is likely that other Irish couples managed pregnancy in similar ways, both within and outside of marriage. Pregnancy, paternity and childbirth were events that interested both women and men, and they had far-reaching consequences beyond the immediate couple too.

CHAPTER TWO

'Every little matter is now in order for the expected stranger': Infancy and childhood

William Drennan was ecstatic. After a nervous wait, he was sure that his wife Sarah was pregnant with their first child. Sarah had been 'very sick' for a few weeks, 'chiefly before and after breakfast', and had been complaining of 'lassitude and weakness'.[1] Writing to his mother in August 1800, William could barely contain his excitement at the prospect of becoming a father; it was, after all, something he had yearned after for so long. With a flourish, he urged his mother to 'congratulate' him, to 'kneel down, and thank an ever good and gracious God for his kindness' to her 'happy, happy, son'.[2] For William, and indeed for many married couples, children were a blessing that made their families complete. In this same letter to his mother, William remarked that he could 'bear the calamities incident to the married state, and even the loss of a child better … than the solitary widowhood of barren marriage'.[3] In William's mind, 'marriage without children was but half marriage'.[4] These comments were particularly pointed, framed as they were by William's knowledge that his eldest sister and confidante, Martha McTier, had been widowed five years earlier in 1795, without ever having children of her own.[5]

Over the next few months, William corresponded frequently with Martha, providing her with updates on Sarah's developing pregnancy. While William's interest in his wife's condition was partly influenced by his work as a male midwife, his letters reveal his excitement about impending fatherhood. So pleased about becoming a father, William confessed that it made 'little difference to him whether the child would be a girl or boy'.[6] The siblings discussed possible names for the new baby; whereas William and Sarah favoured the name 'Ann' (the name of William's mother) if the child were female, Sarah was 'much attached' to the name 'William' if it was a boy.[7] When the child was eventually born on 24 March 1801 at 8 o'clock in the evening, he was a healthy boy and not a 'scraneen' like his parents had feared.[8] They named him Thomas (Tom) Hamilton.[9] Mesmerised by his son, William remarked that the child bore a striking resemblance to his mother, Ann Lennox: 'the little one', he said, even had 'the Lennox lip'.[10] Writing to Martha the day following Tom's birth, William felt satisfied with his lot: 'now', he said, 'I have … a family, a wife and child'. He gifted 'a bottle of excellent port' to his servants to 'drink Master's, Mistress's and Young Master's health' and wrote to Martha that she owed him thanks for having made her an aunt.[11] As he settled down with his little family, William Drennan, like many other new parents, looked to the future. With the birth of children, women and men took on new responsibilities as parents. They were entrusted to rear their children to be happy, healthy, principled and God-fearing members of their communities.

Baptism

One of the first events in the lives of infants whose parents belonged to the Presbyterian church was baptism. The Presbyterian form of baptism, its meaning, and instructions on how it should be administered were outlined in two documents published by the Church of Scotland in the 1640s: the *Westminster Confession of Faith* and the *Directory for the Public Worship of God*. A revised version was published in Ireland in 1825.[12] Although there were some theological differences between Presbyterians over the meaning of baptism, their respective understandings of the rite were fairly similar.[13] Baptism was designed to act as a sign of one's entrance into the 'visible church' (the congregation of believers) and it represented the promise between God and his people.[14] Unlike other religious traditions, Presbyterianism severed the link between baptism and salvation. According to Presbyterian standards, baptism did not ensure one's place in heaven because its efficacy was 'not tied to that very Moment of Time wherein it is administered'.[15] Baptism was therefore not strictly necessary. Presbyterian guidelines made the crucial point that baptism was 'not so necessary, that through the want thereof, an infant dying unbaptized perishes everlastingly'.[16] According to Andrew Holmes, it is this understanding of the efficacy of the sacrament of baptism, one which denied the doctrines of baptismal regeneration and believers' baptism, that distinguished Presbyterians from other religious traditions in Ulster.[17]

The church published guidelines on how baptism was to be administered. These rules covered the eligibility of persons to be baptised as well as the practical elements of the ceremony itself. Baptism was open to all those who professed faith in Christ, as well as the infants of believing parents, or in some cases, parent, if only one was a regular member of the church.[18] Baptism could only be dispensed once in a person's lifetime, and preferably during their infancy. The main rule as to its timing, however, was rather vague. The *Directory* advised only that it should 'not unnecessarily ... be delayed' after birth.[19] Baptism was to be administered only 'by a Minister of Christ' and not 'in any Case by any Private Person'.[20] The ability of midwives to perform an emergency baptism in cases where the life of the infant was threatened, acceptable within the teachings of the Roman Catholic church, was dismissed because it neither had biblical precedent nor did its efficacy ensure salvation.[21] Lastly, the ceremony was to take place publicly, in the meeting house, and before the congregation. The requirement for public baptism, however, became an issue for the laity and church alike. Whereas private baptism was the normal practice in some communities, others (especially in more orthodox communities) insisted upon the ceremony being performed in public.[22] During the 1830s, the Synod of Ulster pressed for a return to public baptism. The church's insistence on this irked some of its members so much that they left their congregations.[23]

The form the ceremony was to take changed only slightly between the eighteenth and nineteenth century, retaining its emphasis on simplicity and rejection of superstition and 'popery'. After giving the minister notice in advance of the baptism, the infant was to be presented by either one or both parents, or in special circumstances by a sponsor or specially elected friend.[24] The minister was then to 'use some words of Instruction' explaining the use and ends of the sacraments, and reminding parents and others of their duties to bring up children in the knowledge of Christ.[25] Importantly, baptism was also used as an opportunity to 'stir up' the faith of all those present so that they would 'make right Use of their [own] Baptism' covenants.[26] The parent or sponsor would then present the child, calling it by name, and the minister would seal the sacrament by sprinkling the child's face with water.[27]

Access to the sacrament of baptism was closely regulated. Church members who were not in good standing were denied this privilege for their children. To be eligible for baptism, parents had to be free from censure and demonstrate evidence of their commitment to the church. It is for this reason that baptism was offered to all infants, irrespective of whether they were legitimate or not; it was the standing of their parent(s) that determined access to the sacrament.[28] The type of offence a person was charged with had no bearing on their eligibility; in the eyes of the Kirk Session all were denied access until they submitted to discipline. Frederick Curry, a member of Ballykelly congregation in County Londonderry, was denied baptism for his children in November 1803 until he produced a certificate exculpating himself from a charge of petty theft.[29] Similarly, Loughaghery Kirk Session in County Down refused to admit Eliza Sproat's child to baptism until she submitted to discipline for having her marriage celebrated by someone other than a Presbyterian minister.[30] In addition to these types of misdemeanours, those who were found lacking in sufficient knowledge of what their role as sponsor would entail were also denied access to this rite. Loughaghery Kirk Session denied baptism to three children in August 1808 because of the misbehaviour of their respective fathers. Their faults included poor attendance at public worship, irregular conduct on the Sabbath, and general 'Ignorance of the principles of the Gospel necessary for parents to know as sponsors'.[31] It was only after the men had been rebuked, and their case published to the congregation, that their children were admitted to baptism.[32]

Not all communities followed this process. Some Kirk Sessions were flexible in their approach and baptised infants whose parents were non-communicants.[33] Moreover, despite the efforts of Kirk Sessions to regulate baptism, 'unworthy' parents sometimes slipped through the net. John Townsley, a member of Ballykelly congregation, had his child baptised in May 1808 despite being 'denied fathers privileges' for maligning and slandering another member of the community. After an inquiry was made as to how he had by-passed baptism regulations, it appeared that the case had 'escaped' the minister's mind and the clerk who certified the baptism had not been present when John first appeared before the Session.[34] As well as the negligent management of Session business, the movement of persons between congregations also enabled some to circumvent the usual rules. In September 1831 Loughaghery Kirk Session directed that Robert Erwin and his wife Margaret be publicly rebuked for the sin of prenuptial fornication. A postscript to the case reveals that, prior to joining the community of Loughaghery, they had both been in 'full communion in Drumlough' and had been 'married & received baptism for two children' by the minister there 'without any cognisance' of their sin.[35]

Given the pressures placed upon parents, why did so many continue to seek baptism? Andrew Holmes has suggested that some parents subjected themselves to scrutiny because they feared for their child's eternal soul, revealing a popular belief in the regenerative effects of baptism not taught by the Presbyterian faith.[36] Certainly, many Presbyterian parents grappled with what the standards of their faith taught them on the one hand, and their own fears for the spiritual welfare of their children on the other. Diary entries by the Reverend Robert Magill, minister of First Antrim (Millrow) Presbyterian congregation, reveal how ministers sometimes bent the rules to placate the needs of the laity. Technically, ministers were only to perform the baptisms of members of their own congregation and had to seek permission before baptising those of other communities.[37] Robert's diaries reveal, however, that sometimes the sickness of infants and fears of parents led ministers to by-pass these rules. In April 1827, Robert recorded how he rode to Crosskennan to baptise the son of Francis Barber, a member of Donegore congregation. His reason for baptising a child that did belong to his own congregation was because it was 'sickly'.[38] This concession was not a usual pattern of his behaviour and seems to have been prompted by the illness of the infant. Just a few months later, Robert refused to baptise the seemingly healthy son of John Fox because he was not a member of his congregation.[39]

In addition to the peace of mind that baptism brought parents, many were happy to proceed with the ceremony because of its social function. Baptisms were times of celebration. In her work on godparenthood and baptism in St Catherine's parish, Dublin, Clodagh Tait suggested that the length of time between birth and baptism was deliberately lengthened to enable families to organise celebrations to coincide with the event.[40] The same procedures appear to have been followed by families in Ulster. We can get a sense of the timing of birth and baptism by examining baptism registers. Presbyterian ministers were instructed by the church to keep a record of the baptisms they performed. These registers were to include the name and place of residence of the child's parents, the mother's maiden name, and the date of both the birth and baptism.[41] Surviving baptism registers for Larne and Kilwaughter in County Antrim, and Loughbrickland and Rademon, both in County Down, indicate that most baptisms took place more than four weeks after birth. This was ample time to prepare for celebrations.[42]

The celebratory side of baptisms was also a source of comment in the *Ordnance Survey Memoirs* for nineteenth-century County Antrim. In the parish of Killead, 'christenings' were described as 'scenes of festivity' that were attended with 'more celebrity' than were weddings. Parents invited 'as many' guests as they could 'possibly contain' and put on a good spread 'with the best they have'.[43] Similar comments were made for other parts of County Antrim. Whereas christenings in the parish of Ballycor were described as 'very joyful occasions', those that took place in Donegore were times of 'mirth and feasting' and were attended by as many guests 'as the house [could] accommodate'.[44] The social side of baptism ceremonies was also commented upon by ministers. Robert Magill recorded in his diary that a company of twenty people drank tea after the baptism of Elizabeth Martin in February 1821, while that of Ann Eliza McCrory, a few months later, was attended by a party of twenty-five persons.[45]

Baptism celebrations were also much more family-oriented than envisioned by the official standards of the church. Loughaghery Kirk Session passed a total of five resolutions detailing the procedure of baptism, four of which were passed within the space of nine years.[46] Most of these resolutions concerned whether baptism should be celebrated publicly in the meeting house, or privately in the family home. Although the Session advocated the use of public baptism, it conceded that there were some circumstances in which private baptism could be administered instead. A resolution passed in January 1818 set out five scenarios in which private baptism was acceptable: in winter season, when the family home was more than two miles from the meeting house; when the sickness of the child, parent or sponsor would render it unsafe to carry the child to the meeting house; if there were two consecutive wet Sabbaths after application; when the sponsor was female (possibly a concession afforded to mothers who were recovering from childbirth); and if any aged or 'tender' members of the family were too ill to attend public worship.[47] Despite these favourable concessions, the Session repined that the congregation seemed 'unwilling to have baptism publicly administered'. In July 1834 and September 1835 the Session passed two further resolutions to reaffirm the stance that public baptism could only be avoided due to illness or when the parents' home was more than two miles distant from the meeting house.[48]

Many families appear to have taken issue with the church's insistence on public baptism because it clashed with their perception of the ceremony as a family occasion, to be kept separate from the prying eyes of the wider community and local Session. In June 1836 William McAuley presented a petition to the Session of Loughaghery asking for baptism to be administered privately in his home on account of his father's inability to attend public worship.[49] For others, baptism seems to have been an occasion reserved for the family only, and the thought of sharing the intimacy of the event with outsiders was unpalatable. The Reverend Alexander Crawford, minister of First Randalstown Presbyterian church, exchanged heated words one Sabbath with a member of his congregation over the issue of public baptism. In a letter drafted by Alexander on the subject, he outlined the reasons for the public nature of the rite and chastised his correspondent for the 'threat of disobedience' to the church. Interestingly, however, Alexander also suggested an alternative location for the baptism to take place, offering the use of the schoolhouse 'for any day you may be pleased to name'.[50] Kirk Sessions made similar compromises. In May 1839 Ballymoney Session allowed baptism to take place 'on the occasional opportunities afforded during the week' as well as before a full congregation on the Sabbath.[51]

Nursemaids and childcare

Parents in eighteenth- and nineteenth-century Ulster were also concerned with the physical welfare of their infant children. Many parents procured the services of paid nurses to help with everyday childcare. There were two main types of nursemaids: wet nurses, who assisted with breastfeeding duties, and dry nurses, who took on a role in general childcare. While writers of advice literature urged new mothers to breastfeed their own children, this was not always a possibility. Some women struggled to produce enough milk to feed their children and were anxious that their babies would not receive appropriate sustenance. Sarah Drennan worried that her newborn son had an aversion to her milk owing to the 'weak bowels' he had inherited from his father. Her sister-in-law, Martha, wrote to her in April 1801 to reassure her that she had 'never heard' of this mystery family ailment and that there was no cause for worry.[52] Breastfeeding took a toll on the health and wellbeing of other women. Anna Crawford, wife of the Reverend Alexander Crawford, suffered terribly with 'sore nipples' while breastfeeding her daughter Olivia. Writing to Anna's sister, Helen, in April 1835, Alexander confided that Anna had 'shed many a tear' as she attempted to feed their child.[53]

Due to the demand for wet nurses, lots of pamphlets were printed with advice on how to choose the best woman for the job. According to the Scottish physician William Buchan, 'Common sense' directed that the best choice of wet nurse was a woman who was 'healthy' and had 'plenty of milk'; the 'proof of a good nurse', of course, was the 'healthy child upon her breast'.[54] Writers reminded parents of the importance of choosing a good nurse. After all, women who 'abandon[ed] their own child to suckle another for the sake of gain' could not be expected to 'feel the affections of a parent towards' the child she nursed.[55] Similar sentiments were shared by other writers. In his *Compleat Family Physician* (1781), Hugh Smythson warned parents that 'Hired nurses' were not only 'insensible' to the cries of infants, but because they were not 'actuated' by 'affection' towards their charges, they would fail to even 'lull them to quiet or soothe their anguish'.[56]

Women who breastfed their own infants might seek the services of a dry nurse instead. Dry nurses assisted with the practical demands of parenthood. In addition to keeping watch over children, feeding, bathing and dressing them, nursemaids could be expected to sleep in the same room as children and soothe them during the night. This was one duty of Eupham Thompson, a servant and nursemaid employed by George Russell in Carnmoney, County Antrim. Eupham, however, does not appear to have attended to her duties religiously. In September 1711 George appeared before Carnmoney Session and 'tabled' a complaint about Eupham's neglectful behaviour. He told the Session that he heard his daughter crying one Sabbath morning and went to investigate. When he reached the child's room, he discovered that she was alone in bed. George searched the house and eventually found Eupham upstairs 'lying naked in bed' with William McCraken, his sixteen-year-old servant.[57]

Whether wet or dry, the character and qualities of a nurse were important factors to be taken into consideration by prospective employers. Nurses could form long-lasting and emotional bonds with their charges, leaving deep impressions on their memories and characters. John Caldwell fondly remembered his nurse, Ann Orr, as 'the very best authority'.[58] He recalled in his memoirs being taken by Ann to the top of a hill one midsummer's eve when he was six years old, 'where the young and the aged were assembled around the blazing bonfires to celebrate' the British victory over the Americans at the Battle of Bunker Hill.[59] Her words to him, 'Look, Johnny, dear, look yonder at the west. There is the land of liberty and there will be your country', were poignantly remembered by Caldwell when he later emigrated to America in the aftermath of the 1798 rebellion.[60] Others who were raised by nurses were not so fortunate. In stark contrast to Caldwell's fond memories stand the comments of Robert James Tennent, who scorned his childhood experience for the 'Success[io]n of nurses' who looked after him following the death of his mother, Eliza Macrone.[61] The loss of his mother shortly after his birth had denied him the benefits of a mother's love, something Robert believed could never be compensated for by nurses.[62]

Finding a suitable dry nurse could be a family effort. Such was the case for William Drennan and Sarah Swanwick. As Sarah entered the final stages of her pregnancy, the couple wrote to William's sister, Martha, for advice. In a letter dated November 1800, William confirmed that he and Sarah were ready 'to advertise [their] speedy want of a hale, heartsome, maid servant to do the office of dry-nurse'.

The prospective candidate, according to Willliam, should be 'young enough to like children, but old enough not to cast them from her arms up to the ceiling'.[63] This letter sparked a flurry of letters on the subject between the Drennan siblings as Martha did her best to find out what she could from other parents in her social circle. Although it may seem strange that it was Sarah's husband and his childless sister who took the lead in these decisions, it should be noted that William's professional background in midwifery and Martha's extensive social connections placed them in a much better position than Sarah to find a nurse. Moreover, Sarah was relatively new to Dublin, having relocated there from England on her marriage to William. Martha did, however, try to involve Sarah as much as possible in the decision-making process, writing to ask her thoughts and directions on the subject, as well as reminding William that, overall, his wife was to be the final judge.[64]

In all, Martha identified three prospective candidates for the job. The first was described as a sober woman of fifty years of age, 'decent in appearance [and] respectable in connections'.[65] Martha, however, ruled her out after discovering that she had been dismissed from her position at the poor house for selling meat intended for its inmates.[66] The second woman interviewed also appeared to be a good fit: she had reared three children of her own, was 'very well looking', relatively young and married.[67] After speaking with her a number of times, however, Martha determined that the woman 'had a something in a pretty eye' which she 'did not like' and ruled her out too.[68] It was the final candidate, Elizabeth (Betty) Miscambell, who eventually proved successful. Described as being twenty-four years old, 'of decent country parents, neither pretty nor ugly' and 'innocent', Betty, as the eldest of five siblings, had first-hand experience in raising children.[69] Her skills did not come cheap, however; Martha told William that Betty would 'not take less than six guineas a year'.[70]

While Betty was chosen as the best candidate, Martha's inquiries into her character had uncovered some potential stumbling blocks. Indeed, as her letters on the matter reveal, Martha's inquiries had been extensive. At their first interview, Betty had presented Martha with the 'discharge' note she received from her last employer, a woman named Mrs David Gordon. The note described Betty as honest and sober, with a 'good temper'. Martha intended to make further inquiries about Betty, noting that she had the address of 'Mrs Rainey of Greenville' who had previously employed her as a housemaid. If she received a positive reference from Mrs Rainey, Martha explained that she would then 'apply for further particulars' about Betty from two other women who had employed her: Mrs Gordon (who had supplied the discharge note) and Mrs Johnston. She would 'transmit' these 'accounts' to William and Sarah and 'then act according to [their] determination'.[71]

Ten days later, Martha wrote again about Betty. She copied into the letter the wording of the discharge note from Mrs Gordon, which was dated 1 May 1800.[72] Her assessment was quite positive. Betty, she said, had lived with the family as a children's maid for eighteen months, during which time she 'behaved herself soberly and honestly'.[73] While she recommended Betty's work as a children's maid, Mrs Gordon was less sure about her abilities to look after an infant, adding that she thought the girl was better suited 'to attend children more grown up'.[74] The reference from Mr and Mrs Rainey was even more problematic. The Raineys reported that they had dismissed Betty from service after finding her upstairs in the garret drinking punch with three female servants and an unknown man. The man in question turned out to be Betty's brother, who she had let stay in the Rainey household without permission. While the Raineys believed that Betty was 'good tempered', they were less sure that she was 'steady enough to undertake the care of a young child'.[75] The Drennans, however, were ultimately happy to take on Betty. By early spring, she was living in their household and appeared to have settled in well. In a letter to Martha in April 1801, William noted that they liked her 'very well'.[76]

As is the case today, first-time parents in this period also worried about the safety of their sleeping babies. These fears were not unfounded; over-laying (suffocation caused by co-sleeping) was one of the most common causes of accidental death of children in early modern London.[77] It was precisely these concerns that prompted William Drennan's mother to send advice about plans for the sleeping arrangements of her unborn grandchild. In a letter to her brother in November 1800, Martha noted that their mother had advised that the child should 'sleep in a cradle at the bed-side, to avoid the possibility of the dreadful accident of being smothered'.[78] In addition to the possibility of placing the new baby in a cradle, Martha added that she had heard that two of their mutual acquaintances had their children 'put up' in settle beds instead.[79] Settle beds were popular pieces of furniture that were an established sight in Irish homes by the nineteenth century. According to Claudia Kinmonth, settle beds were 'dual purpose' items of furniture that served as long seats or 'settles' during the day, and then at night could be 'unhinged outwards and down onto the floor' to make a 'double bed, enclosed on all sides'.[80]

Perhaps following the advice of William's mother, when their son was born, the Drennans chose to have him sleep in a crib that they kept at the bedside. As William told his sister in a letter, sleeping near Tom made it easier for Sarah to breastfeed him at night. Their nursemaid Betty was also 'much too sound a sleeper to have the child at night along with her'. While there were certainly practical benefits to this arrangement, William admitted that he and Sarah had experienced 'nights of bad rest' as a result. In the same letter, William told Martha that 'little Thomas' had interrupted their sleep with 'occasional fits of griping and wakenfulness at night'.[81]

Education and elementary schooling

With the birth of children, women and men took on new roles as parents. The most important of the additional responsibilities that came with this transition was the education of the next generation. Regardless of religious persuasion, authors of advice literature stressed the key role that parents were to play in the education of their children. Daniel Defoe's *The complete family instructor*, published in 1715, drew no distinction between the type of advice given to Dissenters and members of the Church of England on how best to educate their offspring. According to Defoe, the

'Catechising of children, and instructing [them] ... in the principles of the Christian Religion, has been a practice as antient as religion itself'.[82] In common with other mainstream Protestant traditions, Presbyterians believed that it was essential for the laity to be able to engage independently with the Bible to deepen their understanding and commitment to their faith. The ability to read, and less so write, were therefore vital skills, which parents had to ensure their children, both female and male, possessed.

Education began as soon as parents felt that their children were of an age that they had sufficient understanding. In most cases, this was between two and three years old. The Reverend Robert Magill attached such significance to both his children's second birthdays that he composed poems to mark the occasion.[83] In his poem to celebrate his daughter Sarah's second birthday, Robert reflected on how she was no longer an infant, but had reached an age of understanding:

> My little Sarah thou art now
> Upon this 9th of May
> 2 years of age though life at best
> Is like a fleeting day.
> ...
> Thy infant days are quite *forgot*
> Like days of Mortal fame
> ...
>
> I promised by a Sacred Vow
> To train thee in the way,
> That thou shouldst go and early teach
> Thy infant heart to pray.
> That thou mightst early seek and find,
> The Lord of thy immortal mind.
>
> And now my Sarah, may that God
> Whose grass is rich and free,
> For ever bless thee in this Love
> And still provide for thee.

>   Dispelling all thy coming fears
>   And guiding all thy future years.[84]

Robert believed that Sarah was ready to receive God's guidance. As Sarah aged, her education was stepped up a level. A few months after her third birthday, she began attending the meeting-house school with other children of the congregation.[85]

Similar education strategies were followed by other Presbyterian parents. The Reverend Alexander Crawford and his wife Anna also began educating their children as early as possible. Their daughter Christina (born in 1824) was introduced to family worship and psalm singing when she was around eighteen months old. In a letter to her parents in December 1825, Anna recalled that despite Christina's young age and inability to be reasoned with, Alexander and she thought it important to begin training her 'into the custom of waiting on ordinances', noting how Christina joined them 'with her book in hand' during psalm singing.[86] Tom Drennan, the eldest son of William and Sarah, was not only expected by his father to be able to read by the time he had reached four years old, but to do so with feeling and correct pronunciation.[87]

At home, parents used a variety of books that were designed to help their children learn how to read. Picture books were used to stimulate and engage the interest of small children. Anna Crawford wrote to her sister Helen in 1827 asking for 'some little books' for three-year-old Christina, 'with coloured pictures and large type for her amusement as well as to encourage her to read'.[88] Little Tom Drennan was sent to live with his aunt Martha McTier when he was two years old, on account of his delicate health and the expected arrival of another child.[89] Martha revelled in her care-giver role, and directed Tom's parents on what reading materials were suitable for the two-year-old's little collection. In contrast to William Drennan's rather formal approach to reading, such as his instructions that Tom should commit to memory the first two stanzas of William Cowper's 'On the loss of the Royal George', Martha urged the purchase of 'true infantine little books', which contained stories that both amused and instructed their readers with their easy language and capture of the imagination.[90] Martha considered herself especially skilled in choosing books that children would find both delightful and educational. One book she noted was popular among children, and which she wanted William to purchase, began with the words: 'There was a little boy, a <u>very</u> little boy, for if he had been a big boy, etc, etc.'[91] This was in fact a line from Mrs Barbauld's *Lessons for children of three years old. Part I* (published in Dublin in 1779), which was notable for its lively and engaging stories.[92] Another favourite of Martha's was *The renowned history of Giles Gingerbread; a little boy who lived upon learning*, which was sold in Dublin at the time for just two pence, the protagonist of which also learned to read and spell his letters during the story.[93]

From around the age of four years old, parents began to place their children into more formal schooling. Before the introduction of the National Schools System (1831) there were two main options available to parents for the education of their children: attendance at a hedge school or at a Sunday School. For a small fee, hedge schools taught both female and male pupils basic reading and writing skills. John Tennent recalled in his diary having attended two schools alongside his elder sister Margaret during their early childhood. The first of these was in Billy, County Antrim, with a Mr McKewn, where they learned the 'rudiments of reading and writing', and the second in Ballyrobin, with a Mr Richard, where he enjoyed his lessons so much that he was 'happier than a King'.[94] These schools were managed both by lay persons and members of the main religious traditions operating in Ulster at the time. The Reverend James Morgan received his 'elementary education' to the age of fifteen years old under the tutelage of Arthur Devlin, a Roman Catholic, at a village school in Cloghog, County Antrim, and then at a school in Cookstown managed first by a Mr Magouran, also a Roman Catholic, and then by the Reverend Thomas Millar, a Presbyterian minister.[95]

The appearance of Sunday Schools in Ulster, from the latter end of the eighteenth century, has been noted by historians as one of the most significant developments in the provision of education.[96] According to J.R.R. Adams, one of the first Sunday Schools established in Ulster was in the parish of Kilmore, County Down, around

1780.[97] Originally intended as free schools for the labouring poor, Sunday Schools effectively filled the educational void in many communities, providing schooling for the majority of children in the local parish.[98] A Sunday School affiliated with the Presbyterian congregation of Third Cookstown had a total of 431 pupils on its books between May and October 1837. The school was attended by both girls and boys, and the attendance register suggests that most were around eleven years of age.[99] Similarly, the Sunday School attached to the Presbyterian congregation of Loughbrickland was opened to children of the local parish every summer from 1842. At the close of summer 1845, the school had a total of 419 pupils on its books, with an average Sabbath attendance of 313 pupils per week. Like Third Cookstown Sunday School, most of the pupils at Loughbrickland were aged under fourteen years. For most of these students (almost sixty-six per cent), the education they received at the Sabbath School was the only formal education to which they had access. Only thirty-three per cent of pupils on the roll books of Loughbrickland school also attended a day school during the week.[100]

At both these types of schools, children were taught to recognise and pronounce letters, as well as basic spelling. Whereas the 1845 report for Loughbrickland Sabbath School recorded that 108 of its pupils were learning the alphabet and basic spelling, the Cookstown School had a total of 141 pupils registered in classes in which only spelling books were used.[101] Educational guides used for this purpose included those written by the County Antrim school master David Manson, such as his *Spelling Primer*, which was the text used at the village school that taught the Reverend Robert Magill to read and write.[102]

Once pupils had grasped the rudiments of spelling and letters, they progressed to more developed texts for reading and writing. Popular materials included catechisms, short Bible passages and testaments. The *Shorter Catechism* was regarded as especially suitable for young children. The Scottish minister John Willison advocated its use because its short question-and-answer format made it an accessible text for 'young Persons of good Memories ... And for those whose Memories are weaker'.[103] The Reverend Robert Magill also recorded in his diaries the achievements of children in the parish who had learned to read and recite long passages of text from the Bible, as well as from catechisms. In January 1821 Robert noted that 79 children had repeated the whole of the *Shorter Catechism* in the meeting house, while a further 77 could repeat the greater part of it.[104] An additional comment noted that these children were to meet again in May, when a guinea was to be shared among those who could repeat the first twenty psalms.[105]

Girls and boys received a similar standard of early education; reading and writing were regarded as important skills irrespective of gender. It was not until children progressed to more formal education, from around seven years old, that their instruction began to differ. As Toby Barnard has noted, ideas of what 'constituted a fitting education' for children varied according to their social status, finances, gender and intentions for adulthood.[106] Destined as they were for 'domestic and informal roles', girls' education could be 'learned within the family, home or neighbourhood'.[107] John Tennent attended school alongside his sister Margaret until he enrolled at that managed by a Mr McMullan at Roseyards, where he was taught the classics such as Ovid.[108] From this point, John attended school with his elder brother Robert, enrolling at another school with a Mr Ford soon after.[109] No further mention is made of Margaret's education after this point, which may suggest that her schooling was completed. Similar evidence exists for other families. Jane Kennedy, daughter of the Reverend William Kennedy, minister of Carland congregation in County Tyrone, does not appear to have received any education beyond basic reading and writing. In March 1788 her brother Robert expressed his reservations about plans for Jane to accompany their father to visit family in Scotland. The reason for Robert's apprehension was that 'Poor Jane' had been 'deprived of a boarding school education' and he feared that their cousin Sarah would be 'considered as superior' by the wider family.[110]

Grief and loss

For some women and men in eighteenth- and nineteenth-century Ulster, the joys of parenthood were tragically cut short. Rates of child mortality were much higher in this period in comparison with today. Diseases such as measles, worms and croup, as well as a greater susceptibility to epidemics, made early childhood a precarious life stage.[111] While there are issues in estimating mortality rates from the surviving sources, historians, such as Valerie Morgan and William Macafee, have suggested that death rates among children could be relatively high. In early-eighteenth-century Magherafelt, County Londonderry, large numbers of children died before the age of three years, a pattern that was likely the result of epidemic disease.[112] Cholera, which swept Ireland in the early 1830s, had a devastating impact and took the lives of many children. Chronicling this in his diary, the Reverend Robert Magill recorded the death of Henry Gordon, a boy aged two and a half, who had been 'seized' by the disease and died in September 1832.[113] About ten days later, Robert attended a meeting held by the board of health in the market house. At that meeting he heard that ten others had recently died of cholera, four of whom were also children.[114]

Faced with the tragedy of child death, many parents turned to their faith for support. The strong belief held by parents such as the Crawfords in the role of providence enabled them to resign themselves to the deaths as well as the births of their children. Before he was installed as minister of Randalstown congregation, Alexander Crawford had spent time in India as a missionary. In April 1829, together with a pregnant Anna and their three children, he boarded a ship in India and sailed for England.[115] While on board Anna went into labour and Alexander was tasked with delivering the child.[116] In a letter to her father about the birth, Anna thanked God for giving her husband the strength to assist her. His ability to cope was attributed by Anna to the 'Lord [who] has been wonderfully present with his gracious assistance'.[117] A few lines after giving thanks for God's intercession, Anna began to recount to her father the illness with which the infant became afflicted shortly after birth, noting how the baby 'suffered greatly ... with strong convulsions ... till she breathed her last' within just twenty-four hours of life.[118] Anna drew on her faith to cope with the death of her newborn baby:

> This dispensation though peculiarly touching to us, has I trust been greatly blessed to our souls. We were enabled before her death to resign her freely unto the hands of our gracious Saviour to do with her as he saw meet (and since her death we have been greatly comforted by the consolation of the gospel).[119]

While they grieved the loss of their young daughter, the Crawfords found consolation in their belief that the child was safe in the hands of God.

The Reverend James Morell, minister of Ballybay congregation in County Monaghan, was also touched by the pain of child death when his infant daughter died in July 1815. After returning from the meeting house one Sunday, James found his daughter gravely ill. She continued to get worse and eventually died on his knee the next afternoon.[120] James recorded an emotive account of his daughter's final moments in his diary:

> Having commended her soul to God by the most fervent prayers I was capable of ... She breathed her last without any appearance of Pain, with a serene and heavenly smile on her countenance, leaving a confident impression on my mind, that she had tasted of the joy of Heaven, even before her little heart had ceased to beat upon Earth. May my latter end be as peaceful and as serene as hers.[121]

James's description reveals the tensions that parents felt between resigning their feelings to the will of God and expressing their grief after the death of a child. On the one hand, his comment that the prayers he used were those he was 'capable of' is telling of the heartache he felt in that moment. On the other hand, the description of his daughter's death as peaceful, and even beautiful, had much in common with contemporary notions of how to die 'well'.[122] Like the Crawfords, James believed that the death of his daughter had been an act of providence, designed to make him walk more closely with God. This thought continued to console him on the one-year anniversary of his daughter's death. Writing in his diary in July 1816, James noted that his daughter was 'still fresh' in his 'heart & memory'. He hoped that the trials he had received from God were 'enough' to bring him close to God and that 'other trials' would be therefore 'unnecessary'.[123]

The pain of losing a child also had an impact on the marriage of grieving parents. For some, like James Morell and his wife, Letitia, the death of their daughter was a source of tension. Five days after burying his daughter, 'in a retired little spot in the north east side of the burying ground', James noted in his diary that he had 'Spent the evening in labor melancholy at home'.[124] The source of this melancholic mood was Letitia, who felt 'most severely the Loss of her Infant'.[125] In an effort to help Letitia realise the 'great blessing' the event would bring to her soul, James resolved to have family worship every day rather than only on the Sabbath, an activity he noted pleasingly that his wife had participated in.[126] James's comments on their first joint visit to the grave also reveal how each partner had reacted differently to the death: 'We visited this day the grave of our Dear Child, it had been the first time for my Poor wife, and she bore it badly'.[127] While this was not James's first visit to their daughter's grave, it appears that it was for Letitia. Grief then, as today, was experienced differently by individuals.

The Drennan family

William Drennan and Sarah Swanwick went on to have seven more children, four of whom survived to adulthood. Tragically, three of their children died in infancy: Mary Anne (born and died in 1803); John (born in 1804 and died in 1805); and an unnamed boy (born and died in 1808). Their beloved first-born son, Tom, who gave them such joy when he was born in March 1801, died in 1812, much to the grief of the whole family.[128] The Drennans kept a lock of Tom's hair as a memento of the boy they loved. It was enclosed in a 'rectangular crystal locket' that was made to be worn on a fob or watch chain, likely one owned by his father.[129] Engraved on the gold frame was the inscription: 'T.D. Oh my boy forever dear, forever kind, Once tender friend of my distracted mind, Where he is may I be also'.[130] Parents in eighteenth- and nineteenth-century Ulster loved their children. Those who were fortunate enough had the joy of watching them grow from infants to children, then into young adults. Growing up was a precarious life stage; becoming an adult was the next hurdle.

CHAPTER THREE

'I am 16 years of age & I perceive myself growing now wiser & better': Growing up

On 11 October 1788 John Tennent celebrated his sixteenth birthday. He marked the occasion a few weeks later in his diary, noting how he 'perceive[d]' himself 'growing now wiser & better' than he had ever 'been for this long time'.[1] At the time of writing, John was halfway through a four-year apprenticeship with a grocer's merchant named Samuel Givin in Coleraine, County Londonderry.[2] In July 1786, aged just thirteen years, John left his family and began his journey towards adulthood.[3] With each passing year, John reflected in his diary on the ways he had changed since his move to Coleraine, as he made the transition from boy to man. Reflecting contemporary ideas about the differences between childhood and adulthood, John measured his progress towards manhood by his ability to control his passions and desires. In January 1789 he mused once again on his transition to manhood, noting how 'at 12 years of age' he 'knew very little', but now 'at 17', he knew 'rather more' and was 'emerging into [a] man'.[4] As he aged, John outgrew his love of 'childish' and 'idle' pursuits. In April 1790 as he inched towards his eighteenth birthday, John decided against joining the other apprentices who flocked to the 'bowling green' during 'Easter Week'.[5] Whereas he had indulged in Easter 'amusements' many times before, John now mused how 'more sober sentiments [had] taken place of those giddy vain & foolish thou[gh]ts' that had once 'possessed' him.[6] His reading habits, too, underwent changes. John commented in his diary on his dislike of 'Novels & romances', noting how they were the 'worst & dangeroust of books to read in the world' because they 'fill[ed] a persons mind so full of vain imaginations' and 'render[ed] them incable of any rational amusements or any real learning'.[7]

As he entered the final year of his apprenticeship, John took stock of the time he had left. In a diary entry dated 31 December 1799, he reflected on the 'wonderful change' that he had 'undergone' since he started his apprenticeship. Now aged seventeen, he 'scarce' knew himself 'to have been the same person, so altered' that he was 'in stature, knowledge & ideas!'[8] Although he was keen to finish his apprenticeship and 'launch out into the world', John was anxious about what the next phase of his life would entail.[9] He noted how he hoped he was 'duly prepared' for what was to come.[10] It was 'incumbent on every young person', he reflected, 'to follow faithfully, the advice & counsel of their friends'. Youth was an important time; it was during this 'period of a persons life' that they laid the groundwork for either 'their future happiness or misery'.[11]

The follies and jollies of youth

As the period of life between childhood and adulthood, youth was understood to denote the years between the early teens and mid-twenties.[12] In the eighteenth and nineteenth century, concerns were raised about the (perceived) unruliness of the younger generation. While such anxieties were by no means new, they were increasingly expressed in printed form in a genre of writing known as advice literature. Writers in both Britain and Ireland devoted much space to worrying about the waywardness of young people. Describing youth as a 'dark' and 'dangerous' time of life, moralists wrote alarmingly about the grave consequences of unrestrained youthful misbehaviour.

Some immoral behaviours were tarred specifically as youthful sins. Samuel Pomfret, an English Presbyterian minister, remarked in his *Directory for youth* (1722) that 'Youth', like other 'Division[s]' of life was marked by 'peculiar, and predominant Lusts' that 'hang about, that haunt, and dog that season of Life'.[13] The list of youthful sins was long. Pomfret identified twenty that were bespoke to the young, including the pursuit of 'sensual pleasures'; a hatred of 'Instructions, Admonitions and Reproof'; the 'Keeping of ill Company'; 'Lying and inventing Excuses'; taking 'Pride' in their 'Parts' and appearance; 'Time-wasting'; and 'Uncleanness'.[14] Other writers emphasised the vulnerability of young people, especially those who had left the safety of their family home for the first time. Elizabeth Bonhote's *The parental monitor* (1788) stressed that leaving home was a special 'moment of danger' for young men.[15] Once they left the 'fond and watchful care of attentive friends', young men could expect to be 'assail[ed]' with 'Various temptations' that would cause them future 'misery and anguish'.[16] Bonhote advised that young men 'should walk with the most cautious and guarded circumspection, and like a child which has just left off the leading-string, proceed slowly forwards' as they began their journey to adulthood.[17]

For all its negative traits, however, youth was also recognised as having some positive characteristics. While many writers poured scorn on youth as a 'dark age', they also acknowledged that it was a time of opportunity. Despite their natural faults, young people were ripe with possibility: they could, with the right instruction, be taught the ways of piety and be put on the path to a virtuous life. It was for precisely that reason that Presbyterian writers, such as John Willison, directed their texts at younger people. According to Willison, 'the Time of youth' was 'the best Season' for 'laying the foundations of Christian knowledge' and becoming acquainted with the Lord. In comparison with the later stages of life, youth was when the 'heart [was] more tender and tractable' and would 'sooner Kindle into a Flame of Love to Christ' than it would ever 'do afterwards'.[18] Recognising the potential of youth, many other contemporary writers published advice tracts, instruction manuals, poems and anthologies of fables aimed at guiding their young readers on the path to adulthood.[19]

Lusty appetites

Reflecting the broader attempts that were made to guide and control young people, the Presbyterian church courts diverted much of their attention towards curtailing the lusty appetites of their younger members. Kirk Sessions actively monitored the time that young people spent alone and were quick to act when rumours were spread about alleged immodest behaviour. In May 1785 Thomas Black was cited before Cahans Kirk Session in County Monaghan after a 'report' was spread that 'he had gone in an untimous hour of the night to the house of W[illia]m Henderson in order ... to have some conversation' with a girl called Mary Deal.[20] The Session 'called in' Mary and asked her 'how often' she and Thomas 'had such private meetings'.[21] Suspicious that the pair might have been sexually intimate together, the Session questioned Mary about what she and Thomas did during their secret rendezvous, and if he had ever promised marriage. Mary answered that nothing untoward had happened, remarking that she and Thomas had met up 'just twice' and 'that there was no criminal correspondence, nor oath, nor promise' ever made between them.[22] The Session conceded that there was no evidence of 'guilt' (sexual activity). Thomas, however, was not off the hook. The Session decided that he should still be punished for going to see Mary at 'unseasonable times, & especially upon a Sabbath morning'.[23] He was rebuked for his offence and details of the case were announced to the community, in order 'to remove the scandal' caused.[24]

Kirk Sessions also attempted to curtail the lusty impulses of the young by controlling their social spaces. Beds were singled out as sites of potential danger. Like their Scottish counterparts,

Presbyterians in Ireland associated beds with the rituals of courtship and marriage.[25] Proposals of marriage often took place in, on and around the space of the bed.[26] Both the church courts and the wider community actively policed the uses of beds by unmarried women and men. In June 1700 Robert Currie and Jane Heron were called before Carnmoney Kirk Session for their 'very immodest carriage' after they were spied lying in bed together.[27] While both denied that they had committed 'any act of uncleanness', the Session decided that they were both censurable for putting themselves in the way of temptation. Whereas Jane was exhorted 'to study more tenderness in her way', Robert was directed 'to avoid everything w[hi]c[h] may tend to uncleanness'.[28] The bedsharing of three young people in Templepatrick likewise caused much controversy. In June 1701 John Robison, Ann McCanles and Martha Thomson appeared before Templepatrick Session 'confes[s]ing unhandsome carriage' after it was reported they had shared a bed. John denied that he had any 'unhandsome dealing towards any of them' and claimed to have been 'asleep when they came to bed', a point that Martha 'contradict[ed]'.[29] Unsure how to proceed, the Session referred the case to the Presbytery. It was decided to give the trio an opportunity to 'purge themselves by their voluntary oath' that no sexual activity had taken place.[30]

Although the church discouraged unmarried women and men from sharing beds, family members and friends sometimes facilitated the practice and acted as chaperones. Presbyterians in Ulster engaged in a courtship practice known as bundling, whereby couples would sleep together, fully clothed, on the same bed or couch. The practice was designed to enable unmarried women and men to gauge their general and sexual compatibility before marriage. The extent to which bundling was practised in Britain is subject to debate. Whereas English historians are divided as to whether the practice existed at all, it is generally accepted that it was widespread among the poorer classes in Wales and Scotland.[31] Bundling has not gained much attention from Irish historians, but references to the practice do survive in Ulster Presbyterian church records.[32]

A case of bundling came to the attention of Carnmoney Kirk Session in December 1704, when reports were spread that Margaret

Cudbert had lain in bed with John Burns. They were discovered by John Henry who, seeing them, fetched his friend Thomas Baxter to come and watch. Thomas told the Session that John 'took him and said [that] he would let him see a man and woman lie together'.[33] Margaret's mother, Widow Cudbert, appeared in her daughter's defence and told the Session that nothing illicit had happened. Not only did both Margaret and John Burns '[have] their cloaths on', but Widow Cudbert 'and her daughter in law were in the rome all the while they were in bed'.[34] If the pair had engaged in sexual activity, Widow Cudbert implied she would have seen it happen. Despite the Session agreeing that there were 'no grounds to prosecute' Margaret (her mother's chaperonage ensuring that the pair remained chaste), they still decided to censure her 'for unseemly carriage'.[35] Margaret was appointed to stand publicly before the congregation the following Sunday.[36]

Unmarried servants who shared rooms were placed under even more scrutiny because their physical proximity increased the potential for sexual activity to take place.[37] Certainly, some young men took advantage of the opportunities that these shared spaces provided. In August 1758 Cahans Session investigated charges of immoral behaviour that were laid against a servant named Samuel Magill, who was reported to have 'been guilty of some Indecencys' with a fellow servant named Helen Miller.[38] When he appeared before the Session, Samuel admitted that as he was 'coming home from a late wake in the neighbourhood' one morning 'he leaned awhile' on the bed wherein Helen lay asleep.[39] Not content to just sit on Helen's bed, Samuel had taken things a step further and 'laid his hand on her breast above her clothes'.[40]

Living and working in close proximity facilitated consensual sexual activities too. Carnmoney Session was called to investigate the unseemly bedsharing of two unmarried servants in September 1711. George Russell reported to the Session that he had found his servant maid, Eupham Thompson, 'lying naked in bed' with William McCraken, his sixteen-year-old servant.[41] According to George, the pair were lying together in an 'indecent posture', with Eupham's 'arm under William's head'.[42] The intimate and sexually charged potential of the scene was not lost on George, who railed to the Session that 'he knows not what wickedness might have been committed by them'.[43] When Eupham and William appeared before the Session they admitted 'that they were in naked bed together', but denied 'that they were guilty of the act of uncleanness'.[44] Eupham asserted that 'there was no wickedness committed by them' and told the Session that they 'had no ill in mind but did it very innocently'.[45] The Session did not agree. Recognising the sexual dangers of the bed, the Session decided that she should be 'rebukt for her imodesty in lying down in bed with a man' and 'thereby casting herself in the way of a temptation'.[46]

The ribald talk of the young, especially young men, was also subject to church censure.[47] In May 1710 James Strabridge complained to Burt Kirk Session in County Donegal that James McConnal had been telling people that 'he had his will of his daughter Janet in Robert Wallaces Bank' (bank being a Scots word for a hill or boundary-line of a farm).[48] A witness named Paul Barry told the Session that James McConnal had told him that he 'tooke' Janet on his horse to 'Robert Wallaces Bank', where 'he laid her behind a bush & kissed her & afterward sinned carnaly' with her.[49] Janet denied the story and told the Session that everything that James said 'was lies'.[50] It is possible that James had boasted of his sexual exploits for ill purposes. Samuel Work told the Session that James had 'said to him' that 'he could & would keep Janet Strabridge unmarried as long as he was unmarried'.[51] James McConnal's talk, it was suggested, was designed to put other men off from proposing marriage to Janet.

James McConnal offered a different version of events. While he denied that he had told Paul any sexual details, James said that he and Janet had been alone together 'in Robert Wallaces bank' until the middle of the night.[52] James also claimed that the pair were courting, and that he even had Janet's 'hand & promise' of marriage'.[53] In the end, the Session ruled in James Strabridge's favour. They directed that James McConnal should 'acknowledge' his fault in 'wronging Janet Strabridge'.[54] James, however, stuck to his original story and refused to obey the Session's ruling. In July 1710 he caused a scene in church when the minister publicly declared to the congregation that the 'scandalous report' circulating about

Janet had been 'proven false'. James 'stood up' and 'contradicted' the minister, and shouted 'that he could not make a black web white' and 'that there was no witnesses' to his fumble with Janet 'but the horse they rod on'.[55] It would be another two years before James finally acknowledged that he had wronged Janet 'in saying he had his will of her'.[56]

Masturbation

Groups of young men also fell afoul of the church courts when gossip about their sexual experimentation became widespread. Masturbation emerged as a pressing concern among moralists from the middle of the seventeenth century, reaching its height in the century thereafter.[57] The dangers of masturbation were introduced to London audiences in the popular anonymous pamphlet *Onania, or the Heinous Sin of Self-Pollution* (1716), which went through fifteen editions by 1730.[58] While it is not clear if *Onania* was published in Ireland, Irish readers could certainly have got their hands on eighteenth-century Europe's best-selling work on masturbation: Samuel Auguste Tissot's *L'Onanism; ou, Dissertation physique sur les malades produites par la masturbation* (1760), translated as *Onanism; or, a treatise upon the disorders produced by masturbation*. The Swiss physician's pamphlet was 'an instant literary sensation' and 'scores' of editions were printed across Europe, including in Dublin.[59]

Condemned as the sin of 'self-pollution', masturbation was associated with both moral decay and bodily decline.[60] The excessive emission of body fluids (like semen) was believed to bring about the loss of physical strength in young men, and manifested itself in a 'pale, unhealthy complexion with sunken eyes'.[61] Tissot relayed to his readers the cautionary tale of a young man, 'not yet' sixteen years of age, who had 'devoted himself with such fury to masturbation' that 'instead of sperm, he brought forth nothing but blood'.[62] Despite his efforts to treat the young man's inflammation, the boy 'died soon after' from smallpox; a condition that Tissot attributed to 'the shocks' the boy 'gave to his constitution' through excessive masturbation.[63] Such concerns were not just restricted to young men. Young women who masturbated were thought to expose themselves to a range of bodily conditions, including 'hysterical fits', 'incurable jaundices', 'acute pains in the nose', 'violent cramps' and '*fluor albus*' – a term used to describe vaginal discharge.[64] Masturbation impacted their beauty too; the skin would become 'rough', 'the eyes lose their brilliance, and deaden', their 'lips would lose their vermilion hue', and their teeth would lose 'their whiteness'.[65] Writers singled out masturbation as a sin that was especially prevalent among young men, however, and anxieties about its moral and bodily effects were especially heightened in the case of young men on the cusp of adulthood. According to the *Onania*, the 'Practice' was 'not among any so general as it [was] among young Lads and School-Boys'.[66] Given that 'Sexual self-control' was a sign of adulthood and independence, young men who indulged in masturbation not only polluted their bodies but also demonstrated their failure to achieve manly standards.[67]

Masturbation was rarely discussed by Kirk Sessions in Ulster. Of the Kirk Session minute books surveyed for this book, there was just one case in which masturbation was mentioned. In June 1712 Burt Kirk Session in County Donegal met to consider a salacious report that was circulating about Richard Berry. A rumour was spread that Richard had masturbated publicly in a field and was encouraging other young men to partake in the practice.[68] The source of the report was Adam Porter, who presented the church court with five charges detailed in a written 'libel'. The document contained three charges of masturbation, as well two allegations of drunkenness and boisterous behaviour.[69] According to Adam, he and two of his brothers were approached by Richard when they were standing together in their 'sally garden'. Richard asked the three young men if they 'had got mistresses' and then told the group that he was not in 'need' of one himself because 'he had milked himself over the bed-stock by taking his yeard in his hand or between his fingers & thumb'.[70] Richard Porter, Adam's brother, told the Session that Richard Berry 'had told him he eased himself of his seed when he pleased' and that the practice was not sinful, but was sanctioned by scripture.[71] Richard was accused of demonstrating his masturbation techniques too. Adam told the Session how Richard had explained 'what he could do' (masturbate) and then turned away from him. Adam said he perceived Richard 'at some action with his body' and then 'soon after' he turned back to face him and 'shewed [him] the seed' that had 'come from him'.[72]

It was Hugh Berry, Richard's father, who urged the Session to get to the bottom of the 'shameful sinfull & scandalous' report.[73] His concerns were understandable; the accusations made against Richard identified him as the instigator of moral pollution. Moral pamphlets, like *Onania,* printed 'letters' from their readers wherein they recounted their descent into moral and bodily decline. Most recalled having been introduced to masturbation by a male friend. One letter writer told how he and his friends had been introduced to masturbation when they were not yet fifteen years old by an older companion 'who was about 20 Years of Age'.[74] Their story had much in common with that told by Adam Porter. According to the anonymous writer, the older boy asked him and his friends 'Whether ever [they] saw the Seed of a Man?'[75] When they said no, the older boy showed them by masturbating and then ejaculating onto the 'Leaf of a Cabbage'.[76] The letter writer said that this encounter 'stir'd' their 'Inclination', which prompted them to develop a habit of excessive masturbation that lasted about two and a half years.[77]

Other letter writers emphasised how their introduction to masturbation had ruined their lives and halted their achievement of manhood. One anonymous writer explained that they had 'been born of pious Parents, and religiously Educated' but were introduced to the 'vicious practice of Self-Pollution' by 'evil Companions' when they were 'between 15 and 16 Years of Age'.[78] From that point, masturbation became a daily occurrence; indeed, on one occasion, the letter writer noted that they had masturbated 'more than eight times' within the space of one hour.[79] As a result of excessive masturbation, the letter writer developed 'gleets' (a gonorrhoeal infection), which left them unable to marry.[80] While masturbation was considered a moral failing, being the person who introduced others to the practice was regarded as perhaps more sinful still.

Richard Berry denied all the charges made against him. After hearing the evidence, the Session decided that he 'was reproveable' for 'his rash expressions'.[81] Richard was not happy with the Session's decision; before storming out, he told the Session that he hoped that God would 'judge' them as they had him.[82] After some initial resistance, however, Richard did eventually engage with church discipline. In October 1712 Richard told the Session that 'tho he knew his own innocency' of the 'things ... proved against him' he was 'sorry for his rash expressions'.[83]

Apprenticeship

Attempts were also made to control the waywardness of some young people through the apprenticeship system. Apprenticeships were a form of bonded labour that provided for the instruction of young people in crafts and trades in exchange for a fee. Young people who entered service tended to do so between the ages of twelve and seventeen and, once bound, could expect to spend between five and twelve years of their lives in the service of their master.[84] Given the length of these arrangements and the age at which most contracts began, many young people could expect to spend the better part of their formative years – the period of their adolescence – as an apprentice.

Apprenticeship was not, however, an option that was available to every young person in eighteenth- and nineteenth-century Ulster. Unlike England, which had a well-established system of apprenticeship that catered for boys and girls across the social spectrum, in Ulster apprenticeship was largely restricted to young people who lived in towns and, more particularly, to young men who were drawn from the better-off sections of society.[85] Ulster's economy in this period was very different to that of England. In comparison to the rapid urban expansion and large-scale industrialisation taking place in England, which transformed small, rural villages into large, enterprising towns, Ulster's economic development was patchy and uneven, with most activity centred in Belfast.[86] As discussed in the Introduction, young women and men in rural Ulster were employed instead as farm servants, agricultural labourers, or in the domestic linen industry, which was the mainstay of Ulster's rural economy until the late eighteenth century. William Hincks's late-eighteenth-century engravings depicting the manufacture of linen portray women and men working alongside one another.[87] Opportunities for apprenticeship in Ulster were therefore limited, and where they were available – in commercial trades like as those operated by merchants, grocers and shopkeepers – such places were often affordable only to those of the more affluent ranks of society.

Apprenticeship was a route seldom taken by girls from middling-order families. Young women from this section of society were kept at home with their parents until they were ready to marry, and they worked as companions, housekeepers and nursemaids within their natal families.[88] The same was true for girls whose families were of more humble stock. When Margaret (Peggy) Tennent, the youngest daughter of the Reverend John and Ann Tennent, married without her parents' consent, the loss of her housekeeping services and labour drew comment from her brother Robert. Writing to his parents in June 1801, Robert noted how his, 'mother's situation particularly' would be 'affected by an event that goes to deprive her of a companion & of that domestic assistance which I don't know how she can ... do without'.[89] Two weeks later Robert again took up his pen and asked his parents how they were 'reconciled with Peggy's absence' now that 'she must ... live in the house of her husband'.[90]

Although she came from a ministerial family, Peggy Tennent's parents were by no means wealthy. As Jonathan Jeffrey Wright has noted, the Reverend John was a 'man of modest means' and his 'resources stretched to the provision of education and apprenticeships for his sons'.[91] The labour of the Tennent girls was reserved for the good of the family. Of the duties that Peggy carried out for her parents, it was most likely the loss of her assistance during harvest season that affected them most. Letters exchanged between the Reverend Tennent and his sons contain numerous requests for Peggy to return home in time for harvest. In September 1791 the Reverend Tennent required Peggy to return home within three weeks because the harvest was approaching and her help was 'of necessity', adding that he 'would rather need a Shearer more than lose one to Supply her place'.[92] Like many daughters who belonged to middling-order families, Peggy also performed household tasks for her brothers in Belfast while she remained unmarried.[93] The

Tennent letters make frequent reference to the wide range of duties that Peggy carried out for her siblings, from caring for her sister Nancy and brother William when they were ill, to mending and making shirts for her other brothers John and Samuel.[94]

Young men from the middle to upper sections of society tended to be apprenticed into 'respectable' and professional trades, and were trained as apothecaries, physicians or grocers. Not only did these trades demand that apprentices possess more than a basic education, they were also substantially more expensive than hands-on trades, such as blacksmiths or weavers. The more skilled the trade and the longer the training period, the more expensive was the apprenticeship fee. The amounts due for 'respectable' trades could range from a few pounds to several hundred.[95] The Reverend John Tennent, for example, agreed to pay his son's master, Samuel Givin, a premium of fifty pounds, as well as an additional sum of six shillings so that he could attend school.[96] Givin's next apprentice, a boy called Hamilton, paid a smaller fee of twenty pounds.[97] Less common were the fortunes of apprentices like John Caldwell, whose master refused to accept any apprentice fee and offered free board and lodging.[98] The fact that the costs of apprenticeship would have eaten quite heavily into the annual incomes of even members of the middling sort, meant that it was often a route unavailable to persons of the lower orders, who could not afford to pay such fees and costs.[99]

The opportunities open to young people from the poorer ends of society, then, were different. Poorer children who lived in towns, like Belfast, could gain admission to apprenticeship with the assistance of charitable schools or benevolent societies. One such institution was the Belfast Charitable Society (founded 1752). In 1774 the Society opened a Poor House and Hospital and shortly thereafter began admitting children between the ages of seven and twelve. These children were provided with a basic education and then put out as apprentices.[100] The Society sourced apprenticeships for the young people under its charge by posting advertisements in the *Belfast Newsletter*. Typical of most of these adverts was that placed by the Society on 14 November 1817:

> To be Apprenticed out of the Poor House, Several Young Girls, who are well calculated to be Children's Maids, in Gentlemen's Families, being well behaved and taught to read and write. Also, a number of Boys, fit to be taught Trades and to act as Servants. Apply to the Committee at one o'clock on Saturdays.[101]

Those interested in taking on an apprentice were instructed to apply directly to the Charitable Society's School Committee, which met on a weekly basis. The Charitable Society covered the costs of apprenticeship for poor children. When they completed their term, the fee was to be paid back in either cash or kind by the master. On 7 November 1813 Mrs Esther Thomson of North Street, Belfast, applied to the Society to have a girl named Catharine Kane apprenticed to her as a servant. The Society agreed, and bound Catharine for a period of five years. In exchange for Catharine's labour, Esther was to pay the School Committee a sum of three guineas at the expiration of the term.[102] Likewise, Edward Moany of Derriaghy in County Antrim successfully applied to the Society in March 1818 to have James Cahoon as an apprentice muslin-weaver for a period of five years and a fee of three guineas.[103] The Belfast Charitable Society was relatively successful in its efforts of matching young people with potential masters. Published reports reveal that between 1827 and 1843, the Society housed over 3,500 children. Of the 883 children who left the Poor House during these same years, approximately forty-one per cent were put out as apprentices.[104]

Similar institutions operated outside of Belfast.[105] The Vaughan Charity School provided education and training for children in Tubrid, County Fermanagh. Founded in 1780 by George Vaughan, a local wealthy landowner, the school was funded by rent payments from the tenanted land of his estate. Vaughan had originally intended for the school to provide education for approximately 300 poor boys and 200 poor girls, from both Catholic and Protestant families. By the time the school opened in 1787, however, there were not enough funds available to meet these aims and it operated on a more modest scale.[106] Between 1788 and 1800, a total of 119 boys were admitted to the school, of whom the overwhelming majority were Protestant, native to County Fermanagh, and aged between eight and twelve years old. Girls were admitted into the school from 1828.[107] The Southwell Charity school, established in Downpatrick, County Down, in 1733, was governed by a similar set of rules. Like the Belfast Charitable Society, the Southwell School aimed to provide boys and girls with a basic education, so that they were adequately prepared for entrance into apprenticeship. At the time of their entry, pupils were to be between eight and twelve years of age, they were to be the children of parents who either lived in the town of Downpatrick or within the Manor of Downe, and their parents were to be 'of the poorest people' and of 'honest report'.[108]

Young people in these institutions began to be 'put out' as apprentices and servants once they reached adolescence. The Belfast Charitable Society deliberately delayed putting out children as apprentices until they had come of age. According to the 1833 report of its governing committee, children were considered to be neither emotionally nor intellectually mature enough to cope with the demands of apprenticeship before the age of twelve:

> [we have] found from experience that the *best period of life* to sanction [children] being apprenticed, is from the age of twelve to fourteen; for to send them into the world at an earlier age, would be dismissing them from their guardianship *imperfectly educated*, and before they had attained sufficient strength of *body*, and *soundness of judgment & intellect*, to enable them to conduct themselves with prudence & discretion in the *different stages of life* assigned to them.[109]

Lauren Smyth has found that the average age at which children were apprenticed out of the Belfast Charitable Society was thirteen.[110] Once bound, these poor apprentices could expect to spend anything between two and seven years in service.

The types of trades that poorer apprentices entered tended to be manual in nature and labour-intensive. There were, however, gender distinctions in the trades offered. Boys not only entered a wider range of trades than did girls, but their professions of choice also required the learning of specialised skills. Whereas boys in the Vaughan Charity School were put out as gunsmiths, bookbinders, shoemakers and coopers, girls were apprenticed out into 'domestic trades' and became either kitchen-maids, housemaids or servants or performed needlework.[111] This pattern was repeated in the Southwell School. Whereas nineteen different trades were listed for boys enrolled in that school, girls were put out as either bonnet-makers, dressmakers, washerwomen or milliners.[112] In common with their wealthier counterparts, there was also a preference among lower-ranking families to keep girls at home for their labour. Girls enrolled in the Vaughan Charity School were frequently removed from training by their families and friends. In 1844, twenty-year-old Sidney Johnson was removed from the school to care for her grandmother; in 1845, eleven-year-old Elicia Graham went home at 'her mother's request'; Anne Burnett, who entered the school in 1834, was removed by her brother; and in September 1847, sixteen-year-old Susan Benstead was taken by her uncle from the house she had been apprenticed to.[113] The labour performed by these young women was likely too valuable for their families to do without. Girls performed a variety of tasks in rural households, from assisting with childcare, cooking and cleaning, to farm duties. The domestic labour of girls was vital to the success of many Ulster households.

Controlling youthful misbehaviour

Apprenticeship, however, was about more than learning a trade; it was also designed to teach the young how to be adults. When they bound themselves in service, young people signed an apprenticeship agreement. While these contracts contained economic terms, such as fees and costs of boarding, they also set the parameters of the master–apprentice relationship.[114] Masters were ideally to act as surrogate parents to young adolescents under their charge, training them not only to be competent in a craft, but to be respectable members of society.[115] In 1723 the writer Matthew Dutton advised his readers that apprentices should be considered as 'part' of their master's 'family'.[116] Contemporary advice guides warned parents to be judicious in their choice of master. According to *The Apprentices' Companion* (1681), parents should take care to bind their children to a master who 'by his Godly and Prudent Government of his Family' could 'restrain the too forward desires of Youth'.[117] Masters were also to lead by example: those who were 'Pious' would 'encourage … vertuous Inclinations' in their charges.[118] Many parents took this advice to heart. The Reverend David Young, minister of Londonderry Presbyterian congregation, wrote to his son's master and entreated him to 'supply the place of a Parent' and offer moral guidance.[119]

Taking on an apprentice was a risk, and the terms of the contract worked to protect masters from any bad behaviour on the part of their young apprentices. The agreement between Andrew McLaughlin, a bricklayer from County Londonderry, and his apprentice Michael Crossin, serves as a good example. On 26 July 1822 Michael bound himself to Andrew for a term of seven years.[120] While engaged in Andrew's service, Michael promised to 'faithfully serve' his master and obey 'his lawful commands'. Further clauses legally bound Michael to protect his master's business interests. In addition to promising to 'do no damage … to his said Master nor see it done by others', Michael was to never 'waste' his master's goods, 'nor lend them, unlawfully, to any'. He was further prohibited from gambling any of his master's goods or doing anything that caused his master any 'loss'.[121]

The apprenticeship contract set limits on the young person's sexual and social behaviour too. Much emphasis was placed on controlling the lusty energy of apprentices. Like other apprentices in Ulster at this time, Michael Crossin was forbidden from playing 'cards, dice, tables, or any unlawful games'. He was also banned from visiting 'taverns, alehouses, and playhouses'. Sexual activity was also expressly prohibited. When he signed the apprenticeship agreement, Michael promised to never 'commit fornication, nor contract Matrimony' during the period of his apprenticeship.[122] That such prohibitions were explicitly written into the contracts is telling of how society at the time regarded youth. Young people were thought to be especially prone to immoral activities. Apprenticeship contracts were designed to control the 'natural' impulses of young people and ensure that they acted appropriately.

Disputes and abuses

Although their relationships were structured by legal language, masters and apprentices did sometimes form close partnerships, built on mutual trust, attachment and respect. Some masters left their young apprentices bequests in their wills, and others even married their daughters to young men under their charge.[123] Many other apprentices, however, were not so fortunate. Disputes and abuses were a typical feature of service.[124] Common complaints brought against apprentices included idleness, theft and waywardness, whereas masters were most commonly accused of physical abuse or insufficient instruction.[125] Ann Jane Stuart, who was apprenticed to a Dublin dressmaker named Mrs Bartley, frequently wrote to her father to complain about the cruel treatment she received from her mistress.[126] Ann Jane alleged that Mrs Bartley ridiculed her on a daily basis, failed to instruct her properly, and read all of her private letters before she was allowed to send them.[127] In an effort to release his daughter from service, John Stuart wrote to his brother-in-law William Tennent, who had arranged the apprenticeship, and relayed in detail the 'cruel usage' that Ann Jane was receiving from Bartley, calling her a 'wicked inhuman woman'.[128]

Luckily for Ann Jane, she managed to extricate herself from the arrangement. Just over one year later, she wrote to her Uncle William from Dublin, where she was now working as a dressmaker's apprentice to a Mrs C. Little. Her younger sister, Margaretta Stuart, was also apprenticed to this same woman a few years later. Unfortunately for the Stuart girls, however, this new situation does not seem to have been much of an improvement. Ann Jane alleged that Mrs Little had mismanaged the allowance that she had been provided by her uncle. Ann Jane wrote to William to apologise for her perceived 'extravagance' in running up a large bill and laid the blame with Mrs Little instead.[129] Margaretta also held a bad opinion of Mrs Little, believing her to be untrustworthy. Margaretta declined to enter a business partnership with Mrs Little in December 1830, because she feared her mistress would 'take many advantages' of her inexperience.[130]

Poor apprentices fared no better. A common theme that emerges from the records of Ulster's charitable institutions and schools is that apprenticeship for many young people was far from an enjoyable experience. Many simply ran away; in fact, just over one-fifth of young people enrolled in the Vaughan Charity School were recorded as having 'ran away' or 'eloped' from service.[131] While their reasons for absconding are not recorded, we can assume that many were unhappy with their placement. This was likely the reason why William Elliot, a Catholic boy from County Tyrone who entered the school in June 1800, eloped from service. A note beside his name in the roll-book reveals that William was apprenticed out to a 'Doctor Story' in June 1807 when he was fifteen years of age, but returned to the school because 'he would not stay' with his new master.[132]

The Belfast Charitable Society also experienced problems with absconding inmates. After finding that a group of boys had eloped from the Poor House in January 1812, members of the society were sent to search for them at the local 'naval rendezvous'.[133] There, they found three of the missing boys: John Faulkner aged fifteen, and Bernard Scathern and Alexander Stewart, both aged twelve. The governing committee decided to allow the three boys 'to remain where they were' and, after rounding up the others, gathered them together in the hall of the Charitable Society building.[134] Two of the errant boys, named Murryfield and Douglas, 'who had absconded often', were expelled.[135] A boy called Maguire who had run away on a previous occasion and a girl named Elizabeth Kerr were 'punished by solitary confinement'.[136] The Society kept up its strict policy, and in July 1812 dismissed Alexander Doak for having absconded four times, and also James Branagan, who had run away five times.[137] The Society made sure to expel the pair 'publicly in the presence of the rest of the Boys' in order to 'set an example'.[138]

It was not just institutions and charity schools that had problems with runaways. Masters also dealt with absconding apprentices. The *Belfast Newsletter* regularly carried adverts from masters warning others not to employ their fugitive apprentices. On 18 September 1767 John Willson, a skinner and breeches-maker from Rathfriland in County Down, notified the public that two of his apprentices, 22-year-old John Gribben and 18-year-old John Little, had eloped from his service. In addition to fleeing his master's home, John Little had also allegedly stolen goods from other apprentices, namely a 'Prentice's Hat, Shoes, and Buckles'.[139] Some advertisements carried colourful descriptions of wayward apprentices to facilitate their fast capture. In September 1769 William Wark publicly declared his intention to prosecute anyone who hired Henry Drummond, who had absconded from his service in Ballynure, County Antrim. Henry was described as five-foot-eight, 'long visaged [and] very much freckled' with 'red sandy Hair'. The public was advised that when Henry 'went off', he was wearing a 'blue Coat, Waistcoat, and Breeches, with black Stockings'.[140]

Many of the masters who placed these advertisements alleged that their apprentices had eloped for no good reason. Robert Hardy, a breeches-maker from Loughgall in County Armagh, notified the public that his apprentice, Peter McAnnally, had absconded from service 'without any lawful Reason'. Robert also claimed that the lad had 'received above his full Wages' and had refused to return and serve out his time, despite being ordered to do so by two magistrates.[141] Masters were anxious to quell any suspicions that they had treated their apprentices badly, because of the impact that such gossip could have on their businesses. When James Jordan notified readers of the *Belfast Newsletter* in June 1769 that his apprentice, George Stuart, a 'slender' boy with a 'pale Complexion, and pitted with the Small-pox', had eloped 'without any just Cause', he emphasised that his business was still operating to the same high standards. Tacked on to the end of his public notice was a note to his customers, reassuring them that 'Ladies and Gentlemen who please to employ him, may depend on having their Work done with the greatest care and Punctuality, and on the most reasonable Terms'.[142]

While it is true that apprentices could be badly behaved, masters were not free from blame. Snatched references to the abusive and unkind treatment of apprentices appear in the records of charitable societies and schools. A particularly disturbing case of alleged abuse came before the committee of the Belfast Charitable Society in April 1812, when the body of an apprentice named William Lacey was found with 'marks of violence' and a suspected broken back, in his master's house in Carrickfergus, County Antrim.[143] The finger of suspicion was pointed at Matthew Currie, the boy's master. The Society launched an investigation and interviewed several of Currie's neighbours. William Millar, who lived next door, deposed that while he did not see the boy beaten by Currie, he had 'often times … heard late at night the cries of a boy through the wall'.[144] John Mulholland, another neighbour, told the committee that he did 'not know of any ill usage given by Currie to his apprentices' but added that William Lacey was 'very indolent and not willing to work' and that Currie had applied unsuccessfully to the Poor House to take 'him off his hands'.[145] A coroner's inquest was held into the death. Samuel Stewart, the doctor who examined the body, noted that there was an injury to the side of Lacey's head that appeared to have been produced by the 'blow of a blunt Instrument or from a fall'.[146] When he 'opened the head over the place injured', however, Stewart noticed that the 'skull was not fractured'.[147] He subsequently ruled that William's death had been caused by an 'Intermitting fever' and a 'bowel complaint', determining that the boy 'came by his Death, by the usual visitation of God'.[148]

John Tennent's journey to manhood

In July 1790 John Tennent finally finished his apprenticeship. When his master confirmed that his time was out, John recorded in his diary that he felt giddy with excitement to be free. John wrote how his 'whole frame … convulsed' and he could neither 'hardly walk out of the room' nor 'speak' and 'it was a long time before' he 'subsided into tranquillity'.[149] When he 'became more calm', John 'seriously' reflected 'on the many difficulties & hardships' he had 'undergone' during his 'four long tedious years of bondage'.[150] His mind wandered back to the day that he first left home. John recalled a conversation with his father about the step he was about to take. His father asked him, 'John have you seriously considered what you are going to do? Are you determined, & do you think you can serve a strange man four years?'[151] When he answered yes, he would 'be able to serve it well enough', his father 'recommended' him to the 'care of heaven'.[152] This conversation, John noted, 'made so strong an impression upon' him that it 'never left [his] memory' and 'frequently occurred to [him] during [his] apprenticeship'.[153]

Soon after he left Coleraine, John was offered a position with his eldest brother William in the New Sugar House, Belfast. William sent regular updates on John's progress to their parents, noting on several occasions that he was 'strictly Honest but Slow'.[154] While he was living in Belfast, John became involved with the radical and revolutionary Society of the United Irishmen. In 1797 he left Ireland and travelled to France, where he joined the French army as a volunteer. John proved to be a talented soldier; he served in Holland and France and was even nominated for the Legion of Honour. He died in August 1813, aged forty years, on the battlefield.[155]

CHAPTER FOUR

'I felt as if you had suddenly thrown your arms around my neck and kiss'd me!': Courtship

On 23 August 1793 William Drennan sat down at his desk and penned a love letter. The recipient was Miss Sarah Swanwick, an English governess, whom William had met just weeks earlier at an event held at the Dublin home of Sarah's sister. Despite their brief acquaintance, William was head over heels in love. William confessed in his letter to Sarah that while he had long regarded those who 'declare[d] themselves attached at first sight' as 'madmen or fools', he now found himself 'irresistibly compelled to do' what he had once 'condemn[ed]' and announce his feelings.[1] While he had 'done all in [his] power' to 'arm' his 'head against [his] heart', William declared that it would 'form the happiness and honour of [his] life' if his statement of 'attachment' could be met 'with the least return'.[2] To his dismay, Sarah did not immediately reply, leading him to send a second letter on the subject.[3] On 14 September, as William worked on yet another letter, he was delighted to receive not one but two letters from Sarah. William treasured her replies. In another letter to Sarah, William told her that he read her 'Note again, and again' and how he carried it with him everywhere.[4] He not only kept her letter at his 'side during the day' when 'alone', he even slept beside it as a 'companion on [his] pillow' at night.[5] Subsequent letters from Sarah were received with even greater enthusiasm. William told Sarah how he kissed her letters 'again and again', and how he felt a 'flush of joy pass like lightning across [his] chest' as he opened them.[6] Indeed, William not only carried Sarah's letters with him everywhere he went, he also claimed that he could feel her touch emanating from their very pages. On one occasion, he conveyed his 'delight' when he received from Sarah a 'kind … caressing Letter'. As he read her missive, William recalled that he 'felt' Sarah's words 'just in the same way' he would experience a 'gentle pressure' from her hand.[7] On another occasion, William told Sarah how, as he read her letter, he 'felt' as if she had 'suddenly thrown [her] arms around [his] neck and kiss'd' him.[8]

As the stage before marriage, courtship was an important (and exciting) time in the lives of couples. Courtship was a time for lovers to get to know one another and to gauge their overall compatibility for marriage. Finding the *right* partner was serious business. Yet courtship was not just one phase before marriage; rather, it was made up of a series of interlocking stages, each with its own rituals and practices, in which couples were expected to participate as they got to know one another.[9] As a courtship progressed from its early stages towards marriage and became more serious, these practices changed and became more formal.[10] These rituals also varied considerably, and were not practised exclusively by all couples. Geographical location, relative wealth, and literacy shaped the opportunities for love and romance in eighteenth- and nineteenth-century Ulster.

The rural setting of Ulster Presbyterian communities provided the backdrop to the love stories of many young couples. Whereas some young women and men danced together in barns, others met at fair days and festivals, where they played games and bonded over whiskey. As they spent more time in one another's company, couples would give each other small gifts and tokens to mark their progressing relationship. Items like food, jewellery, clothing, and even human hair, were employed as love tokens. Other couples who were separated by long distances, or who were denied the opportunity to spend time in one another's company, exchanged love letters. It was through letters that they expressed their romantic sentiments, sussed out the feelings of their partner, and navigated the route towards marriage. As William Drennan's correspondence suggests, love letters not only carried loving words, they were also regarded as love objects in their own right.[11] Couples stroked, gazed at, sniffed and kissed the letters they received. Courting couples not only employed correspondence to declare their love and intentions to marry, they used the pen and the page to transport themselves to the bedrooms and bosoms of their beloveds.

Meeting and matching

Women and men in eighteenth- and nineteenth-century Ulster met their future marriage partners in lots of different ways. Some were introduced to their partners by family and friends, others met their future spouses at leisure events and entertainments, such as fairs and festivals. Church, school and work were also venues where romances had the potential to spark. Unlike today, however, the geographical scope of where individuals matched with a partner was much more limited. In their study of Irish marriage, Maria Luddy and Mary O'Dowd noted how most people 'looked to their own immediate locality' in their search for a marriage partner; a trend that was very much true of those who lived in rural areas.[12] Of the marriages recorded in the diocese of Ossory between 1739 and 1804, over sixty per cent of individuals married someone who lived in the same county as themselves, and fifty per cent married someone from the same parish.[13] Similar trends marked the courtship experiences of Presbyterian women and men in Ulster.

We can get a sense of where women and men in Ulster met their partners by examining marriage registers kept by the Presbyterian church. Ministers were required to keep a register of persons they married. In order for the registry to be 'accounted sufficient', entries had to contain four main elements: the names of the parties to be married, the names of their parents or guardians, the names of two witnesses, and the parish or congregation in which each party resided.[14] Quantitative analysis of fifteen registers kept by Presbyterian congregations in Ulster revealed that almost fifty-seven per cent of individuals married someone from within their own parish. Persons who travelled farther than their own county in pursuit of a partner totalled less than ten per cent of couples.[15] For the smaller geographical area of townland, the majority of individuals who belonged to the congregations of Greyabbey and Loughaghery in County Down, and Larne and Kilwaughter in County Antrim, married someone from the same townland, in line with trends observed elsewhere in Ireland.[16]

These localised marriage patterns were made possible by an abundance of opportunities for young people who lived and worked in the same geographical area to meet, mingle and strike up courtships. Markets, alehouses and even the journey to and from work offered individuals the chance to meet and begin romantic relationships.[17] Romantic entanglements were not uncommon among young women and men who worked together as servants. In July 1754 Cahans Kirk Session in County Monaghan was called to investigate when the flirtations between two servants who worked for John Lister bordered on the inappropriate after they began sharing a bed. Agnes Kirk, the female servant, told the Session that the young servant man 'came to her bed pretending courtship' and that he even 'lay down in bed with her Sometimes'. The Session quizzed Agnes for further details about their relationship. In addition to bedsharing, Agnes told the Session how the pair often flirted and teased one another as they went about their daily work. She confessed that 'sometimes' as a 'jest' she would even pull the young man 'by the skirt of his coat as he passed by her about his work in the house thro' the day'.[18]

Other young couples met at fair days and festivals that were held to celebrate specific points in the calendar year. John Caldwell recalled in his memoirs the 'delight' with which he 'hailed the annual return of various festivals' in his youth, such as Easter Monday, Midsummer Eve, Shrove Tuesday, Hallow Eve and Christmas Day.[19] According to Caldwell, these occasions enabled him to enjoy 'all the pleasures of unrestrained merriment and romping'.[20] The Easter holidays in particular seem to have been a time of gaiety for many young people. Easter was mentioned specifically in the journal of John Tennent, the grocer's apprentice of the previous chapter, as a time when young people got together to socialise. According to John, during the Easter festival period 'persons of every description' went to the local bowling-green to 'divert themselves', enjoying activities such as cockfighting, running, and playing games.[21] It is likely that one of the games observed, or indeed played, by John was 'Round Ring'. This game was recorded in the *Ordnance Survey Memoirs of Ireland* as popular among the young people who 'flock[ed]' into Ballymoney in County Antrim during 'Easter week'.[22] Played in a field on the western side of the town known as 'the Easter Meadow', the game forced both sexes to mix 'indiscriminately'.[23] After forming themselves into a series of rings, one person would stand outside the ring, run around it, and touch another person. The person they touched would then race to gain the vacant spot. The game was apparently so popular that it was 'kept up with great activity and éclat for several hours each day during the Easter week'.[24]

Attending fair days and festivals not only acted as a popular form of amusement, these events also enabled young people to mix and match, with alcohol often acting as a social lubricant. The *Ordnance Survey Memoir* for Antrim town noted how the annual fairs held in May and November were used as opportunities to hire servants and for general 'amusement'.[25] The events attracted 'very great' numbers and usually ended with 'disgraceful scenes of drunkenness and brawling' after an evening of festivities.[26] Likewise, the report for the parish of Ballycor noted that its inhabitants were 'very fond of attending the summer fairs'. Both sexes 'congregate[d]' at the events and, fuelled by a fondness of 'whiskey-drinking', a 'good deal of immorality' normally ensued.[27] Unsurprisingly, Kirk Sessions often censured Presbyterian women and men for attending these events, especially when their attendance coincided with alcohol consumption and suspected sexual activity. In October

1729 Ballycarry Kirk Session required Rose Carsan to undergo a public rebuke for 'staying all night in Balycarry at the fair & drinking w[i]t[h] idle persons'.[28]

In rural communities, dances held in barns and other farmhouse buildings were also a popular form of amusement for young women and men. The *Ordnance Survey Memoirs* for the parishes of County Antrim made frequent reference to dances as a leisure activity practised by the locals.[29] Dancing was said to be a 'favourite amusement' in Doagh, which boasted a Presbyterian congregation of about 120 families.[30] Dancing was also popular in Islandmagee, another parish with a sizeable Presbyterian population. Here, amusements took the form of 'Punch dances', which were held at public houses and in the barns of local farmers.[31] Young people used these dances as an opportunity to meet and mingle with persons of the opposite sex.

Kirk Sessions regularly censured young women and men for attending what they termed 'promiscuous' or 'irregular' dances. In June 1802 John Pollock, Robert Hutchenson, Martha Knox, Sarah Pollock and William Erwin were 'Severely rebuked' by Loughaghery Kirk Session in County Down for attending a dance.[32] The church feared that these dances would encourage other immoral behaviours, such as sexual activity, and so clamped down on this form of socialising. Sometimes these fears were not unfounded. When Joseph Simrall appeared before Cahans Kirk Session in October 1796 and confessed his 'unregular conduct' in attending 'unregular dancings', it emerged that he was also guilty of 'running away' to marry his wife on the Sabbath.[33] Of especial concern to the Session was the birth of Joseph's child, which was 'born a month before the time' – the implication being that the child had been conceived before marriage.[34] The Session ruled that Joseph was to take an 'oath that he had no criminal correspondence' with his wife before marriage, after which he was to be 'rebuked in public for attending dances and for his running away upon the Sabbath'.[35]

The Presbyterian church did itself provide young people with the opportunity to meet and socialise. The festivities occasioned by the ordination of newly installed ministers provided a focal point for young people to mingle. John Tennent recorded in his diary how he and a group of young men and women had attended a dinner to mark the ordination of the Reverend Matthew Elder, who was installed as minister of First Kilraughts congregation in August 1789. The following day, John joined a riding party to the Giant's Causeway, before ending his jaunt at Dervock fair, where he met his friends and some ladies for tea.[36] The Sabbath also played an important role in the social life of rural communities in Ulster.[37] A popular custom known as ''tween sermon drinking', whereby members of the congregation met between services and exchanged gossip over a jug of ale, provided a regular social meeting point for many people in rural Ulster.[38] Special religious services such as baptism and communion offered young people the chance to intermix and socialise, albeit under the watchful supervision of their families and members of the Session.

Gifts and tokens

One courtship ritual that was practised across Ireland by young couples was gift-giving. A variety of objects were employed by courting couples to symbolise their romantic attachments. Sums of money, items of clothing, household goods, food and locks of human hair were common love objects.[39] Before the increase in popularity of Valentine's Day from the late nineteenth century onwards, autumn was the traditional courtship season in Ireland. Courtship was closely associated with harvest, and women and men in rural Ireland marked the season by exchanging 'harvest knots' made of plaited straw. Marriage divination was also a feature of Hallowe'en festivities.[40] Folklore accounts from County Cavan detail a divination game that was played by Ulster women and men using three saucers. On one saucer was placed a ring, on another a piece of clay, and the final saucer was filled with water. A person was then blindfolded and tasked with choosing their saucer. Whichever saucer they placed their hand upon would tell their future: the ring symbolised marriage, the clay death, the water, emigration.[41]

Other parlour games involved food, particularly nuts. Not only were nuts conveniently available in October, they were also believed to act as aphrodisiacs, making them an appropriate amorous foodstuff.[42] In Whitecastle, County Donegal, nuts were used in divination games to symbolise the strength of romantic attachment between young couples. According to one account, two nuts would be put into the fire, each representing one member of the courting couple. If the two nuts 'burn[ed] brightly together' this was a sign that the couple loved each other. Nuts that failed to 'burn brightly', however, indicated that the couple did not.[43] A similar game was recorded in Lurganearly in County Monaghan, using two hazlenuts. The nuts would be placed in the ashes of the fire and if they burned together the couple would be married. If one of the nuts shot out of the fire, the couple would separate.[44]

The items exchanged in courtship were specially chosen, because different gifts had different meanings. In choosing to send a particular token, the gift-giver communicated a specific message to its recipient, and in return, the recipient indicated their agreement or rejection of this message by either accepting or refusing the gift. Sally Holloway has noted that in Georgian England the exchange of romantic gifts enabled courting couples to 'negotiate the path to matrimony'.[45] The same was true in Ulster. As a courtship developed from initial friendship, through to romantic attachment, engagement and then, finally, marriage, gifts were employed to mark each stage of this progression, serving to confirm, accelerate or terminate the developing relationship.[46] Whereas shirts were regarded as a symbol of friendship, items like gloves were recognised for their association with marriage. Worn on the hands and covering the fingers, gloves symbolised the 'ancient rite of winning a lady's hand'.[47]

The records of the Presbyterian church courts reveal how some women claimed to have been tricked into sexual intercourse by unscrupulous men on the promise of marriage, citing gifts of gloves as evidence. When Grizell Mathison named Thomas Lauchlin as the father of her child in November 1704, she told Templepatrick Kirk Session that Thomas had 'came severall nights to her bed' and had 'promised her a pair of gloves'.[48] Although Thomas had 'once' declined her offer of marriage, Grizell claimed that he had offered to 'give her a pair of gloves' as a token of their commitment.[49] While

Thomas admitted that Grizell had indeed 'sought marriage of him' on a number of occasions, he denied that he had ever 'promised to marry her', nor had he ever 'give[n] her gloves'.[50]

Gifts were also mentioned in a complaint lodged by Alice Maguire, a Catholic woman, who appeared before Cahans Kirk Session in July 1767 to raise concerns about the behaviour of John Makee (a member of Cahans congregation). Alice told the Session that John had hired her daughter as a servant the previous summer. While employed in his service, Alice alleged that John had 'delude[d]' and 'debauched' her daughter, and had even carried 'her off to his sister's house near Clownish' at the expiration of her term of service.[51] As evidence, Alice told the Session that John had given her daughter 'his wife's handkerchief' and his 'sister's garters' as presents.[52] The minutes note how Alice 'with tears' asked the Session to make John 'confess his faulty conduct' and promise to 'quit such wicked practices for the future'.[53] The Session was sympathetic, not least because Alice was a 'papist' and an 'Informer against her own child'.[54] Unfortunately for Alice, when John appeared before the Session, he denied all guilt. Having 'no sufficient proof', the Session ruled that the case should rest until 'God in providence' provided more light on the matter.[55]

For some Ulster couples, gift-giving was central to their courtship ritual. This was certainly the case for the Reverend Robert Magill and his future wife, Ann Jane Skelton. Born in 1788 in Broughshane, County Antrim, Robert was installed as minister of First Antrim Presbyterian congregation in June 1820.[56] He took up residence in a house owned by Samuel Skelton, an agent to Lord Massereene and Ann Jane's father. Robert struck up a friendship with the Skelton family, and would often visit, spending his evenings at their home drinking tea and sharing stories.[57] Robert's duties as minister also meant that he built up an intimate familiarity with the Skelton family. He was a constant figure at the bedside of William Skelton, Ann Jane's brother, as he lay dying in spring 1821. After William's death in June 1821, Robert wore a scarf sent to him by Samuel Skelton in remembrance of his son, and he even composed an epitaph for the tombstone.[58] Ann Jane's siblings also attended the local Sunday School and received tracts as rewards for repeating Bible verses and Presbyterian church materials such as the *Shorter Catechism*.[59]

Given Robert's intimate familiarity with the Skelton family, in both his capacity as minister and family friend, it is perhaps unsurprising that he and Ann Jane began courting. We can chart the progression of their relationship, from friendship to courtship and then marriage, from the types of gifts they exchanged. In December 1821 Robert noted in his diary that Ann Jane had lent him a book. This small token marked the beginning of their friendship and was later repeated by Ann Jane in May 1822 when she made Robert a shirt.[60] From this point onwards, Robert made much more frequent reference to Ann Jane's movements in his diary, as the pair began to spend time in one another's company. In June 1822 Ann Jane stood as a witness to a marriage ceremony performed by Robert.[61] In July, the pair, accompanied by Mr and Mrs Skelton, spent part of the day together in Belfast, and in September they met each other at a wake.[62]

As their friendship progressed to courtship, the tokens that Ann Jane and Robert exchanged became more personal and intimate, reflecting their growing bond. Between July and October 1822, Robert gave Ann Jane a gold breast pin, a psalm book and his own personal Bible, and in return he received from Ann Jane a silver pencil.[63] When Robert left Antrim to spend time in Youghal, County Cork, in connection with the Presbyterian Missionary Society, Ann Jane sealed their romantic attachment by presenting him with 'a ringlet of her hair tied with a blue ribbon' as a 'keepsake' to remember her by during his absence.[64] When Robert returned from Cork in January 1823 the couple's relationship entered its final stages, as they progressed towards marriage. At the end of January, Robert noted in his diary that he 'spoke of marriage' to Ann Jane after dinner one evening in the Skelton household.[65] This progression was also reflected in the types of gifts Robert presented to Ann Jane. For her twentieth birthday in November 1823, he composed a poem and presented her with a ring, an item synonymous with marriage. Two days later he asked Samuel Skelton for permission to marry Ann Jane, and the pair married three weeks later, on 11 December 1823.[66]

Interestingly, the progress of Ann Jane and Robert's courtship was also reflected in the value of gifts he exchanged with the Skelton family, particularly Ann Jane's parents. Mrs Skelton, for example, regularly sent Robert gifts of foodstuffs, such as butter, cheese and eggs.[67] These items were distinct from the 'groceries' the Skeltons provided Robert with in return for a cash payment.[68] Robert himself noted in his diary how he had 'Received the *present* of a cheese from a *friend* to whom [he] gave a *present* of apples.'[69] After his marriage to Ann Jane in December 1823, the items exchanged between Robert and the Skeltons increased in monetary value. Robert presented Mrs Skelton with a gold ring, and gave Ann Jane's two sisters, Ellen and Eliza, a silver thimble each.[70] In return, Mrs Skelton purchased Robert and Ann Jane furniture for their new home.[71] Similarly, as Robert's intimacy with the family increased and his courtship of Ann Jane progressed, he borrowed larger amounts of money from Samuel Skelton. In the early stages of their courtship, Robert borrowed sums amounting to no more than twenty pounds, rising to sixty pounds and one hundred pounds around the same time he proposed marriage.[72] The increasing amounts that Robert was able to borrow reflected the growing trust between him and his future father-in-law.

The most special courtship token a person could gift was their hair. As a physical piece of a person that would outlast their human life, a lock of hair symbolised immortal love and affection.[73] Couples who were separated by long distances would often enclose locks of hair in their courtship letters, offering a piece of themselves to their beloved by which to remember them. This tradition was followed by a young Belfast woman named Hannah McGee during her courtship with Robert James Tennent, the nephew of William Tennent, a wealthy Belfast merchant. Hannah and Robert were young sweethearts, striking up an intimate relationship sometime in 1818, when Hannah was almost seventeen years old and Robert was aged fifteen.[74] Hannah bestowed two locks of her hair on Robert: one in May 1818 and the other in September 1820.[75] Locks of hair were often tied in neat plaits or fashioned with a ribbon, enabling the lock to keep its shape. The recipients of these hairy treasures would interact with the locks both physically and sensorially. The hair could be rubbed, stroked, smelled and gazed upon as the recipient thought about the person from whom the hair had been cut. It is very possible that Robert interacted in this way with the two locks of hair that were given to him by Hannah McGee – one of the locks has the appearance of an undone plait, a faint twist and piece of fabric is visible amidst the unfurled hair.

Despite their young age, it is evident that Hannah was in love with Robert and that she offered these gifts as a romantic gesture. Hannah felt that her parents would not approve of her relationship with a 'harum scarum youth' like Robert, and so the couple conducted their courtship in secret.[76] Despite their desire to keep their attachment hidden, it was Hannah's infatuation with Robert that rumbled their secret romance. In January 1821 Katherine Templeton, a friend of Hannah's mother and an acquaintance of Robert, wrote to Hannah advising her to break off the relationship before it progressed further towards engagement and marriage. In this same letter, she revealed that the love Hannah felt for Robert was visible to all, and that she was by all accounts 'love-drunk':

> I intended speaking seriously to you yesterday ... but I soon perceived you were not in a situation to benefit by it ... [by] the state of intoxication in which you appeared ... you ... would perhaps insist you were perfectly sober, there are however other ways of becoming inebriated besides taking strong liquors. [Y]ours was caused by the victory your passions were gaining over prudence and common sense.[77]

In July 1821 Hannah acted on Katherine's advice and ended her attachment with Robert. Her reasons for doing so were not because her feelings had changed, but because she feared that her 'very many good friends' would inform her father of their secret relationship.[78] Just as she had employed the tradition of gift-giving to cement her relationship with Robert, Hannah likewise used tokens to signify its end. As a parting gift and lasting symbol of their attachment, she enclosed in this same letter to Robert the token of a broken ring.[79]

The choice of a ring was significant, especially when we consider how Robert had once proposed marriage.[80] Hannah's choice of a *broken* ring, however, carried an extra special message. In a letter to Robert in July 1821, Hannah explained how the ring carried happy memories, telling him that she had worn it 'many a day when I was happier than I am at present'.[81] Hannah then broke the ring in two, keeping half for herself and gifting the other half to Robert. This small act symbolised their possible future reunion. Indeed, the ring itself acted as a physical embodiment of Hannah's heart. As she reminded Robert, if their love was never again rekindled, she would 'remain' just like the ring, forever broken.[82]

It is worth noting here that Hannah may have had a lucky escape. While we should not doubt that Robert entertained affection for Hannah, she was not the only woman to have caught his eye.[83] As a young man, Robert engaged in numerous flirtations with various young ladies, some of whom also gifted him locks of their hair. Archived among Robert's family papers are fourteen locks of hair that belong to at least ten different women. Some of the items in Robert's hairy collection are dated precisely, including the day, month and year in which they were received. In many cases the dates overlap, suggesting that Robert may have entertained the affections of multiple women at once. Indeed, during the short period of his flirtation with Hannah, Robert received locks of hair from at least four other women.[84]

Not only were tokens used to make and break relationships, they were also expected to be returned when a courtship failed. The return of gifts both symbolised the termination of a relationship and cut any ties (emotional and material) between the gift-giver and recipient.[85] Similarly, individuals who gladly accepted gifts from would-be suitors without any romantic intention were regarded as duplicitous. William Drennan – the man whose story opened this chapter – engaged in a failed attempt at courtship in March 1798 during a break from his pursuit of Sarah Swanwick. The object of his efforts was a wealthy widow named Sally Scott, who did not return his sentiments. William appears to have been completely unaware of the fact that Sally was not interested in him romantically. Writing to his sister Martha, William claimed that

Sally had given him no clear indication that his attentions were unwanted:

> I am glad it has been done again [i.e. called off], as I am sure in <u>her</u> manner I might have gone on for six months, and the event would probably have been the same; false fancy would have coloured the bubble, and the heart felt itself more deeply betrayed.[86]

William's ignorance can perhaps be forgiven when we consider that despite offering him her 'friendship' and not love, Sally had continued to receive his visits and accept gifts, actions which he believed meant that his attentions were welcome.[87] Indeed, William believed that he was not 'blameable' for how the affair turned out, and criticised Sally for not returning his copy of *Caroline of Lichfield* after their first meeting.[88]

Love letters

Couples who were separated by long distances, or who wanted to keep their romances secret, wrote letters. It was through letters that they expressed their feelings for one another, relayed details of their daily routines, and navigated their way through the complex discussions that accompanied the decision to marry. Analysing who said what, when and to whom in courtship letters can uncover the gendered dimensions of love, power and wealth that underscored the decision to get married.[89] Letters offer a unique opportunity to glimpse into the private and intimate world of a courting couple. It should be noted, however, that letters tell us mainly about those couples who belonged to the middling orders of society, who could afford to learn to read and write. Courtship correspondence rarely gives us an insight into the thoughts and feelings of the servant maids and poorer members of the community whom we encounter much more readily in sources such as Kirk Session minutes.

Historians agree that when it came to discussing love, men were much more vocal than their female counterparts. Commenting on courtship correspondence in eighteenth-century North America, Nicole Eustace has noted that it was men who tended to make public avowals of love. Similar declarations on the part of women were rare.[90] Likewise, drawing on the experience of Mary Shackleton, a young Quaker woman living in eighteenth-century Ireland, Kevin O'Neill has noted that young women were discouraged from being too 'free' in their letters.[91] Yet, just because women were meant to be reserved in how they communicated their affections, this does not suggest that they were by any means passive players in matters of the heart. Women used a tactic in their letters known as 'ritualised courtship testing', whereby they manufactured crises to stress-test their relationships.[92] It was the job of men to overcome these obstacles and prove the sincerity of their intentions. Jonathan Jeffrey Wright's work on the courtship of Eliza McCracken and Robert James Tennent – the owner of the hairy collection already discussed – examined how this played out for one couple in nineteenth-century Ireland.[93]

These patterns are also apparent in the courtship correspondence of William Drennan and Sarah Swanwick. Although elements of their courtship were certainly not representative of the experience of most couples – William was a bachelor aged thirty-nine years at the beginning of their courtship and Sarah lived in England – the economic and social forces that shaped the progress of their relationship would have been recognisable to many of their peers. William first met Sarah, then aged twenty-three years, in the summer of 1793, during one of her annual, six-week vacations at the Dublin home of her sister and brother-in-law, Mr and Mrs William Hincks.[94] According to William, the moment he set eyes on Sarah he felt the unmistakable pang of romantic attachment. When Sarah returned to England at the end of August 1793, William felt compelled to write her a letter declaring his love.[95] That it was William and not Sarah who made the opening declaration of love is hardly surprising, given the etiquette that dictated the writing of love letters. The initial declaration of sentiment was almost exclusively regarded as a male role in the courtship process.[96] What is perhaps most noteworthy about these exchanges, however, is not *what* each party said, but *how* they said it.

From the very outset, William framed his proposal and early letters in the language of unrestrained love, emphasising that his feelings for Sarah were based solely on an overwhelming passion. William used the language of love to normalise, as he said, the 'glaring impropriety' of his letters.[97] Given that they had only met a few times during Sarah's stay in Dublin, William was aware that his declarations of passionate love jarred with the normal progression of courtship. He argued, however, that their separation had intensified his feelings, and that love excused his alleged 'impropriety':

> Has our acquaintance been really so short? Have I not seen you and heard you when here, and thought of you when absent so often as to make me excusable in thinking that ours has neither a slight, nor a short acquaintance. ... The impropriety of this Letter then lessens ... when I think that ... there is no probability of soon seeing you again in Ireland, ... *forum and decorum disappear before the necessity of [d]istances.*[98]

The language of unrestrained love and the by-passing of the usual rules of courtship was justified in William's mind. He loved Sarah; the length of their acquaintance did not matter.

In complete contrast to William's letters, and much to his disappointment, those written by Sarah were much more restrained in both language and tone. William frequently implored her to write 'fully and candidly' about her sentiments and chastised her for her 'precise' and 'prudish' manner of writing.[99] In an effort to break Sarah's reserve, William even sent her directions on *how* to write to him, including instructions on the best time and place to sit down and write, as well as on her posture and clothing. In one letter, dated 26 September 1793, he implored Sarah as follows:

> O Do not keep your little heart in plaits and folds, like one of your quilled and stiffened ruffles, when you sit down to write to me – and do not write to me in the morning – write to me at night, and when all have gone

to rest, and have my Letters before you, and write it in your neat yet negligent night dress, and let your hair float on your shoulders, and give equal freedom to the feelings of your pure and innocent mind and then put out the Light and then cast one short hasty thought (no I did not say, wish) for me.[100]

While we might regard William's instructions as over the top or even intrusive today, we should remember that letter writers used their missives to bridge the emotional and physical distance between them and their intended recipients. Letters not only carried tangible manifestations of their writer's desires, they also created space for these desires to be acted out.[101] Writing these instructions enabled William to imagine Sarah at her desk, giving him access to her private space and enabling him to fantasise about her body. Sarah seems to have obeyed William's instructions to an extent, ending her letters with less stiff forms of address such as 'I am yours', 'Good night', and 'I am your best friend'.[102] No evidence survives, however, that she reciprocated William's elaborate romantic style.

The frustration William felt with Sarah's tight-lipped reserve was not unique to their courtship; rather, it seems to have been a regular feature of the exchanges between other courting couples. For some couples like Robert Tennent, a medical doctor and merchant from Belfast, and his future wife, Eliza Macrone, the difference in the emotional quality of their letters was a source of complaint. In a letter dated April 1800, two years before their marriage, we learn that Robert had accused Eliza of 'coldness and reserve' and that he believed her lack of romantic expression meant that her feelings for him had changed.[103] In reply, Eliza acknowledged that her letters were indeed less expressive than Robert's, but she denied that her attachment to him had lessened:

> You attribute this <u>seeming</u> change to the Freedom (as you express it) you use in writing to me. No. … I am now more conscious of the difference there is between your letters & mine, & perhaps felt a diffidence which communicated itself to my paper, place it to any account

you please but that of an alteration in my sentiments respecting you.[104]

Instead, Eliza admitted that while she harboured feelings for Robert that she would not '<u>blush</u> to acknowledge', she was forced to 'conform to the custom of the world' and remain reticent.[105] It was not lack of affection that inhibited her expressions, but the constraints of traditional etiquette.

Young women like Sarah Swanwick and Eliza Macrone favoured circumspection because they had more to gain from keeping their attachment hidden from public knowledge. Once a man's intentions became widely known, a woman's options began to shrink, leaving her unprotected should a courtship end, or an engagement be called off.[106] Popular literature and poetry aimed at young women encouraged them to remain reticent for this very reason. At the height of his courtship of Ann Jane Skelton, the Reverend Robert Magill copied out a poem composed by the English poet Letitia Elizabeth Landon on this theme, which was reprinted in the *Belfast Chronicle*. We can of course only speculate, but it is probable that the content of the verse struck a chord with his own experience:

> Do any thing but love – or if thou lovest
> And art woman, hide thy love from him
> Whom thou dost worship; never let him know
> How dear he is; flit like a bird before him
> Lead him from tree to tree from flower to flower
> But be not won, or thou wilt like that bird
> When caught and caged be left to pine neglected
> and perish in forgetfulness.[107]

Women kept their cards close to their chest to protect themselves in the event their relationship broke down or a marriage was called off.

In contrast to the candid way in which men discussed love in their letters, they were relatively silent on the subject of wealth. Nicole Eustace has noted that while young men 'doggedly declared their love to women', they 'refused to openly acknowledge the many other goals marriage could help them attain', such as wealth and increased social standing.[108] Women were shrewder in their letters when it came to the practical side of things, and discussed (among themselves at least) the economic and social implications of changing their state from unmarried to married.[109] According to Eustace, whereas men used the language of love to paper over the practical considerations that underscored courtship and tried to convince women it was attachment alone that motivated them, women remained more circumspect, keenly aware of the changes marriage could bring to their social and economic well-being.[110]

The Drennan–Swanwick correspondence reveals the disastrous consequences that followed when a couple failed to properly consider issues of love and wealth in their courtship negotiations. At the time William and Sarah first met, neither of them could be described as very wealthy. William made a living as a struggling physician and man-midwife, barely living off an income of £120 per annum; Sarah made a small income of £60 per annum from her tutoring services at a school managed by her parents in Shropshire.[111] The knowledge of these circumstances, however, did not stall William in his efforts to win Sarah's heart, and he sent his letter of love in August 1793 regardless. Practical considerations were afforded little space in William's initial letter of attachment. After giving Sarah a brief summary of his education and family history, he explained that he had as yet made only a 'proud competence' in his profession, adding that he had been happy to continue in this manner while he remained a bachelor.[112] William attributed his lack of professional success to his bachelor status, which he in turn blamed on his involvement in politics. He told Sarah how his 'interference in politics' had 'injur[e]d' his profession and that he hoped 'an amiable, interesting woman' could produce in him 'that worldly activity for her sake' and give his 'heart a home'.[113] It is likely that William's association with radical politics and the United Irishmen made him an unattractive match for the daughters of many of the middling- to upper-gentry families in Dublin. With Sarah as his wife, William hoped he could refocus his attention on his profession and turn away from politics. The contribution Sarah would make was not measured in material terms, but by her exertions as his loving wife.

Sarah did not, however, share William's enthusiasm for a quick engagement, and returned a 'Letter of pure reason' outlining her objections to the proposal.[114] The most pressing of these – and one she referred to as 'almost insurmountable'– was her lack of fortune.[115] Sarah may indeed have been 'stress-testing' William's resolve by commenting on her less than attractive financial situation. Yet, it is worth noting that she was not a financially advantageous match. Sarah's fortune was expected to be a rather modest £100 on her marriage, with a one-tenth share of her father's farm, which was valued at £3,000, at his death.[116] Sarah had no savings of her own towards marriage, with her income from tutoring used mainly for her upkeep and annual visits to Dublin.[117] In response, William again employed the language of love, arguing that he was already aware that Sarah possessed little fortune, and that it was only for reasons of love he desired marriage:

> I knew, before I wrote to you, that you had little or no fortune … but I could not on that account relinquish all hopes of obtaining a place in that heart which I happen to prefer to riches, and honours, even tho' I were capable of attaining them.[118]

William drew a distinction between love and wealth: he wanted Sarah, not her money. In a letter to his sister Martha in September 1793, William admitted that his 'apparent and real interests' and his 'seeming and substantial happiness' had not coalesced in his choice of Sarah, but that he wanted to marry her nonetheless.[119]

Within the space of three months, however, William changed his mind. In December 1793 he wrote to Sarah to end their engagement, telling her that their union was 'totally impracticable' and that it was more 'prudent' for them to end their relationship now than be 'abandoned to the uncertainty of years'.[120] In complete contrast to his previous letters, William now emphasised the importance of practical considerations. His mother, he claimed, was opposed to the match on financial grounds and so he had to call off the engagement.[121] Despite his protests, rumours abounded that William had ended the affair not from a wish to appease his mother, but from a desire to secure for himself a more financially advantageous match.[122] Indeed, evidence suggests that William may have been under an impression that Sarah's fortune was larger than he had expected, and the realisation that it was not had led him to end their engagement.[123]

From courtship to marriage: William Drennan and Sarah Swanwick

As the courtship of William Drennan and Sarah Swanwick reveals, navigating the route to marriage was no easy feat. Playing the 'game of love' was fraught with difficulties.[124] Couples might attempt to play by the rules, employing gifts and tokens to symbolise their growing feelings, or writing love letters to evidence their attachment, but matters of the heart almost never ran smoothly. In their search for love, Irish women and men not only risked embarrassment, family disapproval and heartbreak, they encountered financial obstacles too.

William and Sarah's love story did not, however, end permanently. About six years later, in August 1799, the pair renewed their courtship, marrying a few months later, in February 1800. It is important to note that the couple married on exactly the same terms as they had initially conceived in 1793 and neither party had increased their relative fortunes. William even penned a letter to Sarah's father, John Swanwick, to apologise for the 'unhappy suspension' of the engagement, and confessed that his 'situation in Life [was] much the same as when [he] first addressed' Sarah.[125] Only speculative reasons can be suggested for why marriage with Sarah was now agreeable, but it is likely that by 1799, in his mid-forties and still a bachelor, William's priorities in marriage had changed significantly. In letters to his sister Martha, William lamented his bachelor status and was depressingly aware that despite all his exertions to increase his prospects, marriage had continued to elude him.[126] William's desire to renew his attachment with Sarah was also accompanied by a new, modest outlook on what he desired from marriage. In a letter to Martha in May 1799, William admitted that he had 'totally lost [his] former ambition' for wealth and status, adding that he was 'sensible not even a little fortune would serve to raise [him] an inch higher' than he was at present.[127] For William, now aged forty-five years old, the practicalities of marriage negotiations and romantic love were compatible concepts in his idea of courtship, enabling himself and Sarah to make the transition from courting to married couple.

CHAPTER FIVE

'Your mother makes me write that she would grudge & grieve to hear of your marriage with any of these base whores': Getting married

In October 1798 troubling reports were relayed to the Reverend John Tennent about the moral character of his eldest son, 38-year-old William. The Belfast gossip network was abuzz with news of the arrival of a woman from Scotland, who claimed not only that she was William's wife, but that he had neglected to 'acknowledge' the children they had together.[1] News of the woman's arrival had spread quickly across Belfast and beyond, reaching as far as Roseyards, County Antrim, where the Reverend Tennent lived. Tracing the source of the rumour in a letter to William, his father explained that he was given the news by a Mr Moore, who had heard it from a preacher named Mr Harper, who had been told about the Scottish woman while drinking tea in the house of Doctor Anderson.[2] Wagging tongues would inevitably carry the report further afield. The Reverend Tennent urged William to 'imediately own' the marriage if the report was true.[3]

Recalling a conversation he had with William 'long ago' that he should 'Marry Some decent Woman', the Reverend Tennent asked if the Scottish woman was the same one that his son had 'betrayed' years previously.[4] Described in a later letter as that 'Unhappy matter', the Reverend Tennent was referring to his son's previous sexual relationship with a woman he met while serving out an apprenticeship in Scotland.[5] Even if the report proved false, the Reverend Tennent advised William to still marry the woman. Considering that she had 'the first & best Claim' upon William for marriage – a reference to both the woman's lost reputation and bearing of his children – the Reverend Tennent urged his son to 'repair the injury [he] did her' by joining in matrimony.[6] Resolving the matter with marriage would benefit William too. Marriage, his father said, would help to 'meet' the 'Blot' on William's character that otherwise 'cannot be easily wiped away'.[7] These sentiments were not, however, shared by William's mother, Ann Patton, a woman who was renowned for her 'sharp' tongue.[8] Furious, she asked her husband to add her comments on the matter separately as a postscript. Appended to the bottom of the letter were the following words: 'your Mother Makes me write that she w[oul]d grudge & grieve to hear of your Marriage w[i]t[h] any of these base whores'.[9]

Presbyterian marriage

In the eighteenth and nineteenth century, members of the Presbyterian community in Ulster were expected to follow the rules of their church in the making of marriage. The Presbyterian church in Ireland traced its right to celebrate marriages to its adherence to the principles of its parent church in Scotland. Presbyterian understandings of marriage and guidelines for its celebration were outlined in two main documents published by the Church of Scotland: the *Westminster Confession of Faith* and the *Directory for the Public Worship of God*. The Presbyterian church in Ireland broadly followed these guidelines and published its own, adapted version in the *Code*.[10] The Presbyterian church taught that marriage was instituted by God for three purposes: 'the mutual Help of Husband and Wife, for the Increase of Mankind with a legitimate issue, and the Church with a holy Seed, and the preventing of Uncleanness'.[11] Marriage was available to all persons, provided that the union was not within the bounds of affinity and consanguinity prohibited by church law, and that the parties to be married were free from prior marriage and not contracted to marry someone else.[12] Presbyterian guidelines also expressed an explicit preference for parental consent in the making of marriage. Both the *Directory* and the *Code* specified that ministers should obtain the consent of the applicants' parents or guardians.[13] Yet, while parental consent may have been *desirable*, it was not strictly *essential* for marriage to take place. Presbyterian guidelines reasoned that parents could neither withhold their consent for 'unjust' reasons, nor could they 'compel their children to marry' against their will.[14]

The procedure for the celebration of the marriage ceremony was detailed in a section of the *Directory* entitled 'The Solemnizing of Marriage'. Ideally, marriages were to be celebrated in the meeting house by the Presbyterian minister of the marrying couple and in the presence of a 'competent Number of Witnesses'.[15] The ceremony could take place on any day, except on a 'Day of publick Humiliation' and preferably not on the Sabbath.[16] Before the marriage ceremony could take place, the *Directory* stipulated that banns of marriage were to be published in each party's respective congregation on three successive Sundays.[17] Individuals who failed to follow procedure were subject to church censure and could be required to remarry according to Presbyterian rules.[18]

Despite these penalties, the church struggled to enforce the requirement of banns. Like other religious communities in Ireland, Presbyterians disliked the public nature of banns and increasingly showed a preference for private ceremonies instead.[19] These changes were in line with a growing preference for privacy in family matters and as we saw, filtered into baptism ceremonies too.[20] Presbyterian marriage registers reveal the shift in preference from public to private ceremonies. Most marriages recorded in the register for Loughaghery Presbyterian church in County Down (1801–44) took place in the natal home of one of the married couple. Of the forty-nine marriages in which a place of solemnisation was recorded, about eighty per cent took place in the parental home of the bride or groom. Only one marriage was recorded as celebrated in the meeting house.[21] The fashion for marrying privately, in the presence of cherished family members and friends, was also favoured by some Presbyterian ministers. When the Reverend Robert Magill married Ann Jane Skelton in December 1823, he took pains to ensure that the occasion remained an intimate affair. His diary entry about the event describes the private and personal nature of his wedding:

> after supper the Rev[eren]d W[illia]m Wray who had spent the day with me walked up stairs in Mr Skeltons to bed as he thought but he was wonderfully surprized when I ushered him into the drawing room where my dear Ann Jane was standing dress[e]d beautifully in white. [H]er sister Ellen and her brother John Standing beside her also her Father and Mother. … we had previously arranged this. I immediately on entering the room requested Mr Wray to proceed with the ceremony … and the marriage was thus celebrated at 11 o'clock at night.[22]

Not only did Robert marry without first notifying the minister who was to perform the ceremony, but the marriage was held in the home of the bride's parents and at what could be considered an irregular hour of the night. His marriage celebration was, however, intimate and family-oriented.

Efforts were made by the church throughout the eighteenth and nineteenth century to placate the changing tastes of its lay members.[23] Various congregations were given the opportunity to vote on whether they wanted to continue with the tradition of banns. It appears that, given the choice, many communities voted to abolish the custom, demonstrating a dislike of the fuss involved.

First Dunboe in County Londonderry voted to abolish banns in April 1802, as did Carnmoney in County Antrim in April 1821 and Rathfriland in County Down in December 1831.[24] When the *Code* was published in 1825, the requirement for banns had been removed from Presbyterian guidelines altogether.[25]

Although the Presbyterian church claimed the right to exercise control over the marriages of its members, its ability to do so was contested. In fact, it was not until 1844 that marriages performed by Presbyterian ministers were recognised as valid in law.[26] These legal difficulties had their roots in the complex relationship between state, church and the making of marriage law. Until the middle of the nineteenth century Ireland was a confessional state, in which access to political power and full civil rights was dependent on adherence to the Established Church, which was Anglican in form. As a dissenting minority, Presbyterians suffered various forms of discrimination, but it was in relation to marriage that this was felt most keenly.[27] The main issue for Presbyterians was the Anglican definition of what constituted a valid marriage. The Church of Ireland defined marriage as a promise exchanged between two individuals in the present tense, that was made in the presence of an ordained clergyman. Presbyterian ministers were not episcopally ordained, and so marriages performed by them were regarded as invalid.[28] Moreover, reflecting broader tensions between the two religious traditions, if Anglican clergymen accepted Presbyterian marriages as legal they would in turn validate the existence of their rival church as a separate, religious body, an acknowledgement that was 'unthinkable' in this period.[29] A series of acts was passed during the eighteenth century to clarify the position of Presbyterian marriage, but it was not until the Marriages (Ireland) Bill became law in 1845 that marriages between two Presbyterians, or between a Presbyterian and a non-Presbyterian, celebrated by a Presbyterian minister, were confirmed as legally valid.[30]

The messy nature of Irish marriage law facilitated the creation of a lively marriage marketplace. Members of the Presbyterian church had their marriages celebrated by Anglican clergymen, Roman Catholic priests, itinerant preachers, and individuals known as couple-beggars – ministers and clergymen who had no formal attachment to a church.[31] In some cases, church members applied to a succession of different celebrants to solemnise their marriages. In April 1708 Burt Kirk Session in County Donegal investigated the 'sinful actions' of Moses Lockart and Rebekah Sterrat, who made a series of aborted attempts to join in marriage.[32] Despite the fact that banns of marriage announcing the union of Rebekah to a different man had been read on two occasions, the couple proceeded with their own plans of marriage. After being turned away by a minister and a Catholic priest, Rebekah attempted to formalise the marriage herself by taking 'Moses by the hand' and saying 'I take the[e] to my lawfull husband untill death part us'.[33] The Session urged the pair to have their marriage publicly 'proclaimed'.[34] Again, however, Rebekah and Moses took the disorderly route and had their marriage celebrated by a 'priest' using a 'forged paper' of Rebekah's mother's consent to the union.[35] A similar case was heard by Cahans Kirk Session in County Monaghan, over 100 years later. In October 1824 Thomas Kerr was disciplined for having his marriage celebrated by a 'degraded' (out of orders) clergyman. The minutes reveal how Thomas had previously tried (and failed) to have his union solemnised by a 'clergyman of the Church of Engl[an]d', as well as a 'Presbyterian Clergyman'.[36]

While the Presbyterian church had no formal authority to determine the legal validity of marriages, what it could do was censure its church members for the irregular ways in which they had joined in marriage. Marriages were determined to be 'irregular' on three main heads: the marriage was not solemnised by a Presbyterian minister; banns of marriage had not been published; or the couple had failed to obtain parental consent.[37] In general, offending parties were directed to undergo church censure, which took the form of either a private or public rebuke. First Dromara Kirk Session in County Down dealt with 145 cases of disorderly or irregular marriage between 1780 and 1805. The celebrants recorded in these cases varied from Catholic priests to 'degraded' Presbyterian ministers and Church of Ireland clergymen. Most offenders were ordered to be rebuked and then remarried by the minister of the congregation.[38]

Private promises

Despite the published guidance of the Presbyterian church on how its members should join in marriage, many failed to adhere to the rules. Against the church's advice that marriage should be celebrated publicly and be overseen by a Presbyterian minister, many couples instead joined in matrimony by exchanging private promises of marriage. When it was discovered that couples had married in this way, the church courts were concerned to find out the wording of the promises that had been used. In eighteenth- and nineteenth-century Ulster, many Presbyterian couples engaged in a form of marriage known as *verba de futuro*, or a promise to marry in the future. Promises made in the future tense were not, however, recognised as a valid form of marriage. Irish law recognised only promises made in the present tense as a valid marriage contract.

Future promises of marriage deviated from church guidance in other, potentially more serious ways, too. In contravention of church teaching that sexual activity should be restricted to the marriage bed, contracting couples sealed their private promises to marry in the future by engaging in sexual intercourse.[39] Several individuals who appeared before Cahans Kirk Session in County Monaghan confessed that they had contracted marriage in this way. In March 1752 Benjamin Green and his wife Elizabeth Bell told the Session that they had sworn 'secretly to another that they would marry some [time] before *actual* marriage' and then engaged in 'fornication'.[40] Some couples even justified their behaviour by arguing that they had incorporated the Presbyterian form into their marriage promises before having sex. In January 1777 Margaret Cunningham told the Session that she and Robert Jackson had 'read the marriage oath in the confession of Faith' on 'the last Friday of last March' and then 'bedded' together 'the following Monday'.[41]

The Presbyterian church courts discouraged the lay community from contracting marriage in this way for several reasons. First, these types of marriage promise were problematic because the church had no power to compel individuals to honour them. When a jilted party appealed to the Kirk Session that a promise of marriage had been breached, there was little (if anything) that the church courts could do. In May 1786 Coronary Kirk Session in County Cavan was called to investigate an alleged breach of promise between Mary Irwin and William Jeffries. The case came to light when banns were read announcing an intended marriage between Mary and a man named John Gilbreath.[42] William complained that he had already 'obtained' from Mary a promise 'of Marriage prior to the publishing' of her union with John Gilbreath.[43] The Session asked William to put his complaint into writing and he returned five days later armed with his evidence.

In his written statement, William claimed that Mary had promised to marry him and no other man on four separate occasions. The first promise, he claimed, took place on 4 September 1784 at the top of 'John Kernaghan's hill' in the parish of Knockbride.[44] It was here, during 'their first meeting', that Mary 'faithfully promised to be true to said Jeffries for one year'.[45] The second promise was exchanged on 'Rob[er]t Anderson's hill' in the presence of Samuel Anderson and Mary's sister, Jean. On that occasion, William promised 'Mary that he would not be engaged to her or any other person for one year'. In return, Mary 'gave him her hand' and said that if he 'would wait for her one year that then she would go with him through the world'.[46] Mary allegedly reiterated her promise to 'marry no other person but [him]' (i.e. William) in a room in the house of 'Manns Morgan' and again at her 'brother David's house on the 24th day of Decemb[e]r 1784', when she offered William 'her hand & promise[d] that she would be true to [him] & no other person'.[47]

The Session called Mary before it and asked her to respond to William's charges. She queried the phrasing of the first promise made on Kernaghan's hill. Mary told the Session that she had actually promised to marry no one (including William) for a period of one year.[48] Mary also denied having made any promises to Willam on Robert Anderson's hill; neither had any 'promise passed between them' in her brother's house in December 1784. Perhaps most importantly, Mary claimed that the promise she had uttered in Manns Morgan's had been made under duress. Mary told the Session how a friend of William's named Hugh McPhillipps had 'pull'd' her by the arm into the room where William was waiting. When 'she struggled against him', Hugh 'took her into his arms

& carried her to the room & thrust her in', after which he locked the door. It was while she was trapped in the room that Willam 'asked her would she not shake hands with him' and say something 'before she would go away'. In order to get out of the room, Mary 'said she would go with him again that time twelve months'.[49]

If true, Mary's testimony undermined the strength of William's complaint on the grounds that her promise was not made freely, as was required. Sensing the potential issue, the Session decided to 'delay proceeding further' on the case until they could 'get farther light in the matter'.[50] Mary, however, did not wait to find out the Session's ruling. She and John Gilbreath married 'with licence … not long after' they appeared before the Session.[51] Unable to determine the marriage as invalid (the marriage having been granted permission by the Anglican Church of Ireland), Mary and John were ordered to acknowledge the 'irregularities' of their union and were rebuked before the congregation for their offence.[52] There was nothing more that William Jeffries could do.

When promises of marriage were not realised, the heartbreak was too much for some to bear. In December 1699 word reached Burt Kirk Session that a young woman named Mary Latimer was 'was going down to ye mosse' at 'night crying & saying that she would drown herself, or kill herself upon the rocks'.[53] The cause of Mary's distress was said to be the breakdown of her relationship. Mary's sweetheart, a man named Robert Killfillan, had recently published his intentions to marry another woman, despite (as Mary claimed) having also made her similar promises. The Session cited Mary to appear before it and quizzed her for details. Mary deposed that Robert had made such promises 'above a dozen times' and that she could give details on 'two remarkable times'.[54] The first memorable occasion had taken place in Robert's house the previous May. Mary told the Session that Robert claimed that 'it was his friends that hindered him to marrie her' but that he had every intention of making good on his promise.[55] Robert also declared his love and attachment for Mary, telling her that he had 'a sore heart' and felt 'almost dead' when they were apart.[56] The second occasion took place in October 1699, '8 days before the fair of Derry'.[57] Mary alleged that Robert had asked her not to hire herself out to anyone because he 'intended to make an end of it' (in other words to marry her) at the fair.[58] Mary also claimed that Robert made a 'vow' that 'he would not marrie another while she lived'.[59]

Robert 'utterly denied' Mary's allegations.[60] The Session 'took pains' with the pair to come to an agreement, but its efforts were fruitless.[61] In a last-ditch attempt to reconcile the couple, the Session urged them 'to agree between themselves'; a resolution which they both said 'they were willing' and would 'try to do'.[62] A postscript to the case, however, reveals that the pair did not resume their relationship. Robert 'went and married another wom[an]' shortly thereafter.[63] It would be almost one year later before he and Mary appeared together before the Kirk Session and confirmed that they had 'take[n] away all differences between them'.[64]

Even if the church courts found in favour of the injured party, church members could simply refuse to obey the ruling. Ballynahinch Kirk Session in County Down handled such a case in January 1788, when a 'purpose of Marriage' was proclaimed between Jean Stuart and a 'young man' from 'the old Cong[regatio]n of B[allyna]hinch'.[65] The Session had received a report that Jean was already promised to 'a young man' from Ballyroney congregation, to whom she had 'solemnly engaged never to marry any other'.[66] Jean confirmed the report was true, but explained that she 'thought herself freed from' those promises on the grounds that the 'young man had delayed his fulfilling his Promise for the space of almost three years'.[67] He had also, according to Jean, 'made application to other young women in a way of courtship'.[68] Unsure how to proceed, the Session referred to the case to the Presbytery of Down for its advice. The Presbytery ruled that Jean should marry the man from Ballroney.[69] Jean did not obey this direction. Instead, she went ahead and married the man from Ballynahinch in a 'clandestine' ceremony.[70]

A second reason why the Presbyterian church discouraged its members from contracting marriage with private promises was because such marriages were tricky to prove. This was especially the case when sexual intercourse was involved. As we have seen, when women became pregnant it was not uncommon for men to deny that they had ever promised marriage. Certainly, some men engaged in sexual intercourse with women on the strength of marriage promises that they had no intentions of ever making good. In December 1788 Scarva Kirk Session referred Thomas Sloan to Down Presbytery after it emerged that he had sex with 'a young woman from Loughbrickland and promised to marry her' despite already being a married man.[71] Other men also appear to have used promises of marriage to get women into bed. In December 1754 William McCrakin was called before Cahans Session when it emerged that he had 'made private promissory oath[s]' to Margaret Gray before he was proclaimed to marry Hannah Eliot.[72] William had even made his proposals of marriage to Margaret while sitting on her bedside.[73]

Given that private promises were exchanged without witnesses, women were faced with the difficult task of proving they had happened. This was the challenge faced by Elinor Beck when she appeared before Cahans Kirk Session in County Monaghan in May 1772 and professed sorrow for fornicating with Walter Neuse. When Elinor told the minister that they were 'promised' to marry, the Session was immediately suspicious because Walter had 'since married' someone else.[74] The Session moved to 'interrogate her on that point' and asked for details of the alleged promise.[75] Elinor provided details of two separate occasions on which promises had been exchanged. According to Elinor, Walter had 'one time ... took her by the hand' and said that he 'would be for her'.[76] On another occasion, Walter had even 'swore by the eternal God that he would never enjoy any but her'.[77] Elinor further alleged that Walter had once asked her whether she would 'quit him' if she received a proposal of marriage that would 'raise her fortune'. When she answered no, Walter made similar promises in turn.[78] It mattered little, however, even if Elinor was able to prove that Walter had made such promises. He was, after all, already married. The Session ordered Elinor to be publicly rebuked for her folly.[79]

Evading parental consent

Although parental consent was not strictly necessary for a marriage to take place, considerable importance was attached to receiving it as part of the normal route to marriage. When consent was not forthcoming, couples responded in a variety of ways to effect marriage. Some simply eloped, choosing to deal with the repercussions afterwards. It was lack of parental consent that motivated Joseph McCracken to have his marriage solemnised by a Catholic priest in December 1719. When he was asked to explain to Carnmoney Kirk Session 'why he married in such a disorderly way', Joseph 'answered [that] he could not obtain his parents consent'.[80] Similar motivations underlay the disorderly nature of Thomas Steenson's marriage in September 1829. When Thomas appeared before Cahans Kirk Session and professed his sorrow 'for the sin of disobeying his Father' and 'marrying without his approbation', he explained that he had only done so because he 'Anticipat[ed] that it' [parental consent] 'would be withheld'.[81]

Although the Presbyterian church courts were unable to determine that the marriages of eloping couples were invalid, they did censure individuals who married in this manner for the irregular course they had taken. The absence of parental consent was highlighted in many cases as the cause of the marriage's irregularity. In September 1713 John Minning and Jean Jamison appeared before Templepatrick Kirk Session and confessed that they had not only engaged in fornication, but that they had been 'married lately' by the Anglican curate of Donegore.[82] The Session decided to 'sharply' rebuke them not only for their sins of fornication and 'irregular marriage', but 'for their disobedience' to their parents.[83] Likewise, in September 1715 Elizabeth McKide was censured by Templepatrick Kirk Session after she had her marriage solemnised by a 'Popish' priest in Newry. Elizabeth's confession emphasised her fault in not obtaining parental consent. As the minutes note, Elizabeth confessed 'her sin of disobedience to her parents in her disorderly marriage'.[84]

Other couples attempted to force their parents to consent to their marriages by engaging in what were known as 'runaway matches'. Young couples would go to the house of a sympathetic friend or relative, where a company of friends would plan to meet them. The entire group would then stay for a night of celebration, sending word the following morning to the girl's parents of her whereabouts.[85] Although these occasions may not have involved sexual misconduct, the association between this behaviour and sexual transgression was enough to ensure that the girl was now viewed as 'compromised' and that subsequent marriage proposals would be out of her reach.[86] A number of young couples were censured by Kirk Sessions for engaging in this practice in eighteenth- and nineteenth-century Ulster. When Mary McKenna appeared before Coronary Kirk Session in County Cavan in 1783 and acknowledged 'her elopement' with Willam Owens, she professed her 'sorrow for staying days with him whereby she gave every person just ground to suspect her charg[e]able of uncleanness'.[87] Similar cases were considered by Cahans Kirk Session in County Monaghan. In March 1785 James Craford appeared before the Session and professed 'his sorrow for taking away his present wife before marriage'.[88] Although James claimed that 'he had no criminal correspondence' with his wife before marriage, he was still rebuked by the Session for his offence.[89]

When parents discovered that their children had married without their consent, many were understandably upset. When two daughters of the Reverend John Tennent and Ann Patton married without first obtaining their consent, the family was torn apart by the rift that ensued. In May 1777 Isabella, then aged twenty, eloped with a man named John Shaw. Her mother was so furious that she banished Isabella from the family home and refused to speak to her again. Despite the attempts of Isabella's brother Robert to reconcile mother and daughter, Ann refused to make up and even declined to see her grandchildren.[90] Indeed, for interfering in the affair, Robert himself earned his mother's displeasure. Writing to his father in August 1799 – almost twenty years after his sister's elopement – Robert repined that as soon as he mentioned Isabella to his mother, she 'not only ... wrap[ped] herself more strongly up in the most inveterate prejudice' but she 'look[ed] upon' him as 'an enemy & treat[ed]' him 'in the most unkind manner'.[91]

The fall-out caused by Isabella's elopement was intensified in June 1801, when Peggy, the youngest daughter of the Reverend John and Ann, followed in her sister's footsteps and married a man named John Stuart without seeking parental consent. When the marriage became public, two of Peggy's brothers corresponded on the affair. It is telling that the issue of whether their sister had secured parental permission was raised first.[92] As in the case of his other sister, Robert attempted to defuse the situation, pointing out to his parents the dangers of disapproving of such marriages. Writing in June 1801, Robert cautioned his mother against disowning Peggy and her husband, noting that he had 'known the most deplorable consequen[ces] spring from this very circumstance'.[93] More importantly, however, Robert reminded his mother that whatever their feeling on the affair, the marriage was one which 'no opposition could now undo'.[94] Neither her disapproval, nor the absence of her consent, made the marriage invalid. That this advice was directed towards his mother was made explicit by Robert in the letter. As he told his father, Robert's reason for 'addressing [his] mother almost exclusively on this subject' was not because he believed his father 'took no interest in it' but from 'a conviction' that he would 'act right not only in this instance, but in every one where there is a moral difference'.[95]

Recognising the friction that elopement caused in families, the Presbyterian church courts did their best to reconcile estranged parents and children. In December 1713 Carnmoney Kirk Session decided to delay the baptism of a child belonging to Margaret Bayly and James Stephenson until they were assured that the couple's parents had consented to the marriage. Margaret's marriage was deemed irregular on the grounds that her husband James was 'one of a different persuasion' (he was not Presbyterian) and that the marriage had been solemnised 'without the consent of her Parents'.[96] The Session appointed an elder to go and speak to Margaret's parents and find out if they 'and she live in amity'.[97] If it emerged that 'all be right betwixt' them, an elder was then to speak to James's mother and find out if she had given her consent to the marriage.[98] Once it was confirmed that all parties had given consent, then the child could be baptised.[99] Thirteen months later, in March 1715, the Session noted that Margaret had 'professed sorrow' for her irregular marriage and that she and her parents were 'reconcil[e]d again'.[100]

Catholic priests and mixed marriages

As well as sometimes having their marriages celebrated by Catholic priests, Presbyterians joined in marriage with Catholics too. This raises several issues about the nature of relationships between Presbyterians and Catholics in eighteenth- and early-nineteenth-century Ireland. The Presbyterian church courts regarded marriages that were celebrated by Catholic priests as problematic, not least because they were technically unlawful. Roman Catholic priests in Ireland did not have legal authority to celebrate marriages between persons who were not Catholic. Legislation passed in the Irish parliament expressly prohibited Catholic priests from presiding over marriages between Catholics and Protestants.[101] The Presbyterian church courts dealt quite seriously with couples who had their marriages celebrated in this way. Many couples were referred by Kirk Sessions to the upper courts for this offence. Of the nineteen cases of disorderly marriage considered by Down Presbytery between 1707 and 1715, eighteen involved individuals who had their marriages solemnised by 'Popish Priests'.[102]

Couples who were married by Catholic priests were also more likely to be sentenced to a public rebuke than were those who had their marriages celebrated by Anglican clergymen. Although the Presbyterian church regarded both celebrants as 'irregular' (they were not Presbyterian ministers), its ability to intervene in marriages celebrated by clergymen of the Established Church were limited. Such marriages were, after all, legally valid. This did not extend to marriages conducted by Catholic priests, which allowed the church to pass down stricter punishment. Between 1760 and 1818, Glascar Kirk Session dealt with ninety-eight cases of disorderly marriage. In sixty of these, the religious affiliation of the celebrant was recorded: three were solemnised by a Roman Catholic priest, fourteen were celebrated by a member of the 'Church of England', and the remainder were attributed to three degraded Presbyterian ministers.[103] In general, individuals who used the services of Catholic priests and degraded ministers were directed to stand publicly for their offence. In comparison, those who had their marriage celebrated in the manner of the 'Church of England' or with an 'Established Churchman' were generally censured privately before the Kirk Session.

Officially, the Presbyterian church disapproved of marriages between Presbyterians and non-Presbyterians. According to chapter twenty-four of the *Confession of Faith,* it was the 'Duty of Christians to marry only in the Lord'.[104] Presbyterians were subsequently directed not to 'marry with Infidels, Papists or other Idolaters'.[105] There are scattered examples of the church courts taking active steps to close off the possibilities of mixed-faith unions. In March 1721 Janet Reed appeared before Carnmoney Session and confessed that she was 'with child' and that the father was a 'Papist' named John Hamel.[106] In response to questions about the nature of their relationship, Janet admitted that the pair had intended to marry. The couple had even 'met in a place' for 'such a purpose' but had failed to go through with the marriage when the celebrant did not turn up.[107] Borrowing the wording of the *Confession,* the Session impressed upon Janet 'how great a sin it was to joyn in marriag[e] w[i]t[h] Idolaters'.[108] Janet insisted that she 'never resolve[d] to marry' John and confessed sorrow for her offence.[109]

A more direct route was taken by Cahans Kirk Session in 1776 when word reached it that Hanna Cleg was planning to marry a 'papist' man named only as 'Maginnis'. The minister went to Hanna's house to stop the marriage and 'warned' her not to proceed. Against the advice of both her father and the minister, Hanna went ahead with the marriage. She was married at 'Three Mile House' by a Catholic priest during 'Mass'.[110] It was reported that Hanna had 'renounced her profession and was baptized' in the Catholic faith during the ceremony too.[111] The union, however, was short-lived. Maginnis soon left the country; his departure, according to Cahans Session, was evidence of God's 'displeasure' with Hanna's improvident marriage. The Session ruled that Hanna was to be publicly rebuked for her breach of the seventh commandment in 'not entering into marriage in a Lawful manner', as well as for the disregard she had shown towards the advice of her father, the minister and the word of God.[112]

Such cases, however, were in the minority. While the church may have disapproved of mixed-faith unions, in practice it rarely took direct action to prevent them. Church members who contracted irregular marriages with a partner who was Roman Catholic generally received the same punishment as those who married in an irregular ceremony with someone of the same religious background. Carland Kirk Session in County Tyrone dealt with forty-nine cases of disorderly marriage between 1780 and 1802, two of which concerned mixed-faith unions. In both cases, the respective church members were sentenced to stand publicly for their faith; a punishment that was in step with how the church treated couples where both parties were Presbyterian.[113] The same was true for church members who engaged in sexual relationships with Roman Catholics. The minute books of the Presbyterian church courts contain numerous examples of Presbyterian women and men who were disciplined for engaging in sexual activity with Roman Catholics. Aghadowey Session directed that Elizabeth McLaw should be publicly rebuked for the sin of fornication with Donald O'Quigg, a 'Papist', in November 1703, and Ballycarry Kirk Session censured Kathrine McGallard for the sin of 'uncleanness' in 1738 after it was discovered that she had engaged in sexual intercourse with a 'Papist' (and suspected married man) named Patrick McFarland.[114] Aside from noting the religious affiliation of the offending partner as Catholic, the punishment handed down by the courts was the same as that in cases involving sexual misbehaviour between two Presbyterians. One party being Catholic made no difference.

The existence of these relationships broadens our understanding of the realities of living and loving across the confessional divide in eighteenth- and early-nineteenth-century Ulster. Presbyterians did not live in isolation from other religious communities. They lived, laboured and socialised with persons of other religious faiths. They also took advantage of the Irish marriage marketplace and sought out the services of diverse celebrants to make their marriages. Love and sexual attraction blossomed across religious lines. Historians generally agree that sectarian tensions between Protestants and Catholics deepened over the course of the nineteenth century. Marianne Elliott has suggested that the spirit of religious 'mixing and co-operation' that marked rural Ulster dissolved during the nineteenth century.[115] As sectarian divisions hardened, attitudes towards mixed marriages grew more hostile. Some couples even chose to emigrate to escape sectarian pressures.[116] The relatively liberal approach of the Presbyterian church to mixed marriage also underwent change. According to Andrew Holmes, the church's attitude 'hardened' from the 1830s onwards, as it grappled with fears that intermarriage would reduce 'the numerical strength of Irish Protestantism'.[117] Such fears were so entrenched that, in 1841, the General Assembly recommended that ministers should no longer celebrate marriages between Presbyterians and Catholics.[118]

Abductions

There were other, morally dubious and legally suspect, routes to marriage in Ireland, such as abduction.[119] According to Maria Luddy, the term 'abduction' referred to the 'practice of carrying off a woman with the purpose of compelling her to marry a particular man'.[120] While it is difficult to determine from surviving sources how widespread the practice was, it is estimated that at least 215 abductions were carried out in Ireland between 1700 and 1802, with a further 1,479 taking place in the period from 1800 to 1850.[121] There were also distinct regional patterns to abduction; the province of Ulster recorded the lowest number of abductions in comparison to any other part of Ireland in the period 1700 to 1850.[122]

Economic motives usually underlay abduction; it was an act of violence that enabled men to force access to a woman's property and land.[123] As James Kelly has noted, abductors generally targeted women of higher social rank than themselves in order to improve their own economic circumstances.[124] Taking an heiress as a wife offered an abductor a substantial material advantage in the form of land, property and inheritance.[125] Yet, there were advantages to be gained from the abduction of women lower down the social scale too. Thomas Power has noted that in the early nineteenth century, the daughters of farmers with portions of between thirty and fifty pounds were also prime targets.[126]

Having been taken away from her parental home by force, it was assumed that the chastity of an abducted woman had been compromised. Marriage to the abductor was thus one way of salvaging a woman's reputation. Rape, terror and intimidation were central to many abduction cases in the eighteenth and nineteenth century.[127] James Kelly has written on the case of Jane Tubman, a farmer's daughter from County Cavan, who was abducted by Edmund McKiernan and a group of men. When Jane grabbed the door to stop herself being carried off, the gang threatened to break her arm. Jane put up a fight, punching and biting her assailants who subsequently gagged and tied her up. She was also raped.[128] Jane eventually escaped her captors; however, her ordeal was not over. Edmund was never prosecuted for the abduction; as Kelly notes, Edmund made it clear that 'if proceedings were initiated against him, he would burn her father's house and take her away again'.[129]

Abduction was subject to serious criminal penalties throughout the eighteenth and nineteenth century. In 1707 a law was passed by the Irish parliament that explicitly addressed the crime of abduction. Titled 'An Act for the More Effectual Preventing the Taking Away and Marrying Children against the Wills of Their Parents or Guardians', the law mandated that anyone who abducted and married an heiress or woman of substance under the age of eighteen without the consent of her parents could be sentenced to prison for three years.[130] The same punishment was extended to any who aided the abduction.[131] More serious penalties were inflicted on those who abducted a woman without her consent. According to the 1707 Act, anyone who abducted or aided the abduction of a woman without her consent could be sentenced to death.[132] The death penalty was reaffirmed in a law passed in 1829, which made the abduction (or aiding the abduction) of a woman against her consent for the purposes of rape or forced marriage a capital offence.[133]

Although abduction was recognised as a criminal offence and therefore fell properly under the remit of the civil courts, the Presbyterian church courts also dealt with cases of alleged abduction. In the early eighteenth century, Burt Kirk Session was called to intervene in several cases where parents complained that young men had attempted to carry off their daughters. The trigger in many of these cases was the announcement that the woman was to marry someone else. In December 1704 James McCrim came to the attention of Burt Kirk Session after it was reported he had gone to the house of Widow Dunlap one Sabbath evening in order 'to take away Janet Dunlap by force after she was proclaimed to Tho[mas] McCarter'.[134] When questioned by the Kirk Session, James claimed that he had only gone to the house in a last-ditch attempt to win the heart of Janet. Indeed, he not only 'went there himself alone', but he had no 'designe of using violence'.[135] The Session appears to have believed James and instructed that he be 'reproved' by the minister for his actions.[136]

A similar rationale was offered by Joseph Barnes when he was accused of attempting to abduct Margaret Wallace in February 1708. The case was brought to the Session's attention when Margaret's parents complained that Joseph, together with four men, had come to their house one night, 'open[ed] their doors' and attempted to 'take away their daughter'.[137] The men in question included John Barnes (Joseph's brother), James Mason, William Long and William Beaty. The minutes reveal how Margaret had rebuffed Joseph's advances in the days before the attempted abduction took place. Margaret told the Session that 'she had given denyal to Joseph ... before he came to take her away'.[138] Undeterred, Joseph went to her house with four of his friends to persuade her to marry him. Although Joseph claimed that he only intended to 'take away ... Marg[aret] if she had been willing', the violent nature of the botched capture, together with him being in company with a group of men, bore all the hallmarks of a real abduction.[139]

That young men denied that their intention to forcibly carry off women is not that surprising, however, especially given the legal consequences of their actions. Indeed, it was likely fear of the legal repercussions of abduction that shaped the responses of the four men who had accompanied Joseph Barnes. When the men were questioned about their involvement, they refused to answer directly; instead, they 'desired Tho[mas] to prove that they were there' that evening.[140] In an effort to resolve the dispute without involving the civil courts, the Session asked Thomas Wallace whether he would be willing to 'not pursue' the men 'at law' if they confessed their fault to him personally.[141] Thomas consented to this arrangement. In April 1708 John Barnes, James Mason

John Tennent (1772–1813) was the son of the Reverend John Tennent, minister of Roseyards Presbyterian church, Ballymoney, County Antrim. He documented his time spent in service in his journal, a source which is used in chapter three of this book.

Unknown Artist, *Portrait of John Tennent,* oil on canvas, *c.* 1810, Ulster Museum, Belfast © National Museums NI

Following pages:
The linen industry played an important part in Ulster's rural economy and the whole family was involved in its production. In 1783, the artist William Hincks created a set of prints that depicted the different stages of linen production, as reproduced below.

Print by W. Hincks from a set of 12 plates illustrating the processes of linen manufacturing in Ireland. London, 1791. © Victoria and Albert Museum, London

Plate IV.

W.m Hincks. delin. et sculp.

KNOW all Men by these Presents That *I John Tennant of Roseyards in the Parish of Ballymoney and County Antrim* am holden and firmly bound unto *Saml Givin of Colerain Mercht* in the just and full Sum of *Fifty Pounds* sterl. good and lawful Money of Great-Britain, to be paid to the said *Saml Givin* or *his* lawful Attorney, Executors, Administrators or Assigns: To the which Payment well and truly to be made *I* do hereby bind *me my* Heirs, Executors, Administrators, and Assigns, firmly by these Presents. Sealed with *my* Seal and Dated the *Ninth* Day of *August* in the Year of our Lord, One Thousand Seven Hundred and *Eighty Six*

WHEREAS *John Tennant Junr of Roseyards & County Antrim* hath by Indenture of Apprenticeship, bearing equal Date with these Presents, put *himself* an Apprentice to the above-named *Saml Givin* for the Term of *Four years* as by the said Indentures may appear: The Condition therefore of the above Obligation is such, that if the *John Tennant* shall faithfully and truly serve the said *Master* during the said Term, without wasting or purloining *his sd Masters* Goods, and observe and perform all other the Covenants and Clauses in the said Indentures mentioned, according to the true Intent and Meaning of them, as the Law doth prescribe in such Cases; that then this Obligation shall be void and of none Effect, or else shall stand and remain in full Force and Virtue in Law.

J: Tennent

Signed, Sealed, and Delivered
in the Presence of

Saml Taylor

Ben Givin

Apprentice contracts were legal documents that outlined the costs and terms of service. John Tennent was bound as an apprentice to Samuel Givin, a grocer's merchant from Coleraine, for a period of four years. His father, the Reverend John Tennent, paid Samuel Givin a sum of 'Fifty Pounds' sterling for his son's instruction.

The Deputy Keeper of the Records, Public Record Office Northern Ireland and National Museums Northern Ireland, Ulster Museum

Opposite:
Apprenticeship contracts attempted to control the youthful impulses of apprentices. Like many apprentices, thirteen-year-old John Tennent was prohibited from engaging in sexual intercourse and from marrying during the term of his apprenticeship. He was also banned from playing cards or dice and from attending taverns, ale-houses and playhouses.

The Deputy Keeper of the Records, Public Record Office Northern Ireland and National Museums Northern Ireland, Ulster Museum

This Indenture

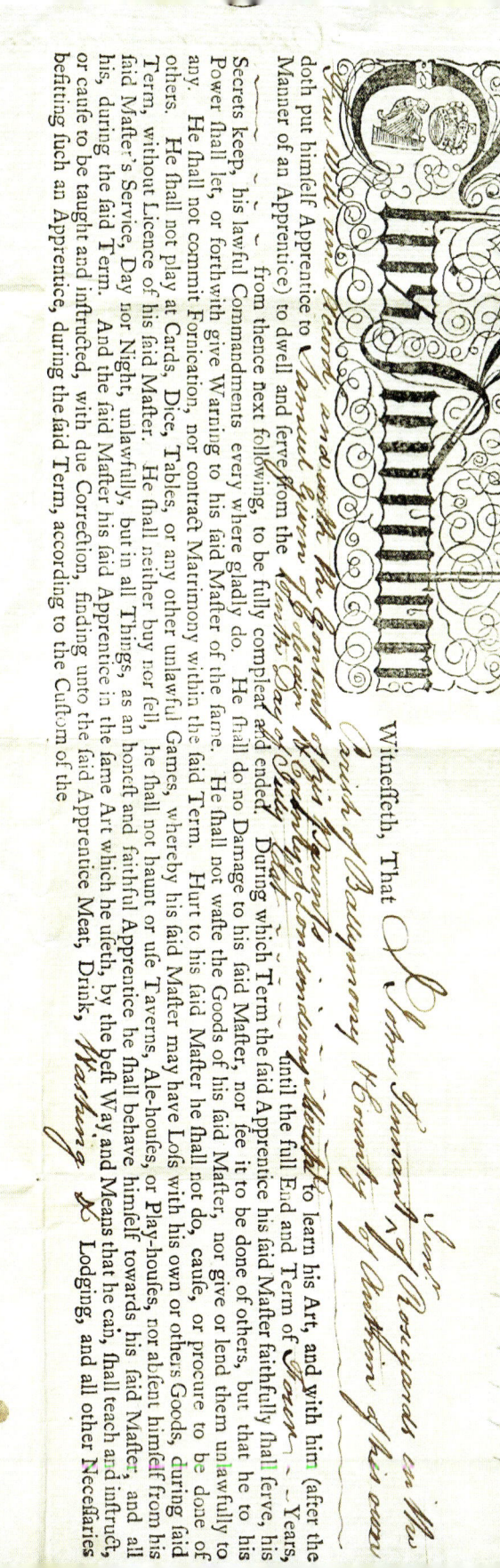

Witnesseth, That John Jennings of Newgrounds in the Parish of Ballymony County of Antrim of his own will and mere Motion and with the Consent of his parents doth put himself Apprentice to Samuel Guin of Ballymony in the County & Kingdom aforesaid Weaver to learn his Art, and with him (after the Manner of an Apprentice) to dwell and serve, from the 16th day of September one thousand seven hundred and Eighty six until the full End and Term of Seven Years, from thence next following, to be fully compleat and ended. During which Term the said Apprentice his said Master faithfully shall serve, his Secrets keep, his lawful Commandments every where gladly do. He shall do no Damage to his said Master, nor see it to be done of others, but that he to his Power shall let, or forthwith give Warning to his said Master of the same. He shall not waste the Goods of his said Master, nor give or lend them unlawfully to any. He shall not commit Fornication, nor contract Matrimony within the said Term. Hurt to his said Master he shall not do, cause, or procure to be done of others. He shall not play at Cards, Dice, Tables, or any other unlawful Games, whereby his said Master may have Loss with his own or others Goods, during said Term, without Licence of his said Master. He shall neither buy nor sell, he shall not haunt or use Taverns, Ale-houses, or Play-houses, nor absent himself from his said Master's Service, Day nor Night, unlawfully, but in all Things, as an honest and faithful Apprentice he shall behave himself towards his said Master, and all his, during the said Term. And the said Master his said Apprentice in the same Art which he useth, by the best Way and Means that he can, shall teach and instruct, or cause to be taught and instructed, with due Correction, finding unto the said Apprentice Meat, Drink, Washing & Lodging, and all other Necessaries befitting such an Apprentice, during the said Term, according to the Custom of the

And for the true Performance of all and every the said Covenants and Agreements, either of the said Parties bindeth himself to the other by these Presents. In WITNESS whereof the Parties above-named to these INDENTURES interchangeably have put their Hands and Seals, the Twelfth ———— Day of August and in the Year of our Lord God, One Thousand Seven Hundred and Eighty Six ———— and in the Twenty Sixth Year of the Reign of our Sovereign Lord George the Third ———— of Great-Britain, France, and Ireland, King, ———— Defender of the Faith, and so forth.

Signed, Sealed and Delivered
in the Presence of

Benjamin Guin
Sam:ll Taylor

John Jennings
Sam Guin

The sd Florence being asked
why she did not cry she said
it was ye divel that hindered
her. Jeames Macky appear:
& declares that his sister told
him that Wm Smith desired
her to go over the water till
she should see what god would
do to her. also his wife would
give her a years wages to
make the thing black.

Wm Smith being present
denyed he said only that he
was owing her a years wages
which his wife desired him
to pay to her.

The Sess: considered ye matter
delayed it till they should have
further light in it.

June 2d 2410 after
prayer sess: did sit at Carnamuddy
before which Wm Smith did
appear & brought in Tho:
Hunter & John Alloe: to
prove Florence Macky a
lyer in that she said he
lay with her in a room
above ye fire.

The sd Tho: & John declare
that they came to Wm
Smiths house from ye fair
of Burnecrenagh at four of
ye clock at night & sat by
ye sd William all night
by ye fire as he waited on
Tho Bill nob, & a little after
they came to him he sent
ye sd Florence to her bed
Item Ann Wood declared
the same to ye above namd
Tho: & John

William Smith brought
in Christian McCarter
who declared that ye sd
Florence stoll a bottle of
aquavite from Wm Smith
& hid it in the byer, ye sd
Christian took up: said
which Wm Smith said
occasiond ye sd florence
to repreach him
Florence Macky being asked
why she did not discover
these things sooner answerd
& said that she would discov
Morrows wife to discover
it, but Marg: Elder being
ded in Tho: Morrows house
she did not discover it.

Tho: Morrow appears
& declared that ye sd Florence
came to his house at that
time very troubled & her
cheeks all bedewed with tears
The sd Florence was asked
if Wm Smith had any discourse
to her at ye time, she sd no
her, tho he would not
for all his horse, she would
cry when she sd she would
cry. The Sess: considered ye
matter parties being removed
judges it fit to relate ye
matter to ye presb: for advice
Item Wm Ramsy ordered
to cite Ja: mcConnal to ye sess
June 5. 2410 ye sd day james
mcConnal appeared not ye
appointment renewed to cite
ye sd Ja: to ye sess: June 22
2410 Item David Scott appointed
to attend ye presb at Donoghedy
June 6. performed.
June 22 sess: did meet
for distributing ye poors
money.
This day James mcConnall sd
would not appear because
he got not 8 days warning
before ye sess: meet. ye business
was delayed till further consid.
Item Sarah Coldwell app:
& being asked if Wm Smith
offerd to commite uncleanness
with her as was reported she sd
he did not offer yet she sd
he was not good.

June 28 2410.
William Ramsay appointed to cite
James mcConnall to appear before
the elder of Burt June 29 2410
June 29 2410 James mcConnall
appeared & being asked if he would
acknowledge his wronging Janet
Strawbridge yet would not submit
or acknowledge his wronging of her
but said it was herself that raised the
scandal by relateing to Anna Rosse
that she & James mcConnal was in
Robert Wallace bank together in the
night time & so was the first raiser
of ye scandal.
Mr Ferguson enquired at Anna Rosse
& Janet Strawbridge ever told her that
James mcConnal & she was in Robert
Wallace bank in the night time
Anna Rosse denyed before witnesses
that ever Janet Strawbridge told her
or that she said to any person that
Janet said so to her.
next session to be July 23 2410

Opposite, top left:
In May 1710, Florence Macky accused her master, William Smith, of rape. In this extract, Florence's brother, James Macky, tells Burt Kirk Session how William and his wife tried to bribe Florence to leave Ireland to cover up her potential pregnancy. William and his wife denied the allegation, arguing instead that they only offered to pay Florence the wages she was owed.

> James Macky appears & declares that his sister told him that W[illia]m Smith desired her to go over the water till she should see what god would do w[i]t[h] her also his wife would give her a years wages to make the thing black. … W[illia]m Smith being present denyed he said so only that he was owing her a years wages which his wife desired him to pay it to her.

Burt Kirk Session minute book, 1676–1719. Image courtesy of the Gamble Library of Union Theological College, Belfast.

Below:
Courting couples might give each other gifts and tokens to symbolise their growing emotional bond. Robert James Tennent (1803–80) had in his possession many such love tokens. Below are two that he received from a young Belfast woman named Hannah McGee. The lock of hair, gifted from Hannah in September 1820, might once have been tied into a neat plait and could have become undone due to excessive touch. When Hannah ended their romance in July 1821, she enclosed a broken ring along with her break-up letter. The ring, she said, resembled her broken heart.

The Deputy Keeper of the Records, Public Record Office Northern Ireland and National Museums Northern Ireland, Ulster Museum

WHEREAS George Stuart, Son of William Stuart of Newry, Apprentice of James Jordan, Hosier, eloped from his Apprenticeship the 10th of April last, without any just Cause: This is therefore to caution the Publick not to harbour or employ said George Stuart after the Date hereof, as I am determined to prosecute them to the utmost Rigour of the Law. Said Stuart is about five Feet four Inches high, slender made, pale Complexion, and pitted with the Small-pox, wears his Hair; had on when he run off dark Fustian Cloaths pretty much worn. Given under my Hand, Newry the 7th of June, 1769. JAMES JORDAN.

P. S. Said Jordan carries on the Hosiery Business as usual. Ladies and Gentlemen who please to employ him, may depend on having their Work done with the greatest Care and Punctuality, and on the most reasonable Terms.

Above:
In April 1769, an apprentice named George Stuart absconded from his master's service. His master was James Jordan, a hosier from Newry in County Down. James posted an advertisement in the *Belfast News Letter* to capture his AWOL apprentice. He was described as being 'five Feet four Inches high, slender made, pale Complexion, and pitted with the Small-pox'.

Belfast News Letter, 9 June 1769, page 1. With Thanks to Irish Newspaper Archives and the *Belfast Newsletter.*

Below:
In November 1761, Henry McGladrye, a shoemaker from County Antrim, posted an advertisement in the *Belfast News Letter* announcing that his wife, Martha, had eloped from the marital home. It was common for spouses, especially husbands, to post these notices in Irish newspapers.

Belfast News Letter, 27 November 1761, page 3. With Thanks to Irish Newspaper Archives and the *Belfast Newsletter.*

WHEREAS Martha Boyd, otherwise Mc. Gladry, wife to Henry Mc. Gladrey near Roughfort in the county of Antrim, Shoemaker, did, on the sixth of this instant November elope from her said husband without any just cause. Now this is to caution the publick not to give the said Martha any credit either in money or goods for I will not pay any debt she shall contract. As witness my hand this 23d day of November, 1761. HENRY Mc. GLADRYE.

and William Long were rebuked by the Session for aiding Joseph Barnes in the planned abduction. In line with the agreement, the three men also 'acknowledged their fault to Tho[mas] Wallace' and asked him for forgiveness. Thomas accepted their apology, and the men were then 'reconciled'.[142] The Session 'ordered' that William Beaty, who failed to make any apology for his role, was 'to be disowned' until he confessed his fault.[143]

While many women were certainly abducted against their will, this was not always the case. Some women colluded in their abductions to force their parents to consent to marriage.[144] When John McDowell was cited before Burt Kirk Session in December 1707 for the abduction of Margaret Elder, he claimed that he had only done so with her consent. The case was brought to the attention of the Session by Margaret's father, John Elder, who complained that McDowell 'had taken away his daughter Margaret w[i]t[h] a designe to marry her'. McDowell, he alleged, had tricked Margaret by telling her he was 'going to be married to Mary Granger' and that he required Margaret to accompany them as a 'maid'.[145] Margaret confirmed her father's account and told the Session that she 'knew not' of McDowell's designs 'to marrie her' and that as soon as she discovered his intentions, she 'desired' him 'to take her home againe'.[146] John McDowell did not deny that he had 'taken [Margaret] away' from her father's house with intentions to marry; indeed, he framed his actions in the language of love by telling the Session of the 'kindnesse' he felt for the young woman. John claimed that Margaret had 'consented to his getting a licence' to marry, and that she had instructed him to buy her shoes and gloves, and to 'take a house' for them in Strabane.[147] Margaret denied that she gave her consent freely, telling the Session that 'she was forced to consent' to the obtaining of the marriage licence out of fear of 'abuse'. She explained that she had planned 'to flee to [the] minister to rescue her' before the marriage was performed.[148] The Session sided with the Elder family. John was rebuked for 'his fault in carrying away' Margaret 'with a designe to marry her' and was ordered to confess his sorrow for the same to John Elder.[149]

William Tennent's marriage

William Tennent did not follow his father's advice and marry the Scottish woman who followed him to Belfast. He did, however, continue to maintain an intimate relationship with her. The woman in question was possibly Anne Henry, who gave birth to six of William's children; the last of these, a daughter named Theresa, was born sometime in 1805.[150] Anne was also not the only woman to give birth to William's children. It is estimated that he fathered at least thirteen children with four different women outside of marriage.[151] William's liberal attitude to sex was the cause of much concern to his ageing parents. His father wrote often to him on the subject and was explicit in his disapproval of his son's lifestyle. Writing in March 1802, the Reverend Tennent chastised William for his disregard of the seventh commandment and reminded him that men should not 'abus[e] a woman as a wife without ye bonets of marriage'.[152] The Reverend Tennent urged his son to reflect on how he might feel if a man 'should behave toward' his 'Sister or Daughter' as he had done with the mothers of his children.[153]

To the great delight of both of his parents, William Tennent did eventually marry, in February 1805, a few months shy of his forty-sixth birthday. His wife was not one of the mothers of his illegitimate children, but a woman named Eleanor Jackson, who was the daughter of a Dublin member of the United Irishmen.[154] Ann Patton, William's mother, was especially pleased with his choice of wife. She directed her husband to add a '2[n]d PS' to their letter of congratulations, a line the Reverend Tennent remarked that 'she positively insisted' that he write.[155] In contrast to her pointed sentiments about William's rumoured marriage with the 'Scottish woman', Ann wanted her son to know how 'happy' and 'thankfull' she was with his choice of Eleanor.[156] As the Reverend Tennent wrote, 'She has found one on whom she can w[i]t[h] pleasure bestow your own picture on w[he]n she is now past wearing it'.[157] Eleanor was not just a suitable wife for William, she was worthy of his mother's approval.[158]

CHAPTER SIX

'She declar'd she study'd to carry as a dutifull wife': Married life

In April 1703 rumours of infidelity, desertion and marital breakdown were circulating around Carnmoney, County Antrim. Reports were spread that 'Thomas Hamilton had deserted his wife Mary Cuningham' and that he had 'gone away' with a woman named Agnes Hamilton. The whereabouts of the runaway couple was at that time, however, 'not known'. 'Information' about the scandal was soon passed to Carnmoney Kirk Session, which called Mary before it to tell what she knew about the affair.[1] When she appeared the following May, Mary confirmed that the report was true and said that she had since heard where her husband and Agnes were living. In its efforts to uncover the cause of the split, the Session 'interrogated' Mary 'what on her part' might have 'provoke[d]' Thomas 'to leave'. Mary was indignant. She 'declar'd' that she had 'gave him none but study'd to carry as a dutifull wife'. Thomas, she said, had deserted her and their family of his own free will, and she was 'both grieved for her family and angry' with him for running off with another woman.[2]

The Session tracked down Thomas and Agnes and called them to appear and give their account of events. Both confirmed that the report was true. Thomas 'acknowledged his sin of living in adultery' with Agnes, as well as 'deserting his own wife Mary Cunningham'. He 'promis[d] subjection' to the Session's ruling. Agnes, 'the adulteress', also 'confess'd sin in living in adultery'.[3] Like Thomas, Agnes also appears to have deserted her family. In addition to adultery, Agnes admitted 'leaving her fatherless children' when she took off with Thomas.[4] The Session ruled that both were to undergo church censure once they demonstrated sufficient repentance. As was usual in cases of adultery, Thomas was ordered to stand publicly before the congregation on three separate Sabbaths, as well as to appear before the Presbytery.[5] Agnes received a similar sentence; however, 'being very big with child' it was agreed that her appearance before the Presbytery should be delayed.[6] Agnes stood before the Presbytery in October, approximately one month after giving birth to Thomas's child. She was ordered to stand publicly before the congregation once more before she could be absolved, on account of the 'aggravating circumstances' of 'her atrocious crime' – likely a reference to the abandonment of her children.[7]

For many couples, the realities of married life deviated sharply from idealised expectations of domestic bliss. Adultery, marital disputes and the breakdown of relationships were as common in the past as they are today. There are, however, some important differences across time. Today, couples who find themselves in unhappy or unworkable marriages can extricate themselves relatively easily from their relationships. If they meet someone new and desire to marry again, they are likewise free to do so. Divorce and remarriage are an achievable legal reality for people in contemporary Ireland. They were not, however, so easily attainable for women and men in eighteenth- and early-nineteenth-century Ulster. Absolute divorce, which cut the marriage tie between two individuals and left them free to marry again, was not widely available; neither was it an easy process to navigate.

The breaking of marriage

The power to dissolve marriage in Ireland was officially vested in the ecclesiastical courts, which represented the interests of the Anglican state. These courts offered two main solutions to Irish couples who desired to end their marriages. Couples could apply for what was known as divorce *a vinculo matrimonii*, meaning 'from the chains of marriage'. This option confirmed that the marriage was null and void and thereby enabled couples to marry again on the basis that the marriage had never existed in the first place. The criteria on which this form of divorce was granted, however, were quite limited. An inability to consummate the marriage, evidence that one or both had been coerced into the marriage, that the marriage was bigamous (one of the parties was already married), or that the parties were within the prohibited degrees of consanguinity or affinity, were considered acceptable grounds.[8]

More commonly, those who sought to end their marriage applied for the second type of divorce offered by the ecclesiastical courts: divorce *a mensa et thoro* (from 'bed and board'). Strictly speaking, this form of 'divorce' was more like judicial separation; couples were permitted to live apart, but they were not granted permission to remarry. Husbands were also bound to continue to support their wives financially, in the form of an annuity.[9] The financial benefit to wives meant that more women than men petitioned for this form of divorce.[10] While the outcome of divorce *a mensa et thoro* was favourable to women, the processes for securing it were not. Until the middle of the nineteenth century, the criteria for achieving a judicial separation were gendered and weighted heavily in favour of men. Whereas a husband merely had to prove that a wife had committed adultery, wives were required to prove adultery in addition to cruel treatment, incest or other 'unnatural practices'.[11]

It was also possible to secure absolute divorce in Ireland by petitioning parliament. According to Diane Urquhart, until 1922 parliamentary divorce was 'the sole legal process' in Ireland that ended a marriage and then allowed remarriage while a spouse was still living.[12] The process was time-consuming, expensive and gendered, and it involved three separate legal suits. The first stage involved a suit known as criminal conversation, also known as 'crim con'. This suit enabled a 'cuckolded husband' to sue his wife's lover for damages in the common law courts.[13] Women were considered the 'marital property' of their husbands and their adultery could be compensated in the form of damages. Wives could not, however, bring these suits against their husband's mistress. Although adultery committed by both parties was considered 'a serious marital offence', it was regarded as even more severe on the part of wives due to its implications for the transmission of property and inheritance.[14] Because complainants had to provide proof of adultery, the cases attracted lots of public and press attention. The proceedings were published in Irish newspapers and in printed volumes. Irish readers were subsequently titillated with lurid details of alleged adulterous activity, including commentary on torn and stained clothing, bedclothes in states of disarray, secret letters, discovered love tokens, and tales of wives caught in the act with their lovers by their shocked and angry husbands.[15]

The second stage in the process was an application to the ecclesiastical courts for divorce *a mensa et thoro* to effect separation. Finally, an application for a private act of parliament to grant divorce *a vinculo matrimonii* was made.[16] The minimum cost for obtaining a parliamentary divorce was between £450 and £500 and, in some cases, it could reach up to £5,000.[17] The costs of parliamentary divorce meant that it was a route that could be afforded only by the wealthy. Between 1730 and 1800, only eleven private divorce acts were presented to the Irish parliament. The gendered operations of the law also meant it was an option that was overwhelmingly pursued by men. Diane Urquhart has argued that the gendered grounds of divorce constitute 'one of the most striking and long-lived examples of the sexual double standard'.[18] No Irish women and just four Englishwomen divorced in the period before 1857.[19] In that year, the Divorce and Matrimonial Causes Act was passed, which transferred the legal processes of divorce from parliament to a court-based system in England and Wales. The act made obtaining a divorce faster, cheaper and less cumbersome, and resulted in increasing numbers of women applying for divorce.[20] Ireland, however, was excluded from this legislation and it continued to follow the parliamentary route into the twentieth century.

Members of the Presbyterian church in Ulster had other options; they could also seek divorce through their church. The Presbyterian church made explicit room for absolute divorce in its standards. According to the *Westminster Confession of Faith*, divorce with the option of remarriage was possible in cases of adultery and 'wilful Desertion'.[21] Unlike the gendered criteria that underpinned petitions for divorce in the ecclesiastical courts or before parliament, divorce was theoretically available to Presbyterian women and men on equal terms. Presbyterian belief and practice were underpinned by the concept of fault divorce, which granted the right to divorce and remarry solely to the aggrieved partner. Presbyterian standards directed that, irrespective of gender, individuals whose partners had committed 'Adultery after Marriage' were able to sue for divorce and marry another 'as if the offending Party were dead'.[22] Similarly, in cases where adultery or fornication had been committed before marriage, the 'innocent Party' had 'just occasion' to dissolve the contract.[23]

Even though the Presbyterian church had mechanisms in place for divorce and remarriage, very few women and men actually made use of them. Irish Presbyteries, the middle-level church court empowered to grant divorce, seldom considered divorce petitions. A survey of twelve Presbytery minute books for the period 1700 to 1840 reveals evidence of just fourteen such petitions.[24] These relatively low numbers partly reflect the fact that the legal status of divorces granted by the Presbyterian church were hazy at best.[25] As we know, the ability of the Presbyterian church to make (and break) the marriages of its members was contested across the eighteenth and nineteenth century. The low numbers are also indicative of the broader Irish distaste for public divorce proceedings. As was the case with divorces offered by the ecclesiastical courts, the relatively low numbers of petitions reflect 'the social stigma' of divorce in Ireland.[26] Maria Luddy and Mary O'Dowd point out in their history of Irish marriage that many couples preferred to handle the breakdown of their marriages 'as discreetly as possible' and made their own arrangements to end their marriages outside of the formal options that were available.[27]

Runaway wives and eloping husbands

The easiest, and perhaps most favourable, option for individuals who were caught in unhappy marriages was simply to walk out the door and never return. While some appeared to be dismayed or claimed they were taken unawares by the departure of their spouse, many others colluded with their partners and agreed to separate using this method.[28] This is what appeared to have happened in the case of James Kirkwood, a member of the Presbyterian congregation of Finvoy in County Antrim. In July 1814 James appeared before the Presbytery of Route and appealed for access to church privileges. Finvoy Kirk Session had refused to admit James as a member after he contracted a second marriage, likely within the lifetime of his first wife.[29] James explained that his first wife had 'deserted him' a 'short time' after their marriage.[30] Despite making 'repeated solicitations' for her return, his wife 'could not be prevailed on'.[31] Unable and unwilling to reconcile, James and his wife then mutually agreed to separate. According to James, the pair 'gave under their hands with mutual consent' that they 'were to have no further intercourse nor after claim'.[32] On the strength of this promise, he then 'married another wife'.[33] The Presbytery directed that James was to be rebuked for the manner in which his first marriage had been solemnised, it having been celebrated by an 'irregular clergyman', and that he then be restored as a member.[34] The bigamous potential of his second marriage was not commented upon.

That desertion was prevalent in Ulster society is indicated by newspaper coverage of abandoned husbands and wives. Readers of Irish newspapers would have been familiar with elopement notices placed by aggrieved spouses to advertise the departure of their partner from the marital home.[35] These advertisements were overwhelmingly placed by husbands, who cautioned the public that they would not pay any debts accumulated by their wayward wives. Mary O'Dowd has noted that there were about '900' such notices placed by husbands in the *Belfast Newsletter* between 1750 and 1800.[36] The majority of these notices were placed by men who lived in Counties Antrim and Down, which were areas of dense Presbyterian settlement.[37] As Luddy and O'Dowd have argued, these geographical patterns were significant, given the grounds on which the Presbyterian church permitted women and men to break the marital tie.[38] Typical of most notices was that placed by Henry McGladrye, a shoemaker from County Antrim, in November 1761, who advertised that his wife Martha had 'elope[d]' from their marital home 'without any just cause'.[39] Henry 'caution[ed] the publick' not to extend Martha 'any credit either in money or goods', and he said he would 'not pay debts she shall contract'.[40] Like many elopement notices, Henry's emphasised his wife's 'wilful desertion' from the marital home.

While the purpose of these notices was to disclaim legal responsibility for a wife's debts, husbands also took the opportunity to punish and shame their wives for eloping.[41] Men sometimes cast aspersions on their wives' moral characters by insinuating that they had been unfaithful. In June 1799 a notice was placed by William Pearley from Lurgan in County Antrim, to caution the public 'not to credit' his wife Elizabeth, who he claimed had not only 'absented without any just cause' but had 'behaved very improperly'.[42] Other men emphasised the unnaturalness of their wives' behaviour, pointing to how they had abandoned not only their marital home, but their motherly responsibilities too. In January 1754 Samuel Cord told readers of the *Belfast Newsletter* that his wife, Agnes, not only 'threatens to ruin' him by 'contracting Debt', but that she had 'left with him two Children, one of which was sucking her at the Time of her Departure'.[43]

Wives seldom posted in response, but when they did, they denied that they had absconded from the marital home freely. Some wives said they had been driven from the marital home by violence.[44] When David Cuddy advertised that his wife, Jane Kirk, had eloped and 'taken away sundry of his Goods', Jane decided to reply to his notice for her own 'Vindication'. Jane told readers of the *Belfast Newsletter* that her husband David had 'used her on all Occasions in a cruel unbecoming Manner', and that he had 'often threaten[ed] to kill her'.[45] She was in 'such Fear' of her husband that she was unable to 'sleep in the House with him' and had even appealed to her 'Neighbours to lie in the same House' for her protection.[46]

Other women, such as Jane Marshal, were fired by a desire to clear their characters. Jane's husband, a man named John Marshal, had published a notice in January 1768 in which he claimed she had absconded from the marital home and never returned. While John had offered no reasons for her departure, his notice cast doubt on her sexual character. According to John, he 'firmly resolved never after to treat' Jane 'as his Wife ... for Reasons he doesn't like to publish'.[47] As Jane herself remarked, the ambiguity of her husband's notice was damaging: 'he most cruelly and unjustly impeaches [my character] with some nameless Imprudence, artfully couched under those Reasons he does not like to publish'.[48]

Jane then offered her version of events. She alleged that she was the victim of a nefarious plan, concocted by her husband, to make her appear as an absconding wife. Jane told readers of the *Belfast Newsletter* that she and John had 'mutually' set out from their home in Mullaghmossagh, County Tyrone, on 29 December 1768, on a visit to her father's home, near Lisburn in County Antrim.[49] On 4 January 1769 the pair set off again on the journey home, 'riding on the same Horse'.[50] Two miles into their journey they came across 'a small Cabin where Spirits were sold'.[51] It was then that John informed Jane that 'he had left a Pair of Gloves' behind and asked her 'to stay there till he would return for them'.[52] Jane said she 'obeyed his Order's and stayed at the cabin 'till near 12 o'Clock at Night'.[53] John, however, never returned. Feeling 'ashamed' that her husband could 'treat [her] with such Disrespect', she began to walk 'along the Road ... in hopes he would come up'.[54] It was a cold winter's night; Jane said that the 'Snow was deep' and feeling 'fatigued' she broke down 'some Furz Branches' and 'sat down under a Hedge by the Road Side'. Here she stayed until the next morning.[55] According to Jane, she 'never' again 'laid [her] Eyes upon' her husband, nor did she 'ever hear' from him again.[56]

Jane then challenged John to 'declare what Part' of her 'Conduct' had 'induced him to treat' her with 'such unexampled Barbarity' and to 'publish it to the World'.[57] Confident that she had no case to answer, Jane dared him to 'expose' her 'to all the world'.[58] Her tone was biting:

> But how can I be charged with Elopement? Nay, rather applaud me for Obedience. Did you not desire me; did you not order me to stay till you would come for me? I obeyed. You never came. If so, where is my Transgression? If I am guilty, Obedience to your Commands is the only Crime of her who has now the Misfortune to be JANE MARSHAL.[59]

Advertising one's marital misfortunes was undoubtedly a risky strategy, for both parties involved.

The consequences of desertion were regularly dealt with by the Presbyterian church courts. Presbyteries were often called upon by Kirk Sessions to give advice in cases of church members who either desired to remarry or had remarried without permission during the lifetime of their absent spouse. Such marriages were, after all, technically bigamous and thus theoretically subject to criminal punishment. Until the early nineteenth century, the punishment for bigamy was death or transportation. The law was subsequently amended in 1829, reducing the maximum sentence to transportation for seven years.[60] The Presbyterian church treaded carefully in its assessment of desertion cases, balancing the guidelines of the church with the law of the land. Following Presbyterian guidelines on 'wilful desertion' as grounds for divorce, the church courts inquired into the reasons and timeline of desertion and remarriage. In October 1807 Clontibret Kirk Session asked the Presbytery of Monaghan for advice when Margaret McKeifer, a member of its congregation, asked to marry again. Margaret had been married fourteen years previously to a man named Robert Allister.[61] Within one year of their marriage, Robert had deserted Margaret 'without a cause'.[62] In addition to wilful desertion, he had also committed adultery with Margaret's sister, Jane. Robert had since migrated to America, where it was believed he had married at least three more times.[63] The Presbytery was sympathetic. Weighing up her husband's transgressions, together with Margaret's 'prudent sober behaviour', it ruled that it was 'lawfull' for her to remarry.[64]

Cases of desertion and remarriage were even more complex when errant partners suddenly returned, or word was received that spouses believed to be long dead were in fact alive. In February 1823 Ballyblack Kirk Session sought the advice of Down Presbytery when it emerged that Hugh Gebby 'had married a second time not knowing' that his wife 'was still living'.[65] Hugh was employed as a soldier and in 1805 was 'sent abroad' on service.[66] In 1806 Hugh received a letter from his wife, written from a London hospital, where 'she was confined by sickness'.[67] This was the last communication he received from his wife. According to Hugh, 'From this date till 1815 he got no Letter from her nor any account of her, tho' she had opportunity at any time of knowing where he was & writing to him'.[68] When Hugh returned to England in 1815, he received a letter from his 'brother in Ireland' stating that it 'was said & believed' that his wife was 'dead'.[69] 'Resting on this testimony of her decease', Hugh then remarried.[70] As his wife had been missing for almost nine years, Hugh was legally within his rights to remarry. According to common law, it was possible for an individual to remarry if their spouse had been missing for a minimum of seven years; errant partners were, at this point, deemed to be legally dead.[71] Hugh's wife was not, however, dead. Less than two years later she appeared at Hugh's house 'in straitened circumstances', before quickly disappearing again. Hugh told the Session that he had no idea where she had gone and that she had 'not since returned'.[72] The Presbytery was sympathetic to Hugh's predicament. Taking into consideration his particular 'circumstances', it ruled that Hugh 'should not be excluded' from church membership. His second marriage was considered by the Presbytery to be lawful.

Infidelity

Of all the offences that the Presbyterian church courts dealt with, adultery was regarded as among the most heinous. Not only did adultery undermine the purpose of marriage, it was considered as grounds for divorce by the Presbyterian church and it was also an offence that threatened the safety and harmony of the wider community. As the Irish Presbyterian minister John McBride expounded in his 1702 pamphlet, *A Vindication of Marriage*, adultery not only threatened the 'Common-wealths [that] arise from, and are preserved by Marriages', it 'shakes their Foundations [and] converts conjugal Love into mutual Hatred'.[73] The unhappiness that festered in adulterous households had the potential to bleed out into the surrounding community and fill 'whole Houses … with Reproaches and Feuds', resulting in 'publick Miseries and Destruction'.[74]

Adultery was not just punishable in the Presbyterian church courts, it was also an offence that was prosecuted in the Irish ecclesiastical courts. Between 1700 and 1711, twenty-three cases of adultery were heard by Killaloe diocesan court, making it the second-highest most recorded offence after fornication.[75] As we have already seen, adultery was invoked in 'crim con' (criminal conversation) cases – civil actions initiated by husbands against the men with whom their wives had committed adultery. If successful, men who initiated 'crim con' actions were awarded financial damages. While the rationale for assessing damages changed over time, factors such as the plaintiff's loss of honour, the loss of his wife's 'comfort and society', and the happiness of the marriage prior to the breach, were all considered.[76] Niamh Howlin has noted that some men in early-nineteenth-century Ireland were awarded damages in the amount of £5,000.[77] Interestingly, 'crim con' suits survived as a legal process in Northern Ireland until 1939 and in the Republic of Ireland until 1981. According to Diane Urquhart, 'crim con' in the Republic was 'far from a nineteenth-century relic'; in the ten years before it was abolished, six cases were lodged by Irish complainants.[78]

Although the Presbyterian church considered adultery a serious moral infraction, cases were seldom considered by Irish Kirk Sessions. In a sample of sixteen Irish Kirk Session minute books across the period 1700–1844, adultery accounted for just four per cent of cases.[79] Such small numbers do not, however, mean that adultery did not occur. As an illicit sexual relationship, adultery naturally took place in secret. Couples who engaged in adulterous affairs did their best to keep their trysts hidden from public knowledge, not least because they feared the volatile reaction of their families, friends and neighbours. When Cahans Kirk Session in County Monaghan twice dismissed a charge of adultery that was levelled against Margaret Macrea and John Wales, the community's anger was palpable. The case first appeared before the Session in November 1755, when 'a flagrant report' was circulated that John was 'guilty of adultery' with Margaret.[80] Two witnesses appeared in their defence. A servant in John's house 'declared she never saw them guilty of it'.[81] Margaret's husband, William Scot, also testified that 'he believe[d] the whole report' was 'false'.[82] On the strength of these testimonies, together with the fact that the pair's 'character was not bad formerly', the Session dismissed the charge.[83] One week later, the Session reopened the case because 'the affair' was 'still making great noise in the country'. Once again, the Session dismissed the charge on the basis that there was 'no evidence'.[84]

One year later, in November 1756, the Session was forced to renew its investigation. John Lister, an elder of the Session, noted that the 'noise about the affair' had 'broke[n] out again with more violence than ever'.[85] Margaret was recalled to the Session. This time, however, she admitted that the report was true. According to Margaret, since her last appearance before the Session she had been much 'trouble[d]' by her 'lies'.[86] She subsequently confessed her sin to her husband, who had grown concerned about her 'very pensive' state of mind.[87] Margaret told the Session she had 'concealed' her guilt out of 'pity' for John Wales, who had 'exprest [his] great penitence' in 'private converse with her'.[88] To credit her story, Margaret offered the Session times, dates and places of their intimate trysts. She said they had engaged in sexual intercourse three times: 'once in John Wales's garden, another time in his stable & a third time in her own bed on a Sabbath morning' when her husband was away.[89] John 'stiffly denied' the allegations and continued to refute the truth of the reports.[90]

Given the hostile reaction of the community of Cahans to the rumours, it is unsurprising that Margaret and John did all they could to undermine each other's testimonies. Margaret's version of events portrayed John as the more culpable party. She told the Session how John had tried to 'seduce her' with 'long protestations of his love' and that he had even 'proposed selling his farm' so that they could run off 'to America' together. Their sexual encounters were also framed in language that painted John as the instigator. Whereas Margaret claimed that John had 'tossed her down and was guilty with her' in the barn, she said that he had 'seized her in her own bed & was guilty with her' in her own home.[91] Like many other men who denied allegations of sexual misconduct, John Wales attempted to undermine his accuser's credit by attacking her sexual reputation. John Dunn appeared on his behalf and testified that Margaret had behaved very freely with him in the past. According to John Dunn, 'above 3 years ago', he and Margaret were 'tossing & playing' on the floor together. As he rose up, he said to Margaret, 'You are a lusty girl! It's a pity someone would not get you with child.' Margaret, he said, had 'replied that she thought more affront of lying under the blame of having none than to try another man'. John Dunn essentially implied that Margaret was neither averse to having sex with another man, nor did she think it problematic to pass off another man's child as that of her husband.[92] John Wales also brought to the Session's attention a report that Margaret had been caught 'in the act of fornication ... above ten years ago' in County Tyrone – a story that could allegedly be confirmed by Margaret's 'own mother-in-law'.[93]

Faced with two contrasting stories, the Session referred the case to the Presbytery. John was given the opportunity to purge himself of guilt by taking the 'Oath of Purgation'. He was given '6 or 8 weeks' to consider the option.[94] In the meantime, Margaret was censured by the Kirk Session, not for adultery, but for 'her great sin of lying before God & the eldership' that the report was untrue.[95] She was publicly rebuked for this sin before the congregation.[96] As it turned out, John refused to take the Oath.[97] In October 1757, almost two years after the matter was initially referred to the Session, the elders decided to 'wait some time' for new evidence that could 'discover the real truth of [the] affair'.[98] While Margaret's story had not been proved true, her rebuke for lying indirectly confirmed her version of events. It is likely that John refused to co-operate because he feared the repercussions of his actions.

Cases of adultery that came before the courts were usually discovered when pregnancy occurred or when the behaviour of the parties roused the suspicions of others.[99] The Presbyterian church courts relied on community members to actively police one another's behaviour. Presbyterian women and men used their eyes, ears and tongues to watch, listen to and then report on the misbehaviour of their neighbours. Church members closely scrutinised the conduct of their neighbours and were quick to report anything that they considered suspicious. It was the prying eyes of neighbours that led Ballycarry Kirk Session in County Antrim to investigate an alleged tryst between David Weir, a married man, and Isobel Morton. They had been seen by Elizabeth Neilson and Michael Sweetman emerging from a ditch looking guilty and dishevelled. According to Elizabeth, she and Michael were 'siting together at the foot of Thomas Grels' yard, when they spied David and a woman coming 'over the ditch'.[100] Their attention had been alerted, not least because the woman had attempted to hide her identity by 'put[ting] her head behind Michaels back'.[101] Asked how she knew the man was definitely David Weir, Elizabeth said that she recognised him 'by the colour of his wig & cloathes & his voice'.[102] She was also sure it was him, having previously worked for David as a servant.[103]

Michael Sweetman's evidence, presented as a signed document, was even more damning. He claimed to have heard David and Isobel use each other's names in conversation. According to Michael, he 'heard' Isobel 'say will you make a fool of me & your selfe Mr Weir'.[104] Michael also said that he heard David say 'Bell [Isobel] rub the mules [soil] off thy back' – a statement that not only identified the couple but suggested they had been lying down together in the ditch.[105] Perhaps even more incriminating, Michael said that when he saw them emerging from the ditch, David had 'his hands under the henches of his coat as if he had been put[t]ing the buttons in his breeches'.[106]

Suspicious spouses sometimes weaponised the gossip network to expose their partner's suspected adultery. When rumours were spread that Jane Magill had engaged in an adulterous affair with James McCabe, it emerged that the source of the rumour was James's own wife, Mary McCabe. In June 1768 Jane complained to Cahans Kirk Session that three of her female neighbours had 'spread a report that there was some appearance of ... criminal correspondence' between her and James.[107] The women in question were named as Mary Wat, Elizabeth Gray and Mary McCabe. All three were cited to appear before the Session. Mary Wat confessed to spreading the report, but 'asserted strongly' that she had only done so at the direction of Mary McCabe.[108] She further admitted that she 'never saw anything or knew anything faulty' between James and Jane.[109] Elizabeth Gray also pointed the finger at Mary McCabe, who she said had 'complained to her' that James 'kept too much company with the Magills'.[110] Mary McCabe was last to be called. While she denied that she had said anything to Mary Wat about a suspected affair, she 'confessed she had said so to Elizabeth Gray'.[111] Mary McCabe then advised that another witness, a man named William Rowland, 'could say more'.[112] The Session ruled that there was 'nothing' from the evidences presented 'to condemn either James McCabe or Jane Magil' and deferred the matter 'until William Rowland' could 'be brought before them'.[113]

William's evidence was circumstantial at best. He told the Session that he had witnessed the pair 'standing' together 'at the foot of James McCabe's garden' the previous August.[114] Although it was 'dusky' and 'dark', William said that the two 'stood so nigh each other that he took them for one person'.[115] He further alleged that his appearance had spooked the couple, raising his suspicions that something untoward was going on. William told the Session that when James noticed him approaching, he 'went into his garden', putting distance between himself and Jane. When James realised who William was, he was reportedly relieved. William stated that James said to him, '"is that you Billy, I was afraid it was James Magil?"'.[116] While the Session agreed that the 'circumstances looked most doubtful' and were 'to be suspected', there was not enough evidence to prove guilt. Like the gossip circulated by the three women, William's evidence was insufficient.

Kirk Sessions required accusers to be able to prove their claims because individuals sometimes fabricated charges of adultery to ruin the reputations of those they accused. Malice allegedly underlay the charges of adultery laid against James Young and Margaret Lyk by George Keefe in November 1705.[117] George claimed to have caught James and Margaret in the aftermath of an 'indecent' act.[118] When asked by the Kirk Session to elaborate, George explained that he saw them 'coming out of a room' together with red faces, a constitution that 'he suppos'd' was caused by 'heat or shame'.[119] Margaret vehemently denied George's accusation. She told the Session that not only had she never been 'alone' with James in 'that pantry', but that he 'never frequented her house' any more often 'than the rest of the neighbourhood'.[120] James Young was likewise enraged at the accusation. According to the Session minutes, he 'resent[ed]' the charge to such a degree that he 'threat[e]ned to take Kelso with a warrand' (pursue the matter civilly).[121] After a thorough investigation, the Session ruled that George had made the story up. Remarking that George was 'convict of horid prevarication', the Session decided that the charge was a 'malicious aspersion'. George was ordered to 'appear before the congregation and acknowledg[e] his sin' in falsely accusing James and Margaret.[122]

Marital violence

Unhappy marriages also manifested in arguments and disputes between warring couples.[123] At times, these marital disputes were violent. In April 1703 James Boyd appeared before Route Presbytery and angrily accused it of having granted his wife, Margaret Kerr, a divorce.[124] The couple's marriage was anything but harmonious. James was a repeated philanderer and had been 'convict of divers adulterys'.[125] He had also declined to co-operate with church discipline, and refused to allow his family 'be orderly or be catechized'.[126] The marriage was also violent; it was known to the Presbytery that Margaret was 'being beaten grievously' by her husband.[127] While the

Presbytery had not awarded Margaret a divorce, they had 'granted her a testimoniall'.[128] Also known as a 'testificat' or 'certificate', a testimonial served as proof of a church member's good behaviour and standing. Testimonials acted as passports to church privileges, and they were essential letters of introduction for women and men who wished to join a new congregation.[129] It was likely the violent nature of the marriage that prompted the Presbytery to grant Margaret her testimonial. As the Presbytery noted, 'knowing' that James 'grew so abusive' to Margaret and that 'she fear'd for her life in his company', it had given her the testimonial 'that she might be admitted a member in any Christian congregation'.[130]

Cases of marital violence, however, were seldom presented to the church courts. Only a handful of such cases appear in the minute books of Irish Kirk Sessions and Presbyteries.[131] The low numbers of such cases in no way suggest that domestic violence was not a feature of Ulster society during this period. In their book on Irish marriage, Maria Luddy and Mary O'Dowd unearthed a 'substantial' number of murder and manslaughter cases involving spouses. Between 1772 and 1925, at least 713 cases of spousal murder and manslaughter were recorded in Irish newspapers, with an additional 85 attempted murders recorded over the same period.[132] Marital violence was also commonly dealt with by civil authorities. Spouses who alleged that their partners were violent could present their case to a justice of the peace or magistrate and ask that the violent partner be bound over to keep the peace.[133]

While the Presbyterian church courts may have dealt with relatively few cases of marital violence, those that did come to their attention did so because of their severity. The Presbyterian church got involved in disputes between wives and husbands only when they crossed the threshold of 'acceptable' levels of violence. Such a case was handled by the Presbytery of Monaghan in 1711, when a series of charges relating to marital abuse, public intoxication and threatening behaviour were levelled against the Reverend Robert Darragh, minister of First Monaghan congregation.[134] In addition to numerous allegations of alcohol misuse and quarrels with members of the Presbytery and lay community, Darragh was accused of keeping 'very bad order' in his family. According to the libel lodged against him, Darragh was renowned for 'frequent[ly] brawling' with his wife, Anne Fixter, despite her being 'und[er] affliction', and for 'scolding, beating and abusing' his servants.[135] His domestic terror was said to be so bad that his family was 'reported' to be on the brink of breaking up.[136]

As was usual in libel cases, the Presbytery called upon witnesses to substantiate the charges against the minister. James Maxwell appeared in February 1712 and told the court of the marital abuse he witnessed. James relayed to the Presbytery details of an argument that broke out between Darragh and his wife five years previously. James had been present at the house, having been hired to thatch the roof of Darragh's room. He told the Presbytery that Anne and Darragh 'fell out' one Friday to such a degree that 'worship was neglected in the family'.[137] Unable to control his passions, Darragh followed 'his wife from one room and corner of the house to the other scolding her'.[138] Not only was Darragh unable to keep his fury in check, but he likewise failed to make peace with his wife. The row between the pair continued into the weekend and lasted until at least the following Monday. Indeed, James admitted that it could have lasted even longer, telling the Presbytery 'how long after [the Monday] he cannot tell'.[139] James also testified that such rows were not uncommon between the pair, and that three years previously, Darragh had 'beat his wife down to the ground' – a fact that both parties had admitted.[140]

The point at which individuals and communities decided to intervene in violent marital disputes depended on several factors. In her work on wife-beating and marital violence in eighteenth-century England, Joanne Bailey has argued that there were many reasons why people were hesitant to get involved. Some individuals decided not to intervene on the grounds of 'self-preservation', the 'vicious' reputation of the husband being enough to ward off neighbourly interference.[141] Others may have felt that their interventions were 'pointless'.[142] When women failed to follow the advice of their neighbours and leave their violent partners, communities were much 'less likely to intervene' again in the future.[143] The social rank and status of offending men also played a part. As Janay Nugent has noted for communities in early modern Scotland, the 'consequences of challenging the privacy of one's social superiors could be severe'.[144] The Reverend Darragh's reputation for brawling certainly inspired fear in those who dared to testify against him. The Presbytery of Monaghan recorded in its minutes that it had heard a 'common report' that Darragh had 'terrif[ied] persons' who were called as witnesses in his case.[145]

Aside from his temper, Darragh's role as minister also imbued with him natural authority and privilege. It is likely that many in the community of Monaghan were simply too afraid to challenge their minister. Darragh, himself, was combative and obstructive throughout the Presbytery's investigation. While the witness testimony in the case only began to be collected from February 1712, the case had initially appeared before the Presbytery almost two years earlier, in June 1710. The Presbytery of Monaghan had been directed by the Synod in June 1710 to investigate 'into some scandalous reports' that were circulating about Darragh. Efforts to do so, however, were hindered when Darragh refused to co-operate.[146] Indeed, Darragh's fractious relationship with church authority was among other charges that were levelled against him. At a Presbytery meeting in January 1708, Darragh had allegedly behaved with 'much insolence' and used 'many hectoring and abusive words' towards those present. Indignant at being questioned about his behaviours, Darragh was said to have declared that he knew 'what belongs to [his] post' and threatened to 'twist' the noses of those who spoke against him, exclaiming in a 'furious manner' that he was 'a man as well as a minister'.[147]

Those living in proximity to the Darragh household were certainly aware of the abuse that Anne endured. They were also clearly uncomfortable with the knowledge that their minister was abusive. When Walter Bell told the Presbytery that he had witnessed Darragh's abusive behaviour first-hand, he described how the sight had impacted him at a visceral level. According to Walter, he went to Darragh's home to discuss the baptism of a child. As he entered the house, he saw Darragh 'beat a woman on the head' who he 'believed' was Mrs Darragh.[148] Walter, however, did not intervene. Instead, 'being ashamed to see it' he 'immediatly turn'd and came out' of the house.[149] Other witnesses told the Presbytery that Anne had directly appealed to them for help. James Maxwell, for example, deposed that Anne had 'appealed' to him 'to judge whether she was a fitt object to be beaten or not'.[150] While James did not divulge what he had answered (if indeed he had answered her question at all), he does appear to have told others of the abuse. William Adam, another witness in the case, told the Presbytery that James had relayed to him details of the domestic discord that swamped the Darragh household. Believing that William had some 'influence' over Darragh, James agreed to send for William whenever he 'observed any further disturbance' between the couple.[151] On one such occasion, William along with a man named Cornelius Rowan went to the Darragh household. There they were met by Anne who, 'in tears', 'appeall'd to them … whether she was a person fitt to be beaten by her husband'.[152] Again, Anne's appeals for intervention appear to have gone unanswered. According to William, Darragh answered Anne's question himself, and replied that 'he would be master in his own house'.[153]

Darragh's comments were couched in the language of patriarchy, drawing on contemporary beliefs that men were the rulers of their own households. Similar rationales were invoked by Darragh in response to charges that he had likewise beaten and abused his servants. John Randell, another witness, testified that 'brawling, abusing and beating' was the 'ordinary current of [Darragh's] way'.[154] Randall told how Darragh had once beaten a servant named John Smith with a pitch fork, and when challenged by the Kirk Session on the propriety of the punishment, he replied that 'it was no man's business and that he would chastise his family as he pleased'.[155] The charges brought against Darragh in relation to the abuse of his wife and servants were eventually proved. At a meeting of the General Synod in Belfast on 17 June 1712, a motion to rule that Darragh was guilty carried *nemine contradicente*, no one disagreeing.[156] He was subsequently deposed from office.[157] Anne Fixter, however, did not live to see her husband reprimanded for his abusive behaviour. Described throughout the case as being 'under an affliciton', she died sometime before November 1711.[158]

Thomas Hamilton and Mary Cunningham: Happily ever after?

Mary Cunningham and her husband Thomas Hamilton, the estranged couple whose story opened this chapter, do not seem to have ever reconciled. It likewise appears that Thomas and the woman with whom he eloped also failed to achieve a happy ending. Shortly after Agnes Hamilton gave birth, Thomas applied to Carnmoney Kirk Session for permission to have the child baptised.[159] He was not, however, the only person to make that application. According to the Kirk Session minute book, Agnes's father, with whom she was currently living, also requested baptism for the child.[160] In response to the Session's query as to 'what duty he design'd to do' for his child 'either for soul or body', Thomas 'promis'd' that he would 'sometime' in the future 'see some way to its maintenance'.[161] Robert's promises to maintain the child were not good enough. Described as a 'poor contemptible soldier' with 'no place of constant abode', Thomas was anything but the ideal father.[162] Reflecting on his financial situation, the Session decided that because there was 'no great probability' that Robert 'would make conscience of discharging' his duty to the child, that it was best for Agnes to 'hold it up' for baptism instead.[163] Given that it was traditionally the responsibility of fathers to present their children for baptism, the denial of this role spoke volumes about Thomas's failure as a man, and as a father.[164] Married life did not always live up its expectations, but those who attempted to find happiness outside of it were not always successful in their efforts either.

CHAPTER SEVEN

'And now I'm left alone of worldly company': Widowhood

In the early hours of the morning of 14 September 1832, the Reverend Robert Magill's life changed forever. He was awoken out of his sleep by the sounds of his 'Dear Wife', Ann Jane, vomiting. Turning to her husband, Ann Jane said that the vomit was 'sweet to the taste' and then she 'began to purge alarmingly'.[1] Robert 'rose hastily' from the bed. He offered Ann Jane 'a little punch', but she was 'unwilling' to take it.[2] In a panic, Robert raced to Ann Jane's father's home and 'awoke the family', who quickly gathered in the Magill household.[3] Three medical professionals were called, one of whom administered 'injections of arrow root, laudanum, and brandy' to Ann Jane.[4] None of these treatments had any effect. Ann Jane was to become another victim of the cholera epidemic that swept through Ulster that same year.[5] Looking on as his 'beloved wife' approached 'the hour of her departure', Robert watched helplessly as she succumbed to her illness.[6] After six hours of 'suffering', Ann Jane died, her head resting in the hands of her grief-stricken husband. Owing to the ongoing epidemic, the funeral arrangements were made in haste. By 2p.m. Ann Jane was 'coffined', and at 3.30p.m. the funeral procession made its way to the graveyard. By 5.30p.m. Ann Jane was laid to rest 'in the grave on the south side of' where her two brothers, Samuel and William, also lay.[7] Recording the events of that fateful day in his diary, Robert made sure to add an important postscript: 'NB I Kiss[ed] my Dear Ann Jane twice before she was coffined'.[8] These final kisses sealed what had been, to that point, a loving and happy marriage of almost ten years in duration. Aged forty-four years, Robert Magill was now a widower.[9]

Today, rising life expectancies mean that people are much more likely to become widowed in old age. Contemporary figures put life expectancy in Northern Ireland at seventy-eight years for men and eighty-two for women.[10] While it is difficult to estimate mortality figures in pre-Famine Ireland from surviving sources, life expectancy was generally much lower. In the two decades before the Famine, life expectancy in Ireland was approximately thirty-eight years.[11] In some parts of the country, it was even lower. In a demographic study of Carrick-on-Suir, County Tipperary, Leslie Clarkson found the local population in 1799 had a low life expectancy, of less than thirty years of age.[12] These figures had a knock-on effect on the size and shape of Ireland's population. Chris Gilleard has noted that Ireland had a relatively youthful population in the nineteenth century. Fifty per cent of the population was aged under twenty years in 1821; the corresponding proportion of those aged sixty years or over was much smaller (approximately 6.5 per cent).[13] By the time of the 1841 census, Ireland's population had grown even younger, marking it out as different from its neighbours across the Irish sea.[14] Comparatively, Ireland had fewer older people and more younger people than either England, Scotland or Wales.[15]

People in Ireland could therefore expect to become widowed at ages that we would consider today to be quite 'young'. Key to understanding widowhood in the eighteenth and nineteenth century is an appreciation of what it meant to be a 'younger' widow.[16] In Carrick-on-Suir in 1799, for example, more than half of all widows were aged under fifty-five years.[17] This was not that out of step with the equivalent data recorded elsewhere. In the Netherlands, the average age at death for married men and women in the nineteenth century was fifty-five years and fifty years, respectively.[18] Likewise, in pre-industrial England, two-thirds of widows were aged under sixty-five years old.[19] Life expectancy did, however, extend as individuals reached significant milestones in the life cycle. Once women surpassed their child-bearing years, they were more likely to outlive their husbands. Clarkson has estimated that the average age at which women in Carrick-on-Suir became widowed was fifty-four years, and that most could expect to live for another fifteen years.[20] For many individuals, their widowhood could potentially outlast the duration of their married lives.[21]

The widow at the door

Becoming widowed impacted women and men in different ways. For many women, the loss of a husband had a tangible impact on their ability to support themselves and their children. The Presbyterian church played an important role in alleviating the distress of poor widows. Believing that it was its Christian duty to alleviate the suffering of the less fortunate, the church did its best to support orphans, the sick, the poor and the aged. Of these categories of 'deserving' poor, however, it was the figure of the distressed widow who figured most prominently in popular imagination as being in need of relief. The belief that widows, specifically, and not widowers, were in most need of charitable aid was underpinned by a gendered conception of poverty and widowhood. Contemporaries considered the sufferings of the widow to be greater and more long-lasting than those experienced by her male counterpart. At the root of her distress was the loss of her husband's economic support, in the form of wages, labour and protection.[22] The widow, especially if she had young children, was unable to supplement these sources of income by her own efforts, leaving her impoverished through no fault of her own. In contrast to the plight of the widow, that of the widower was regarded as much less severe. Widowhood left him bereft of his wife's 'service' support, which included tasks such as the management of the household and childcare; jobs that could be fulfilled by female family members or hired domestic servants.[23] The ability of the widower to continue his labour, largely unaffected, meant that he was perceived as less 'deserving' of aid than were widows.[24]

Support for widows was organised at a local level by the Kirk Session through the raising of poor-money funds. The amounts distributed to the poor depended on both the wealth of each individual congregation and the willingness of the laity to contribute to the fund. Poor monies were raised by means of weekly or monthly collections, which were then distributed either as a monetary sum or in the form of goods or services. Records relating to the distribution of poor relief in the community of First Dromara in County Down reveal how, in addition to small monetary sums of one shilling, individuals received items such as clothing or help towards the payment of coffins and funeral expenses.[25] Other communities were more specific in what type of assistance they gave to the poor. The congregation of First Antrim (Millrow) in County Antrim established a committee in 1821 for the specific purpose of clothing the poor. Robert Magill, the minister of that congregation, visited poor householders of the community in order to form a 'correct idea of their wants'.[26] His visits between November and December 1821 culminated in the distribution of 130 articles of clothing to those identified as in need of assistance.[27] At a meeting held in December 1821, Robert noted how twelve widows received items that included blankets, petticoats and shoes.[28]

To receive poor relief, the needy had to make known their situation and enter a claim for aid. Although the Kirk Session and minister did sometimes give aid to passing beggars who asked for alms at the meeting-house door, most individuals had to apply directly for assistance.[29] Widows were common recipients of such aid. A sample of poor lists compiled by six Ulster Presbyterian congregations for the period 1780–1840 reveal how one-fifth of poor relief recipients were described as 'widows'.[30] In some communities, widows received regular relief from the poor money fund. In 1780 a woman named 'Widow Cry' made fifteen applications to

First Dromara Kirk Session for assistance.[31] Widow Cry continued to rely on the church for help. In the ten-year period between 1780 and 1790, she made a total of 100 applications to the Kirk Session for charitable relief.[32]

Other Presbyterian communities established organisations that were designed to support the poor. Killinchy Presbyterian congregation in County Down launched an initiative of this type in January 1800 in order to tackle the 'high price of provisions and the melancholy situation of the poor.'[33] A subscription was to be paid on the first day of each month, into the hands of a 'Superintending Committee' that was then, on the third day of each month, to pass the collected monies on to a 'General Committee.' The monies raised were intended to purchase provisions such as meat and potatoes, as well as a store 'as near the centre of the Congregation as possible' in which to house the items purchased.[34] The store, which was based at the Kirk Session house, was to open at least one day per week, and persons who wished to make a claim for relief were to come and state their case. To receive provisions from the Committee, poor persons were required to have the validity of their claim authenticated by three individuals from their townland of residence.[35] The Committee established means-based criteria on which to assess claimants. Applicants were judged against eight standards: the age of the person making the claim; their mode of industry; how many children they had and the ages of the oldest and youngest; which children lived with them and were 'burthensome'; whether any family members were afflicted with disease; the length of time they resided in the parish; and the name of the church to which they belonged.[36]

The poor were to be divided into four 'classes or rates', which determined the frequency with which they were to receive provisions. Those in the first class were to receive provisions weekly, those in the second class every fortnight, those in the third class every three weeks, and those in the fourth class every four weeks.[37] All classes were to receive the same amount of provisions, which were to alternate between one stone of oat meal or one bushel and a half of potatoes, together with twelve herrings.[38] In order to ensure that no mistakes were made in the distribution of relief, each claimant was to be awarded a ticket, signed by the president of the Committee, mentioning their name, place of residence, and how much they were to receive. This ticket was to be presented each time the claimant visited the store.[39]

As with other forms of poor relief, widows were common recipients of aid in Killinchy; in 1801 widows accounted for just under one-third of all claimants there.[40] The certificates of widowed claimants provide evidence of the tough financial circumstances that many faced after the death of their husbands. Forty-year-old Widow Glencooss struggled to support herself and her ten-year-old daughter, having lost 'the power of her arm'.[41] Widow Dumphy, a 41-year-old Roman Catholic woman, likewise required support, being in 'a Bad state of health'. She had two children, aged seven and nine years old.[42]

Some widowed women on the Killinchy list appear to have taken on responsibility for the upbringing of children that were not their own. Widow Marshal, who was placed in the first class of claimants, was described as being fifty years of age with four children, ranging from three and a half years to nine years of age. Likewise, Widow Lenighan, who was also in the first class of claimants, was sixty years of age with four children, ranging in age from five to fourteen years. Her two eldest children were described as 'very unhealthy' and were afflicted with 'falling sickness', meaning they were 'not fit for service'.[43] Given the ages of these two women, it is likely that they were not the biological mothers of the youngest children under their care. It is possible they may have been stepmothers and had inherited parental responsibility through marriage. It is also possible that they had stepped in to provide childcare for other female relatives. Irrespective of biological tie, widows with young children would have felt the burden of their upkeep keenly. In their study of widows in Carrick-on-Suir, Clarkson and Crawford noted that up until the age of ten, children were a 'drain on the family budget'. It was not until they started earning or left home to enter service that children began to offset the costs of their upkeep.[44] Widow Lenighan not only shouldered responsibility for all four children in her household, the ill-health of the eldest two had prevented their entering service and deprived her of any potential income.

The minister's wife

In addition to financially supporting poor widows, the Presbyterian church also made provisions for the widows of its ministers. Meetings held by the Synod of Ulster in the early part of the eighteenth century regularly heard petitions from ministers' widows and their families for financial assistance. The death of a minister, perhaps more so than the death of men involved in other middling-order professions, impacted most heavily on his widow, because her links with the wider community, which had been cemented by her husband's ministry, were dissolved at his death.[45] The minister's wife could not continue her husband's occupation, and in many cases she lost both her spouse and her home when she became widowed.[46]

Cynthia Curran's research on middle-class widows in Victorian England has revealed that men of the emergent middle classes, such as ministers, were relatively unable to provide for their families after death. A sizeable proportion of clergymen in England were paid less than one hundred pounds per annum, an amount that was considered 'barely adequate to maintain a middle-class lifestyle', never mind make assurances for their families in the event of their death.[47] The situation was more concerning for Presbyterian ministers in Ulster, who earned considerably less than their English counterparts. Ministerial salaries in Ulster were intimately connected to the fortunes of their congregations. In the 1790s, Presbyterian ministers in Ulster could expect to receive an average of forty pounds per annum in stipend from their communities, which was itself irregularly paid.[48]

Presbyterian ministers were keenly aware of the financial impact their deaths would have on their wives and families. After being involved in a coach accident on his way home from meeting one evening in June 1822, the Reverend James Morell took out a life insurance policy at the Royal Exchange Office for £1,000. Mulling over the event in his diary, he observed that although it was 'wrong to speculate on life' he 'thought it prudent to secure something' for his family.[49] Similarly, the Reverend James Morgan of Belfast recorded in his diary the anxiety he felt for his family when he endured periods of sickness:

> My feelings are much exercised about my family – a much loved wife, and five dear children. The promises of God to the widow and the fatherless are enough to sustain my spirit, but I have not been enabled so to rest upon these as to be raised above anxiety.[50]

James Morgan was later to hold the position of chairman of a board of the Amicable Assurance Society and encouraged other Presbyterian ministers to join such schemes to 'save' their wives and families from financial distress.[51]

Over the course of the eighteenth century, various schemes were proposed by the Synod of Ulster to deal with requests from the widows of ministers for financial assistance. In 1717 it proposed that widows and orphans were to continue to receive the minister's proportion of *regium donum* – a fixed annual payment that was paid to the Presbyterian church by the government. While the amounts that ministers received depended on the branch of the church to which they belonged, at the close of the eighteenth century the annual payment was no more than thirty-three pounds.[52] Widows of ministers, however, were only entitled to this payment while the congregation remained vacant. Once a new minister was put in place, her entitlement stopped.[53] The question of how to support the minister's widow and their children once a new minister was installed was left open. Subsequent efforts to redress the issue exposed further deficiencies in the scheme, such as the remarriage of widows and the eligibility of orphaned children.[54]

It was not until 1750 that the Synod established a more permanent and extensive fund that better met the needs of the widowed and orphaned.[55] The scheme, which was proposed by Mr William Bruce, an elder of Wood Street congregation in Dublin, had three main features. First, every minister was required to pay forty shillings annually out of their proportion of the *regium donum* as a subscription to the fund. Second, on his death, the widow of every minister who had paid into the fund was to receive a lifetime annuity of between twelve and thirty pounds per year. If, however, a widow died within eight years of receiving her annuity, the payments were to revert to the children of her marriage for the remainder of the eight-year payment period. Children left orphaned by the death of their father were also to receive the annuity for a term of eight years. Third, steps were also taken to account for the remarriage of the minister's widow. From the time of her remarriage, one part of the annuity was to be given to her, and the other distributed among the minister's children. In the event of the deaths of the minister's children, however, the whole annuity was to return to the mother.[56]

Between the implementation of this scheme in 1751 and the incorporation of the Presbyterian Widows' Fund by act of parliament in 1809, the regulations of the Fund remained largely unchanged. Several alterations were, however, made to the raising of funds. The amount of annuity that widows received was reduced to twenty-five pounds per annum.[57] James Seaton Reid has noted that it was discovered that Bruce's 1750 scheme had underestimated the number of ministers' widows. In order to meet the needs of annuitants, it was necessary to reduce the amount of money awarded to each one.[58] Also, on joining the scheme ministers had first to pay the full amount of one year's royal grant and, from then on, a fixed annual subscription of forty shillings. Depending on the rate of *regium donum* that ministers received, they were also required to pay an additional membership fee on top of the required subscription. This meant that ministers who received the top level of £100 in *regium donum* were required to pay an additional £3 per annum, while those who received the lowest amount (£50) paid an extra thirty shillings per year.[59] Finally, ministers who remarried had to pay an extra one-off premium on top of their annual subscription fee. Ministers marrying for the second time were required to pay one years' annuity, which in 1809 was twenty-five pounds; those marrying for the third time were to pay two years' annuity (fifty pounds); and so on in proportion to every succeeding marriage contracted.[60]

The payment of annuities to widows and their children was also brought under much stricter control. The minutes of the Synod reveal that its treasurers were concerned about frauds and abuses of the Fund. The minutes detail the curious case of the widow of Mr Hugh Nisbet (died in 1778), minister of the congregation of Ballymote in County Sligo. The Synod, operating under a suspicion that the marriage of the late minister and 'the woman who calls herself Mrs Nisbet' was 'collusive & made chiefly with a Lucrative view' of deriving emolument from the Fund, refused to admit her as an annuitant.[61] In order to prevent the unlawful approbation of monies, a series of overtures was passed requiring Presbyteries to make returns of the number of eligible widows and orphans who were living within their bounds.[62] A regulation passed in 1809 required the receipt of a certificate proving that an eligible widow was alive, or, if she was dead, the date of her decease and name of the persons entitled to receive the annuity.[63] In addition to these measures, resolutions were also passed that held the potential to invalidate a widow's claim to the Fund. Ministers who resigned their pastoral charges to take up secular or professional employment were not permitted to remain a contributor to the Fund and forfeited the right of their widows and families to receive any benefit from its monies.[64] Similarly, any ministers who left Ireland to reside abroad also surrendered their membership of the Fund.[65]

One of the obvious benefits of the Fund was that any minister attached to the Synod of Ulster was eligible to join. Efforts were made to join ministers of the General Synod and their non-subscribing counterparts of the Presbytery of Antrim under this scheme.[66] Factors such as age and state of health, which are important for modern life assurance policies, were not accounted for, enabling cover to be extended to every widow whose husband had paid into the Fund. Returns made by the treasurer of the Fund between 1791 and 1814 reveal the enormous growth in both capital raised and monies paid out to the widows of ministers. In 1791 the capital of the Fund stood at £11,682 12 shillings 3 pence, with a debit of £809 12 shillings and 4 pence being paid to a total of sixty-four annuitants.[67] By 1814 the number of annuitants had grown to seventy-six, withdrawing from the Fund £2,930 per annum. The total capital of the Fund had also increased rapidly, to just over £27,000.[68]

Despite the improvements to the scheme, the Presbyterian Widows' Fund was never able to address the underlying problems that wives endured after the deaths of their husbands. Complaints were regularly presented to the Synod about the failure of congregations to settle their stipend arrears. Before a new minister could be installed, any outstanding stipend was to be paid to the previous minister's widow or his children. Many congregations either overlooked this regulation or chose to ignore it completely. In June

1781 a representative from the Presbytery of Tyrone requested the advice of the Synod respecting a disagreement between the widow of Mr Kerr and the community of Minterburn in County Tyrone. The congregation was keen to settle a new minister, but efforts were stalled by Mrs Kerr's claims that the congregation was in arrears. At length, the Synod agreed with Mrs Kerr and recommended that the congregation, 'see speedy Justice done to' her.[69] The Synod noted in June 1782 that the congregation and Mrs Kerr had 'condescended to compromise their differences' and came to a settlement.[70] Other disputes did not end so amicably. In 1810 the Synod threatened the congregation of Fintona in County Tyrone that it would be deprived of church privileges if it did not pay what was owed to the family of the late minister, Mr Moorhead.[71]

The reason widows of ministers pursued the recovery of these monies was because the amount owed was usually substantial enough to assist them after their husbands' death. The stipend owed to a minister was often irregularly paid and short of the fixed amount agreed at ordination.[72] The steps taken by the family of the Reverend John Smyth, minister of Loughbrickland congregation in County Down, to secure the payment of arrears in stipend are fully understandable when one takes into account that the congregation owed just over £230, a sum with a modern value of over £10,000.[73] In addition to the problems that some widows encountered in recovering stipends, others met difficulties in securing their annuity from the Fund. The Synod dealt with complaints from widows who had not received their annuities. In June 1803 Mrs Barr, widow of the Reverend Isaac Barr, minister of Moywater (Killala) in County Mayo, presented a memorial to the Synod in which she outlined her 'distressed state'. She was subsequently awarded an emergency payment of £75 out of the first settlement of royal grant to be paid that year.[74] Delays in the payment of annuities led some to initiate legal proceedings. In 1792 the Synod resolved that anyone who commenced lawsuits to recovery their annuity would be subject to financial penalties. Any expenses incurred by the Fund because of a suit would be deducted out of the annuity to which the plaintiff was entitled.[75]

While the blame for delays in payments rests partly with the church courts, the mobility of widows following the deaths of their husbands also played a part. The returns made by Presbyteries to the Synod on the number of widows who were residing within their bounds reveal that some women left the care of the Presbytery without notification. Mrs Caldwell, wife of James Caldwell, minister of Usher's Quay in Dublin, first appeared on the Widows' Fund in June 1783, under the care of the Dublin Presbytery. She appeared on the next two returns made by this body in 1784 and 1786, and then somewhat more sporadically thereafter. Between 1790 and 1794, and 1796 and 1798, no reference was made to Mrs Caldwell; finally in 1800 she was reported as living in Strabane in County Tyrone. The Presbytery of Dublin repeated in 1801 and 1806 that it believed she 'was still living' and referred her case to the Presbytery of Letterkenny, which should have taken her into its care. There is no mention of her by this latter body at all, however, and in 1817 she reappeared once more on the Widows' Fund lists for Dublin Presbytery.[76] Where Mrs Caldwell had been for those intermittent years, and why she had not claimed her annuity, is unclear. Other women went even further afield. Mrs Turbitt, widow of James Turbitt of First Donagheady congregation in County Tyrone, migrated to Scotland, while Mrs Davis, widow of the Reverend Jacob Davis of Drumachose congregation in County Londonderry, was believed to have emigrated to America.[77]

In a somewhat sad turn of events, there are references in the minutes of the Synod meetings to instances of when the location, and even fate, of widows was unknown. In 1784 an inquiry was ordered to find out if Mrs Cochran, a widow listed on the Fund, was living or deceased.[78] Similarly, in 1794 the Synod resolved to pay the annuity of James Jackson, late minister of Ballybay congregation in County Monaghan, into the hands of a guardian, 'for the use of the younger children', as his widow had made no claim, nor was it known whether she was alive.[79] Mrs Jackson was eventually located; in 1796 the Synod noted that she was now the sole claimant of her husband's annuity.[80] Where she had been for the past two years, and why she was living apart from her children, are questions that remain unanswered. It can be suggested, however, that widowhood ushered in profound shifts in both the identity and place of the minister's wife in the wider community. The widow's ties with the congregation, which were the product of her husband's ministry, were loosened at his death. A new minister would most likely also bring with him a new wife, supplanting her role in the community. Becoming widowed brought about both economic and social marginalisation for the minister's wife.

Lonely households

If widowhood ushered in changes to women's financial circumstances, the same could be said for men's household arrangements. Men who became widowed at relatively young ages, especially if they had children, were forced to make difficult decisions to support the smooth running of their households. Such was the case for the Reverend Robert Magill, who we encountered at the opening of this chapter. When his wife Ann Jane died in 1832, he was left to care for their only surviving child, seven-year-old Sarah. Becoming widowed brought about major changes to the composition of Robert's household. In the days following the death of Ann Jane, his daughter Sarah went to live with his father- and mother-in-law, Mr and Mrs Skelton. Robert recorded in his diary on 10 January 1833 that Sarah had spent the previous night at home for the first time since September, having stayed with her grandparents since her mother's death.[81] This arrangement was also not temporary; Sarah continued to divide her time between the homes of her grandparents and father.[82] Robert's fatherhood responsibilities were likely difficult to manage on top of his extensive visiting and ministerial duties. His mother's relocation from the townland of Kinbally in County Antrim, where she had resided since April 1825, to the neighbourhood of Millrow in November 1832, also seems to have been prompted by her son's widowhood.[83] When Ann Jane was alive, the family took regular trips to visit Robert's mother.[84] She probably moved closer to her son to assist with the care of Sarah.

The sharing of childcare and the temporary placement of young children into the homes of relatives was a strategy employed by other men. William Tennent placed his three-year-old daughter Letitia into the care of his mother-in-law and daughter's namesake, Letitia Jackson, after the death of his wife Eleanor in 1806. His diary entries for the months following Eleanor's death reveal how

Letitia travelled back and forth between Monaghan and Belfast, spending time with her father and grandmother.[85] Similarly, when Eliza Macrone, the wife of William's brother Robert Tennent, died just weeks after giving birth to their son, Robert James, in 1803, he placed the child in the care of a 'Ma Jackson'.[86] That such arrangements were not only approved of, but also expected, can be seen in the comments of the Reverend John Tennent, minister of Roseyards congregation and the father of William and Robert, about the placement of his grandchildren with relatives and nurses. Speaking of Robert James, he concluded that, 'best no doubt [Robert's] care for the infant must be ... those in whose keeping it is might Suffice for some time'.[87] Similarly, after the death of Eleanor Jackson, the Reverend Tennent wrote to William inquiring after the whereabouts of Letitia, recommending that she remain a year or two with her maternal grandmother.[88]

Becoming widowed not only left Robert Magill bereft of his wife's childcare services, more importantly, it robbed him of his companion in life and of Christ. Robert wrote about how much he missed Ann Jane in his diary. In April 1833 he added the following dedication to his 'dear and beloved wife' on the front page of one of her music books:

> She was a faithful and affectionate Partner and a warm hearted generous Friend ... Her religious vows ... were scripturally clear, and evangelically correct ... The affection and Love she felt for me I shall never forget for never was affection more sincerely true, never was Love more faithfully devoted.[89]

Robert felt the loneliness of widowhood keenly. Family get-togethers were especially difficult. On 31 October 1832 Robert drank tea with his daughter, Mr and Mrs Skelton (Ann Jane's parents), and his sister-in-law. Despite spending his evening in their company, he reflected on 'how lonely compared to former days' their meeting had been.[90] Other diary entries were poignantly short, such as that on the anniversary of his marriage: 'It is 9 years this day since I was married.'[91] Other entries reflected his melancholy, such as when he recorded moving his bedstead out of the room he had shared with his wife for the previous seven years and placed it in the front room.[92]

In the weeks and months following Ann Jane's death, Robert compiled a list of her belongings, which included items such as clothing, tableware and pillowcases. Carrying on the tradition of gift-giving that he had employed in his courtship of Ann Jane, Robert bestowed the items on family and friends.[93] He gave Mrs Skelton a pair of boots, a bonnet and a ring.[94] To Mary and Margaret, his two servant girls, he gave a gift of two gowns, and to John Ring he bestowed a coat, in return for his kindness at Ann Jane's funeral.[95] That such gifts were exchanged in an effort to honour his wife's memory and mitigate his loneliness can be inferred from a verse inscribed on a gold watch he presented to Ann Jane's sister, Eliza:

> Accept This Pledge of my esteem
> Eliza friend sincere
> I give it for thy sister's sake
> A name for ever dear
> Her day of life is pass[e]d away
> Her bed is in the tomb
> Then let this watch still bring to mind
> Thy day of final doome.
> R. Magill.[96]

The timing of his gift was also significant: 18 November 1832 coincided with his late wife's birthday. Robert made a note to this effect in his diary: it 'being the anniversary of Mrs Magill's Birthday. Had she lived she would this day have been 29 years of age.'[97]

For other men, becoming widowed not only brought increased parental responsibilities, it also coincided with a change in the composition of their households. In early April 1782, after battling a chronic complaint, Martha Bailie, the wife of the Reverend William Kennedy, minister of Carland congregation in County Tyrone, died.[98] The couple had been married for roughly twenty-three years and had seven children, all living at the time of their mother's decease: John, Robert, Andrew Thomas, William, Elizabeth, Jane and Martha.[99] Information on the age of their children is limited, but it is likely that most of them were under eighteen years of age. We know that their second son, Robert, was eighteen when his mother died; a declaration signed by his father certified that he was born on 29 November 1764. We know also that William was an 'infant', from a letter communicating news of his death from smallpox in the months following his mother's decease.[100] We can infer from comments made by the Reverend Kennedy about their schooling that Andrew, Jane and Martha were relatively young, perhaps less than twelve years old. Whereas 'Andie' was with a Mr Wier learning arithmetic, the two youngest girls were at school learning 'to write and figure'.[101]

In the weeks following his wife's death, two female relatives moved into the Kennedy household: Aunt Huggins and Cousin Nancy (Ann) Huggins.[102] With William left a widower with five children living at home, it is likely that these two women moved in to assist him with childcare. They both remained in the Kennedy household for approximately six years, suggesting that their arrangement was not made solely to comfort William as he grieved.[103] Although Aunt Huggins and Cousin Huggins contributed towards the household in terms of rent and money towards goods, their company was greatly valued by William.[104] Writing to his son Robert in April 1782, William referred to Aunt Huggins as 'a good well minded friendly woman', and he praised Cousin Nancy's pleasurable company, which had 'help'd to bear [him] up'.[105] In his eyes, there was 'no better young woman; few as good' as Cousin Nancy.[106]

Supplementing the role that Martha Bailie had played in managing household affairs was his eldest daughter, Elizabeth. That Elizabeth was a young adult can be inferred from a comment made by her father that she had 'come to the time of life to be a housekeeper' and he commended her for having such a turn of 'oeconomy' (economy [sic]).[107] Indeed, Elizabeth showed such skill in this position that her father decided 'it would be an affront to set upon another in that place'.[108] As far as William Kennedy's surviving correspondence tells us, this extended household arrangement seems to have been a happy and enjoyable one, free of family discord. In a letter to his son Robert in November 1783, William boasted that 'perhaps there's not a family in the kingdom enjoys more domesticated peace' than his did at Gortnaglush in County Tyrone.[109]

It was not just 'younger' men who were forced to adjust to the new position of widower. Such was the case for the previously mentioned Reverend John Tennent when he himself became widowed at the age of seventy-eight. On 2 August 1805 his wife of forty-seven years, Ann Patton, died. Reverend Tennent was heartbroken by her death. In a letter to his son Robert, the Reverend lamented that 'holy providence' had taken from him 'the Light of mine eyes' and that now he was 'left alone of worldly company'.[110] When his eldest son William's wife died in 1806, John empathised with his son's distracted state of mind. In a letter to William, the Reverend Tennent wrote that his mind too had been 'raging like a wild Bull in a net' after the death of Ann.[111]

In the days following Ann's death, Reverend Tennent wrote to both sons asking their advice on how he should spend the remainder of his 'time without distracting or distressing care about [this] world'.[112] He told William that he did not know how he would cope without the company and services of his wife, who had shouldered the burden of looking after their household.[113] It is likely, too, that Reverend Tennent felt lonely after the death of Ann. In a letter to William, he confessed that he had always believed that Ann would survive him, and in that case she would 'have had [the] pleasure of enjoying a little terestial [sic] *paradise*' with William and Eleanor at their home in Mount Vernon, Belfast.[114] Such an arrangement would not only have ensured that Ann was taken care of, but that she would have had company too.[115] To relieve himself of the burdens of managing the household and land alone, as well as likely to mitigate his loneliness, the Reverend Tennent outlined to William what he believed were his only two options. He could sell his property and take rented lodgings for the remainder of his life, or he could sell off part of his land and harvest, retaining the house for himself, with the use of two cows and a horse.[116] None of these options was realised, however, as by the beginning of 1806 the Reverend Tennent still retained charge of his household.

In February 1806 a third scheme was proposed. The Reverend Tennent suggested that his daughter Margaret (also known as Peggy), her husband John Stuart and their children, could move into his home and live together as one household.[117] In a letter to

William in February 1806, Reverend Tennent stated that he had resolved to 'disenta[n]gle' himself from any 'trouble' about his property and, imagining that Peggy and John Stuart would 'wish to be here', wrote them a letter in which he sketched out what part of the house and land he was willing to offer them.[118] It appears, however, that John Stuart was not pleased with what was offered, replying that the 'part of [the] House from [the] Kitchin & downward would not suit him'.[119] Reverend Tennent believed that the matter was at an end, but after some persuasion from Peggy and a concession on his father-in-law's side that he might allow them the 'temporary use of [the] kitchen', John Stuart agreed to think on the proposal.[120] William did not approve of his father's scheme. Reverend Tennent likewise grew unsure about the arrangement. Writing to William, he conceded that he too was not fond of his son-in-law, but that as the scheme had a 'reasonable prospect of a comfortable alteration', he had 'conde[s]cended to [Stuart's] gratification for a year or two … to admit him & her here'.[121] In May 1806 Peggy and her daughter moved in with the Reverend Tennent, with the expectation that John Stuart would join them in a few days' time.[122]

It is very likely that were it not for his becoming widowed, the Reverend Tennent would not have contemplated entering this type of co-resident arrangement. An earlier scheme for co-residence, proposed by his son Robert in 1802, was rejected because the Reverend and his wife wanted to retain their independence.[123] Three years later, however, now aged seventy-eight years and a widower, John Tennent was keenly aware that he would need some degree of care and support. As he admitted to William, becoming widowed had left him alone and fearful for the future:

> I'm now left alone in comparison w[he]n my dear was w[i]t[h] me … And how shall I endure w[he]n I think on times past now & then these thoughts are like to strike me to [the] very heart. this is an affliction & [I] must bear it.[124]

Indeed, the reason he regarded the option of taking rented lodgings as so distasteful was that it would render him 'comfortless' without any of his children to come and attend to him in illness or old age.[125] The change in status from married to widowed seems to have made the Reverend John Tennent reflect on his own mortality and failing health, prompting him to suggest the joint living arrangement between himself, his daughter and his son-in-law.

Reverend Robert Magill: Married twice – and buried twice?

Robert Magill eventually remarried. After almost six years of widowhood, on 11 June 1838 he married Ellen Liggat in a ceremony conducted in the parlour of his home by the Reverend Henry Cooke. His daughter Sarah was among those present to witness the marriage.[126] Diary entries made by Robert in the months preceding the marriage reveal how he and Ellen spent increasing amounts of time together, as their relationship grew more serious. Like his courtship of Ann Jane seventeen years earlier, Robert recorded in his diary how he spent time with Ellen's family and friends, as well as at the religious services and community celebrations they both attended.[127] Gift-giving was likewise central to their courtship ritual. Robert recorded the gifts he bestowed on and received from Ellen and her family, including foodstuffs and books.[128] His daughter Sarah also participated in the tradition of gift-giving with the Liggat family, cementing their new family ties. On 2 January 1838 Robert noted how Sarah had given Ellen 'a book entitled texts for every day in the year' and that she had received from Abraham, Ellen's brother, a 'needlebook and a New years gift of Silver' to the value of 2 shillings and six pence.[129] The marriage, however, did not last long. Robert died just nine months later, on 19 February 1839, aged fifty years old. Robert was buried in Templepatrick.

His story, however, did not end in a Templepatrick grave plot. Robert has since become known as the man who was 'married twice and buried twice'.[130] Believing that he was buried in Templepatrick 'against his expressed wishes', First Antrim congregation exhumed his body and interred it in a plot beside his first wife, Ann Jane, and their infant son William John.[131] Widowed from her in 1832, Robert now rests eternally beside his beloved first wife, Ann Jane.

CONCLUSION

In May 1804 James Hoey, a member of Coronary Presbyterian church in County Cavan, appeared before the Presbytery of Monaghan and asked to be readmitted to church ordinances.[1] The cause of James's exclusion from the privileges of church membership lay in the suspected bigamous nature of his second marriage, a union that had taken place while he was still technically married to someone else. James claimed that his first wife, a woman named Fanny Sharp, had 'eloped from him without just cause' shortly after their marriage had taken place.[2] Considering himself free to marry again (desertion being one of two grounds for Presbyterian divorce), James did just that three months later, and he and his second wife (unnamed) had gone on to have six children together. The case was temporarily returned to Coronary Kirk Session for investigation, before it was considered once more by Monaghan Presbytery a few months later. The finer details of James's story had changed somewhat in the interim, but the overall thrust was the same: Fanny had eloped 'without a just cause' and James had remarried shortly thereafter.³ An additional child had also been born to the marriage; as of September 1804 James and his second wife shared seven children.⁴ James did not, however, receive a clear ruling. Hesitant to decide, the Presbytery voted to 'Leave the matter' as it stood in the hope that 'the Lord would cast light on it'.⁵ While the Presbytery did not elaborate on what further information it required, it likely wished to corroborate James's story and check not only that Fanny had deserted the marriage, but that she had done so wilfully.

Six years later, in September 1810, James appealed once more for admission to privileges. In the intervening period, he and his wife had welcomed another child, making a total of eight. In addition to James's claim that Fanny had 'eloped … without a reason', he now added that she had done so after committing adultery (the other ground on which Presbyterian divorce could be granted).⁶ James further claimed that Fanny had since 'went to America' and it was 'reported' that she was now 'dead'.⁷ These additional details failed to sway the Presbytery, however, and James's case was returned once more to Coronary Kirk Session, which was directed to 'investigate it further'.⁸ It is unclear if James's request for church privileges was ever granted.

This book set out with two main aims: to tell the story of Presbyterian family life in Ulster and to explore what the Presbyterian example can tell us about the Irish family more broadly. The story of James Hoey's repeated (and apparently unsuccessful) attempts to gain readmission to church privileges thus provides a fitting example with which to conclude. From the cradle to the grave, the family lives of many Presbyterians in Ulster were intimately connected to their church. While the province of Ulster underwent considerable social, economic, political and demographic changes across the period covered, for many of its Presbyterian inhabitants their church retained an important place in their everyday lives. James Hoey's six-year appeal for readmission is a case in point. We cannot know for sure what underlay his dogged desire for church privileges. James may have wished for his children to be baptised and welcomed into the church community; perhaps he desired the Kirk Session to formally recognise his marriage; or possibly he felt a deep, personal desire to be reconciled to the church of his faith. All or none of these reasons might be true; what his case does signal, however, is the importance of community membership. While not all church members may have shared James's desire for reconciliation (or his tenacity), it is precisely because of that relationship that the Presbyterian archive exists at all. It is an archive of family life: its births, marriages and deaths, and all the events that happened in between these important milestones.

Stories like that of James Hoey tell us about much more than Presbyterian families in Ulster. His story, like that of the many other Presbyterians described throughout this book, adds to our knowledge of the Irish family too. The religious demography of Ulster, together with its socio-economic profile, has meant that historians have tended to dismiss the province as unrepresentative of the wider Irish picture.[9] Presbyterians – a religious minority, concentrated in the province of Ulster and with strong Scottish connections – have also generally been regarded as very different from other inhabitants of the island.[10] While Presbyterians may have been a religious minority, their records offer much more than a marginalised and unrepresentative picture of Irish family life. The individuals and families discussed in this book were indeed bound by a shared religious tradition, and religious belief was by no means unimportant in shaping the contours of Presbyterian family life in Ulster, but the community had much in common with families from other confessional backgrounds in Ireland. The respective experiences of those whose stories are presented in this book varied considerably; age, birth order, gender, wealth and individual personality all played a role in determining the everyday rhythms of their lives, as it did for families throughout Ireland, not just in Ulster. Indeed, to speak of a specific 'Presbyterian' experience of family life would imply that the lives of women and men mirrored one another by virtue of their attachment to the Presbyterian church, which would obscure both the variety of individual experiences and the varying degree to which women and men formally adhered to church principles. It would also overlook those who identified as Presbyterian but who had 'no formal link with the church', a 'sizeable group', which, according to Andrew Holmes, could have comprised up to one-fifth of the Presbyterian population in Ulster.[11] To do so would also contribute to the continued side-lining of Presbyterian families in Irish historical scholarship.

As outlined in the Introduction, recent scholarship has argued for the inclusion of Ulster in histories of Irish sex and marriage. My own work and that of Maria Luddy and Mary O'Dowd has revised the view that Presbyterians were radically different from other religious communities in Ireland with respect to their sexual behaviour. In other work, I have also championed the use of Presbyterian family papers to advance knowledge of topics such as childbirth, youth and adolescence, courtship, marriage, parenthood and siblinghood.[12] The sources drawn together in this book extend this argument to the Irish family more broadly. Historians have traditionally been hesitant to draw conclusions about Ireland using Ulster evidence. The same can be said for Presbyterian sources. This book, however, points to the richness and unique value of sources such as the Presbyterian archive to histories of the Irish family and family life in Ireland. The patchy and uneven survival of Presbyterian church records is undoubtedly an issue, but an archive of similar material does not exist to the same degree for any other religious community in Ireland.

As many have long lamented, the destruction of the Public Record Office in Dublin in 1922 has had a lasting impact on the ability of historians to reconstruct aspects of the Irish past.[13] Among the records lost were a major portion of those belonging to the Irish ecclesiastical courts, which were managed by the Anglican Church of Ireland. These courts existed in every diocese across the island until the dissolution of the Church of Ireland in 1869. The ecclesiastical courts were used by women and men from across the religious and social spectrum (including Presbyterians and Roman Catholics), and they dealt with issues that impacted every element of family life in Ireland, from the making and breaking of marriage to family disputes and paternity claims – aspects of family life that are likewise covered by Presbyterian sources. Rich in detail, the minute books of the Presbyterian church courts in Ulster therefore capture aspects of family life in Ireland that are otherwise out of reach to historians.

While the Presbyterian church courts were established for the primary purpose of regulating the behaviour of the lay community, their records provide an insight into how Presbyterians interacted with members of other religious communities in Ulster. Presbyterians did not live in religious isolation. Not only did some Presbyterians whose stories appear in this book have their marriages solemnised by clergymen of the Church of Ireland and Roman Catholic priests, they married adherents of other religious denominations too. Presbyterian women and men worked for, and worked with, members of other religious traditions. Those with sufficient resources also hired persons from across the religious spectrum. The stories of their working lives and their working relationships are captured in the minute books of the Presbyterian church courts. Throughout this book, we see how these sources enable us to access the worlds of individuals who left behind few records of their own experiences: the agricultural labourers, childminders, servants, spinners, wet nurses and weavers who formed the backbone of Ulster's rural society between 1690 and 1830, the 'long eighteenth century'.

Moreover, just as Presbyterians might seek recourse in the civil courts or the ecclesiastical courts, so too did members of other religious communities approach the Kirk Session for help in times of crisis. Worried parents from different confessional backgrounds might ask the Presbyterian church courts to intervene if they suspected their children were being treated badly by their Presbyterian masters, and Kirk Sessions might even make sure that parents of other persuasions had consented to their child's mixed marriage. The Presbyterian archive then, is not just a record of the Presbyterian experience, it also captures Ulster society more broadly.

The real value of the Presbyterian archive, however, lies not merely in the fact that it exists, but in what historians of the family can *do* with it. In 2024 Maeve O'Riordan and I set 'a new agenda' for the history of the Irish family. Recognising that the Irish family is, and always has been, marked by rich diversity, we advocated for the study of Irish families from alternative viewpoints.[14] We argued that there have always been 'many ways of doing family' in Ireland, and in order to 'appreciate the complicated and messy realities' of families in the past, we called for Irish historians to wrestle free their understanding of family as being tethered to a 'traditional' norm.[15] The sources drawn together here model this approach in action. James Hoey's story is a case in point. As we have seen, for six years James petitioned the church courts to readmit him (and his family) to the privileges of church membership, their exclusion having been caused by his contracting a second marriage. According to James's account, the desertion of his first (and we can assume legally recognised) wife signalled the termination of that marriage, leaving him free to start again. James's family story, however, has a longer (and more instructive) history than the six years captured in the minute books of the church courts.

At his first appearance before the Monaghan Presbytery, we learn that James had fathered six children with the woman he considered to be his wife. The minutes of the Presbytery also reveal James and his wife welcomed at least eight children into their family, two of whom were born during the six-year period that the case was under consideration. If we estimate that a child had been born to the marriage every year, James and his new wife may have been living together as husband and wife for at least twelve years. And it is quite possible that they had done so for far longer. That James and his second wife had not only lived together for such a long period of time but continued to add to their family indicates a societal tolerance, if not acceptance, of his marriage. At the same time, the church's continued hesitancy to readmit James to church privileges is evidence of how individual family practices could stand in stark contrast to what was expected by church standards, as well as the law. James's second marriage could, after all, be labelled bigamous. In addition to signalling the importance of church membership, James's repeated efforts to gain readmission may be indicative of his belief that his second marriage (and the family that it produced) was not at odds with the standards of his faith.

James Hoey's story is therefore useful to historians of the Irish family because it underlines the complex realities of family life in Ireland. In the past, Irish families came in many different forms. Whereas some were produced inside of marriage and others were made outside of its boundaries, very many more lay somewhere in the space between. Family relationships were likewise just as complex. Dynamics among family members changed over time, flexing in response to changes in family composition brought about by births, marriages, desertions, remarriages and deaths. Presbyterian sources offer valuable lessons for those interested in the history of the Irish family. They remind us to think expansively and creatively about the family, and they offer a lens through which to rethink the Irish past. Taken together, the stories of Presbyterian families told in this book not only deepen our understanding of the intimate worlds of women and men in long-eighteenth century Ulster, they also provide a unique window through which to consider the broader Irish picture. The Presbyterian archive is ripe with potential, and more historians should recognise its value.

A NOTE ON THE BIBLIOGRAPHY

This book is not the first to focus on the Presbyterian community in Ulster. What sets it apart, however, is its focus on the family and the cycle of life. Much has been written about the institutional history of the Presbyterian church in Ireland, and the political, intellectual and theological developments that shaped Presbyterianism on the island from the seventeenth century onwards.[1] Historians have also written about how Presbyterians practised their religion and understood their beliefs. Work by scholars such as J.M. Barkley and, especially, Andrew Holmes has enriched our understanding of how the laity engaged with communion, baptism and the processes of church discipline.[2] Research has also been undertaken on the social backgrounds of Presbyterians in Ireland. Of note is Robert Whan's study of Ulster's Presbyterian community between 1680 and 1730. Whan reconstructed the social lives of the various 'layers' of Presbyterian society, including its ministers, gentry, servants, craftsmen and the poor.[3] A book-length study of the family lives of Presbyterians that covers the eighteenth and early nineteenth century has yet to materialise. Indeed, Whan concluded his book by noting that 'a gap still remains' in knowledge about the lives of Presbyterians between the end of the period covered by his study and the work of Holmes and others from the late eighteenth century onwards.[4]

A number of historians have also used Presbyterian sources to elucidate broader themes in Irish histories of marriage and the family.[5] Jonathan Jeffrey Wright, for example, has made extensive use of the papers of the Tennents – a prominent Presbyterian family, who also feature in this book – in his work on nineteenth-century Belfast, as well as in several essays on courtship and adolescence for the same period.[6] Merchant and middle-class Presbyterian families are the focus in research by Jean Agnew for the seventeenth century and Alice Johnson and Shannon Devlin for the nineteenth century.[7] Presbyterian church court records have been used by historians of marriage and sexuality. Maria Luddy and Mary O'Dowd consider cases of disorderly marriage and sexual discipline in exploring attitudes to the making and breaking of marriage in eighteenth- and nineteenth-century Ireland.[8]

A study of Ulster family life, using Ulster Presbyterian sources, however, had not existed for the period covered by this book, which builds on existing scholarship in two ways. Covering the approximate period 1690 to 1830, it offers the first comprehensive study of Presbyterian family life in Ulster. It follows Presbyterian families from the cradle to the grave to explore how members of this religious community navigated the cycle of life and the trials and tribulations of family life. It considers Presbyterian family life across the social spectrum, extending our knowledge of families from the lower to the middling sections of Ulster society. Furthermore, the book breaks new ground through its innovative gendered approach. Save my own work, very few published studies have seriously considered gender in relation to the Ulster Presbyterian community.[9] In 1999 Roisin Browne completed a statistical survey of church discipline for the period 1640–1740, and in 2022 Frances Norman considered the sexual agency of Presbyterian women in the eighteenth century.[10] Andrew Holmes explained that the 'comparative neglect of a gender dimension' in his book owed much to 'constraints of evidence', highlighting a 'chronic lack of information' about the involvement of women in the church during the eighteenth century, and the male bias of sources for the nineteenth century.[11] Several historians have, however, considered the experiences of Presbyterian women. Myrtle Hill, Janice Holmes and Andrea Ebel Brozyna have examined the role of women in relation to missionary work and periods of religious revival.[12] And while historians of Scottish Presbyterianism, such as Leah Leneman and Rosalind Mitchison, have succeeded in bringing to light the experiences of women, a history of the everyday lives of female members of the Ulster Presbyterian community had yet to be written.[13] A gendered approach, however, is not reserved for the writing of women's histories; it is important to remember that men too have gender.[14] Women and men did not live in isolation from each other in Ulster and their histories should not be disconnected. Men emerge from the Presbyterian archive as gendered subjects and in their family roles as husbands, fathers and brothers. In this book, therefore, I have offered a fresh insight into the family lives of Presbyterian women *and* men who lived, loved and laboured in Ulster across the 'long eighteenth century'.

ENDNOTES

Introduction

[1] Public Record Office of Northern Ireland (hereafter PRONI), MIC1P/37/4/9, Carnmoney Kirk Session minutes, 9 March 1713; 29 March 1713; 5 April 1713.
[2] PRONI, MIC1P/37/4/9, Carnmoney Kirk Session minutes, 19 November 1710; 1 December 1710; 10 January 1711; 25 January 1711; 20 February 1711; 26 March 1711; May 1711; 13 June 1711; 12 July 1711.
[3] PRONI, MIC1P/37/4/9, Carnmoney Kirk Session minutes, May 1711; 26 March 1712.
[4] PRONI, MIC1P/37/4/9, Carnmoney Kirk Session minutes, 26 March 1712.
[5] PRONI, MIC1P/37/4/9, Carnmoney Kirk Session minutes, 26 March 1711; 26 March 1712.
[6] PRONI, MIC1P/37/4/9, Carnmoney Kirk Session minutes, 8 April 1713.
[7] PRONI, MIC1P/37/4/9, Carnmoney Kirk Session minutes, 8 April 1713.
[8] PRONI, MIC1P/37/4/9, Carnmoney Kirk Session minutes, 30 March 1715.
[9] PRONI, MIC1P/37/4/9, Carnmoney Kirk Session minutes, 5 April 1713.
[10] PRONI, MIC1P/37/4/9, Carnmoney Kirk Session minutes, 8 April 1713.
[11] PRONI, MIC1P/37/4/9, Carnmoney Kirk Session minutes, 30 March 1715; 15 April 1715.
[12] PRONI, MIC1P/37/4/9, Carnmoney Kirk Session minutes, 15 April 1715.
[13] PRONI, MIC1P/37/4/9, Carnmoney Kirk Session minutes, 10 March 1723.
[14] See Patrick Fitzgerald, 'Scottish migration to Ireland in the seventeenth century', in Alexia Grosjean and Steve Murdock (eds), *Scottish communities abroad in the early modern period* (2005), 27–52; T.C. Smout, N.C. Landsman and T.M. Devine, 'Scottish emigration in the seventeenth and eighteenth centuries', in Nicholas P. Canny (ed.), *Europeans on the move: studies on European migration, 1500–1800* (Oxford, 1994), 76–112: 77; S.J. Connolly, 'Ulster Presbyterians: religion, culture, and politics, 1660–1850', in Tyler Blethen (ed.), *Ulster and North America: transatlantic perspectives on the Scotch-Irish* (Tuscaloosa, 1997), 24–40: 24–6.
[15] Robert Whan, *The Presbyterians of Ulster, 1680–1730* (Woodbridge, 2013), 1.
[16] Raymond Gillespie, 'The early modern economy, 1600–1780', in Liam Kennedy and Philip Ollerenshaw (eds), *Ulster since 1600: politics, economy and society* (Oxford, 2013), 12–26: 21–2.
[17] S.J. Connolly, *Religion and society in nineteenth-century Ireland* (Dundalk, 1985), 3.
[18] Connolly, *Religion and society*, 3.
[19] A Kirk Session minute book survives for Usher's Quay Presbyterian church in Dublin. My thanks to Clontarf and Scots Presbyterian church and Hilary Fairman for facilitating access. See Usher's Quay Kirk Session minute book, 1726–66. See also Steven C. Ffeary-Smyrl, *Dic-

tionary of Dublin dissent: Dublin's protestant dissenting meeting houses, 1660–1920 (Dublin, 2009); S.J. Connolly, *Religion, law and power: the making of Protestant Ireland, 1660–1760* (Oxford, 1992), 160–1.

[20] Connolly, *Religion and society*, 3.

[21] Connolly, *Religion, law and power*, 160. See also David Hempton and Myrtle Hill, *Evangelical Protestantism in Ulster society, 1740–1890* (London, 1992).

[22] S.J. Connolly, *Divided kingdom: Ireland, 1630–1800* (Oxford, 2008), 249; Connolly, *Religion, law and power*, 147.

[23] See Charles Ivar McGrath, 'The Penal laws: origins, purpose, enforcement and impact', in Kevin Costello and Niamh Howlin (eds), *Law and religion in Ireland, 1700–1970* (Cham: Switzerland, 2021), 13–48.

[24] Robert Whan, 'Irish Presbyterians and the quest for toleration, c. 1692–1733', in Costello and Howlin (eds), *Law and religion in Ireland, 1700–1970*, 157–84: 159–60.

[25] Whan, 'Irish Presbyterians', 160; Ian McBride, 'Presbyterians in the Penal era', *Bullan* 1 (1994), 73–86: 73–5.

[26] Patrick Griffin, 'The people with no name: Ulster's migrants and identity formation in eighteenth-century Pennsylvania', *William and Mary Quarterly* 58(3) (2002), 587–614: 591.

[27] D.W. Hayton, 'Presbyterians and the confessional state: the sacramental test as an issue in Irish politics, 1704–1780', *Bulletin of the Presbyterian Historical Society of Ireland* 26 (1997), 11–31; Whan, 'Irish Presbyterians', 161.

[28] See J. M. Barkley, 'Marriage and the Presbyterian tradition', *Ulster Folklife* 39 (1993), 29–40.

[29] Whan, *Presbyterians of Ulster*, 199.

[30] Connolly, 'Ulster Presbyterians', 27.

[31] See Chapter 7 in this book and also Whan, *Presbyterians of Ulster*, 171–7.

[32] See for example, R.F.G. Holmes, *Our Irish Presbyterian heritage* (Belfast, 1985), 63–6; W.G. Brown, 'A theological interpretation of the first subscription controversy (1719–1728)', in J.L.M. Haire et al (eds), *Challenge and conflict: essays in Irish Presbyterian history and doctrine* (Antrim, 1981), 28–45.

[33] See David Stewart, *The Seceders in Ireland, with annals of their congregations* (Belfast, 1950); R.F.G. Holmes, *The Presbyterian church in Ireland: a popular history* (Dublin, 2000), especially, 49–83; and Adam Loughridge, *The Covenanters in Ireland* (Belfast, 1984).

[34] Andrew R. Holmes, *The Shaping of Ulster Presbyterian belief and practice, 1770–1840* (Oxford, 2006), 30.

[35] R.F.G. Holmes, *Our Irish Presbyterian heritage* (Belfast, 1985), 1–4; Holmes, *Presbyterian church in Ireland*, 9–12.

[36] Church of Scotland, *The confession of faith: and the larger and shorter catechisms. First agreed upon by the Assembly of Divines at Westminster, and now appointed by the General Assembly of the Kirk of Scotland, to be a Part of Uniformity in Religion between the Kirks of Christ in the Three Kingdoms. Together with the directions of the General Assembly concerning Secret and Private Worship: And the Sum of Saving Knowledge, with the Practical Use thereof* (hereafter cited as *Confession*) (Edinburgh, 1744), 59. See Holmes, *Shaping of Ulster Presbyterian belief and practice*, chapter 6: 'Communion and discipline'.

[37] Holmes, *Shaping of Ulster Presbyterian belief and practice*, 189.

[38] The Presbyterian Church in Ireland, *The constitution and discipline of the Presbyterian church: with a directory for the celebration of ordinances, and the performance of ministerial duties, published by the authority of the General Synod of Ulster* (Belfast, 1825) (hereafter cited as Presbyterian Church in Ireland, *Code*), 94.

[39] Holmes, *Shaping of Ulster Presbyterian belief and practice*, 204.

[40] J.M. Barkley, *The eldership in Irish Presbyterianism* (Belfast, 1963), 30–3.

[41] Union Theological College (hereafter UTC), Burt Kirk Session minutes, 22 March 1700.

[42] Holmes, *Shaping of Ulster Presbyterian belief and practice*, 169; 192–4; Blaikie and Gray, 'Archives of abuse', 70.

[43] PRONI, MIC1P/37/4/9, Carnmoney Kirk Session minutes, 1686–1748 and 1786–1821.

[44] PRONI, CR3/8/1, Loughaghery Kirk Session minutes, 1801–1844.
[45] Andrew R. Holmes, 'Community and discipline in Ulster Presbyterianism, c. 1770–1840', in *Studies in Church History*, 40 (2004), 266–77: 267.
[46] Leanne Calvert, '"From a woman's point of view": the Presbyterian archive as a source for women's and gender history in eighteenth- and nineteenth-century Ireland', *Irish Historical Studies*, 46(170) (2022), 301–18: 305; Leanne Calvert, '"I am friends wt you & do entertain no malice": discord, disputes and defamation in Ulster Presbyterian church courts, c. 1700–1838', in Costello and Howlin (eds), *Law and religion in Ireland, 1700–1970* (Cham, Switzerland, 2021), 185–210: 191; Andrew Blaikie and Paul Gray, 'Archives of abuse and discontent? Presbyterianism and sexual behaviour during the eighteenth and nineteenth centuries', in R.J. Morris and Liam Kennedy (eds), *Ireland and Scotland: order and disorder, 1600–2000* (Edinburgh, 2005), 61–84: 65, 69–70; Holmes, *Shaping of Ulster Presbyterian belief and practice*, 166–72.
[47] J.M. Barkley, 'The Presbyterian minister in eighteenth-century Ireland', in J.L.M. Haire (ed.), *Challenge and conflict: essays in Irish Presbyterian history and doctrine* (Antrim, 1981), 46–71: 48.
[48] Barkley, 'Presbyterian minister', 48.
[49] Barkley, 'Presbyterian minister', 48.
[50] Calvert, '"I am friends wt you & do entertain no malice"', 197–202.
[51] See UTC, Burt Kirk Session minutes 12 August 1707; 27 May 1709; PRONI, MIC1P/37/4/9, Carnmoney Kirk Session minutes, 15 February 1707; 27 May 1709. For work on witchcraft and magic in Ireland and among Presbyterians see Andrew Sneddon and John Fulton, 'Witchcraft, the press, and crime in Ireland, 1822–1922', *Historical Journal* 62(3) (2019), 741–64: 741–2 and Andrew Sneddon, *Witchcraft and magic in Ireland* (Basingstoke, 2015).
[52] Whan, *Presbyterians of Ulster*, 165.
[53] Liam Kennedy and P.M. Solar, 'The rural economy, 1780–1914', in Liam Kennedy and Philip Ollerenshaw (eds), *Ulster since 1600: politics, economy and society* (Oxford, 2013),160–76: 163; Gillespie, 'Early modern economy', 22–4.
[54] W.H. Crawford, *The impact of the domestic linen industry in Ulster* (Belfast, 2005), 87.
[55] W.H. Crawford, 'Women in the domestic linen industry', in Margaret MacCurtain and Mary O'Dowd (eds), *Women in early modern Ireland* (Edinburgh, 1991), 255–64: 255; Judith Ridner, *The Scots Irish of early Pennsylvania. A varied people* (Philadelphia, 2018), 16
[56] Ridner, *Scots Irish*, 17.
[57] Hinck's prints are reprinted in W.H. Crawford, *The impact of the domestic linen industry in Ulster* (Belfast, 2005).
[58] Mary O'Dowd, *A history of women in Ireland, 1500–1800* (Oxford, 2004), 139; Brenda Collins, 'Proto-industrialization and pre-famine emigration', *Social History* 7(2) (1982), 127–46: 130.
[59] Collins, 'Proto-industrialization', 130.
[60] PRONI, MIC1P/37/4/9, Carnmoney Kirk Session minutes, 22 November 1719; 25 November 1719.
[61] PRONI, MIC1P/37/4/9, Carnmoney Kirk Session minutes, 22 November 1719; 25 November 1719.
[62] PRONI, MIC1P/37/4/9, Carnmoney Kirk Session minutes, 22 November 1719.
[63] Kennedy and Solar, 'Rural economy', 165.
[64] O'Dowd, *History of women*, 139.
[65] O'Dowd, *History of women*, 139.
[66] O'Dowd, *History of women*, 137.
[67] O'Dowd, *History of women*, 138.
[68] See Benjamin Bankhurst, *Ulster Presbyterians and the Scots Irish diaspora, 1750–1764* (London, 2013), chapter one.
[69] Peter E. Gilmore, *Irish Presbyterians and the shaping of Western Pennsylvania, 1770–1830* (Pittsburgh, 2018), 6.

[70] Ridner, *Scots Irish*, 29.
[71] Kennedy and Solar, 'Rural economy', 164–5.
[72] Kennedy and Solar, 'Rural economy', 166.
[73] Kennedy and Solar, 'Rural economy', 166.
[74] Kennedy and Solar, 'Rural economy', 167.
[75] Kennedy and Solar, Rural economy', 168.
[76] Holmes, *Shaping of Ulster Presbyterian belief and practice*, 26.
[77] Alice Johnson, *Middle-class life in Victorian Belfast* (Liverpool, 2020), 2–3.
[78] Holmes, *Shaping of Ulster Presbyterian belief and practice*, 27.
[79] Holmes, *Shaping of Ulster Presbyterian belief and practice*, 27.
[80] Holmes, *Shaping of Ulster Presbyterian belief and practice*, 172.
[81] Holmes, *Shaping of Ulster Presbyterian belief and practice*, 173–4.
[82] Holmes, *Shaping of Ulster Presbyterian belief and practice*, 173–4.
[83] Holmes, *Shaping of Ulster Presbyterian belief and practice*, 172.
[84] Leanne Calvert, '"He came to her bed pretending courtship": sex, courtship and the making of marriage in Ulster, 1750–1844' in *Irish Historical Studies* 42(162), 244–64: 258; Holmes, *Shaping of Ulster Presbyterian belief and practice*, 171.
[85] Presbyterian Church in Ireland, *Code*, 67.
[86] UTC, Burt Kirk Session minutes, 31 July 1711.
[87] UTC, Burt Kirk Session minutes, 31 July 1711.
[88] UTC, Burt Kirk Session minutes, 31 July 1711.
[89] PRONI, CR5/5/B/5/1, Bangor Presbytery minutes, 13 May 1766.
[90] PRONI, CR5/5/B/5/1, Bangor Presbytery minutes, 13 May 1766.
[91] PRONI, CR5/5/B/5/1, Bangor Presbytery minutes, 13 May 1766.
[92] PRONI, CR5/5/B/5/1, Bangor Presbytery minutes, 13 May 1766.
[93] PRONI, CR5/5/B/5/1, Bangor Presbytery minutes, 13 May 1766.
[94] PRONI, CR5/5/B/5/1, Bangor Presbytery minutes, 13 May 1766.
[95] PRONI, CR5/5/B/5/1, Bangor Presbytery minutes, 13 May 1766.
[96] Church of Scotland, *The form of process in the Judicatories of the Church of Scotland; with relation to scandals and censures: to which is subjoined, several acts and overtures of the General Assemblies* (Glasgow, 1763) (hereafter *Form of process*).
[97] Church of Scotland, *Form of process*, 5; Presbyterian Church in Ireland, *Code*, 67.
[98] Church of Scotland, *Form of process*, 9; Presbyterian Church in Ireland, *Code*, 67.
[99] Church of Scotland, *Form of process*, 6–9; Presbyterian Church in Ireland, *Code*, 67–8.
[100] Church of Scotland, *Form of process*, 10–15; Presbyterian Church in Ireland, *Code*, 68–9.
[101] Church of Scotland, *Form of process*, 10–15; Presbyterian Church in Ireland, *Code*, 68–9.
[102] Presbyterian Church in Ireland, *Code*, 65.
[103] Holmes, *Shaping of Ulster Presbyterian belief and practice*, 169; Presbyterian Church in Ireland, *Code*, 64.
[104] Presbyterian Church in Ireland, *Code*, 78.
[105] Leanne Calvert, '"Came to her dressed in mans cloaths": transgender histories and queer approaches to the family in eighteenth-century Ireland', *History of the Family* 29(1) (2024), 115.
[106] UTC, Burt Kirk Session minutes, 2 August 1702; 6 September 1702; 2 October 1702; 22 November 1702; 25 December 1702; 29 December 1702.
[107] UTC, Burt Kirk Session minutes, 29 December 1702.
[108] UTC, Burt Kirk Session minutes, 18 April 1715.
[109] UTC, Burt Kirk Session minutes, 18 April 1715.
[110] Holmes, *Shaping of Ulster Presbyterian belief and practice*, 168.
[111] The fragile nature of many minute books means that access to the originals is restricted, and researchers must use microfilm copies. Others are closed to the public. At the time of writing, it was not possible to access the minute book of the Reformed Session of Antrim, 1789–1802, which has been closed to public consultation in PRONI since 1996. The archive reference, for this minute book is PRONI, CR5/9/2/1/1, Minutes of the Congregation of Antrim 1789–1802.

[112] Holmes, *Shaping of Ulster Presbyterian belief and practice*, 168, 172–4; Calvert, '"He came to her bed"', 250.
[113] Holmes, *Shaping of Ulster Presbyterian belief and practice*, 168–9.
[114] Holmes, *Shaping of Ulster Presbyterian belief and practice*, 306.
[115] See Frances E. Dolan, *True relations. Reading, literature and evidence in seventeenth-century England* (Philadelphia, 2013); Tim Stretton, 'Women, legal records, and the problem of the lawyer's hand', *Journal of British Studies* 58(4) (2019), 684–700; Natalie Zemon Davis, *Fiction in the archives. Pardon tales and their tellers in sixteenth-century France* (California, 1987); See also Margo Todd, *The culture of Protestantism in early modern Scotland* (New Haven and London, 2002), 16–20.
[116] See Calvert, '"Came to her dressed in mans cloaths"', 115–16.
[117] Robertson, 'What's law got to do with it?', 162.
[118] See Margo Todd, *Culture of Protestantism in early modern Scotland*, 16–20.
[119] Zemon Davis, *Fiction in the archives*, 4.
[120] Julie Hardwick, *Sex in an old regime city. Young workers and intimacy in France, 1660–1789* (Oxford, 2020), 8.
[121] Hardwick, *Sex in an old regime city*, 7–10.
[122] Wright, *'Natural leaders'*, 8–9.
[123] Shannon Devlin, *Siblinghood and sociability in nineteenth-century Ulster* (Liverpool, 2025), see 10–11.
[124] See Sally Holloway, '"You know I am all on fire": writing the adulterous affair in England, c. 1740–1830', *Historical Research* 89(244) (2016), 317–39.
[125] Devlin, *Siblinghood*, 11.
[126] PRONI, D2003/B/4/5/1, Records of the Crawford family, volume ii, 4.
[127] PRONI, D2003/B/4/5/1, Records of the Crawford family, volume ii, 4.
[128] PRONI, D2003/B/4/5/1, Records of the Crawford family, volume ii, 4.
[129] See Leanne Calvert, '"Your marage will make a change with them all … when you get another family": illegitimate children, parenthood and siblinghood in Ireland, c. 1759–1832', *English Historical Review* 137(587) (2022), 1144–73; Katie Barclay, 'Illicit intimacies: the imagined "homes" of Gilbert Innes of Stow and his mistresses (1751–1832)', *Gender and History* 27(3) (2015), 576–90; Kate Gibson, '"I am not on the footing of kept women": extra-marital love in eighteenth-century England', *Cultural and Social History* 17(3) (2020), 355–73.
[130] See Rebecca Earle, 'Introduction. Letters, writers and the historian', in Rebecca Earle (ed.), *Epistolary selves: letters and letter-writers, 1600–1945* (Aldershot, 1999), 1–18; James Daybell, 'Introduction', in James Daybell (ed.), *Early modern women's letter writing, 1450–1700* (Basingstoke, 20021), 1–15.
[131] Katie Barclay, *Love, intimacy and power. Marriage and patriarchy in Scotland, 1650–1850* (Manchester, 2011), 27.
[132] Barclay, *Love, intimacy and power*, 27. See Leanne Calvert, '"Do not forget your bit wife": love, marriage and the negotiation of patriarchy in Irish Presbyterian marriages, c. 1780–1850', *Women's History Review* 26(3) (2017), 433–54.
[133] Barclay, *Love, intimacy and power*, 27
[134] See Calvert, '"Your marage will make a change with them all"', 1144–73 and Emma Marshall, 'Absent parents, sick children, and epistolary relationships in England, c. 1640–c.1750', *History of the Family* 30(1) (2025), 44–71.
[135] Hannah Barker, 'Soul, purse and family: middling and lower-class masculinity in eighteenth-century Manchester', *Social History* 33(1) (2008), 12–35: 15. See also Irina Paperno, 'What can be done with diaries', *Russian Review* 63(4) (2004), 561–73.
[136] See Leanne Calvert, '"What a wonderful change have I undergone … So altered in stature, knowledge & ideas!": Apprenticeship, adolescence and growing up in eighteenth- and nineteenth-century Ulster', *Irish Economic and Social History* 45(1) (2018), 70–89: 81.
[137] Barker, 'Soul, purse and family', 15.
[138] See Calvert, '"What a wonderful change have I undergone"', 81.

[139] See Kathryn Carter, 'The cultural work of diaries in mid-century Victorian Britain', *Victorian Review* 23(2), 251–67.
[140] Leanne Calvert, 'The journal of John Tennent, 1786–90', *Analecta Hibernica* 43 (2012), 69–128: 71.
[141] S.J. Connolly, *Priests and the people in pre-Famine Ireland, 1780–1845* (Dublin, 1982), 187–8.
[142] *Ordnance Survey Memoirs of Ireland*, eds Angélique Day, Patrick McWilliams, Nóirín Dobson and Lisa English (40 volumes; Belfast, 1990–8) (hereafter cited as *OSMI*), Island-magee, vol. 10, 36.
[143] *OSMI*, Island-magee, vol. 10, 36.
[144] *OSMI*, Island-magee, vol. 10, 37.
[145] *OSMI*, Island-magee, vol. 10, 37, 40.
[146] Connolly, *Priests*, 190.
[147] Paul Gray, 'A social history of illegitimacy in Ireland from the late eighteenth to the early twentieth century' (unpublished PhD thesis, Queen's University, Belfast, 2000), 296; Diane Urquhart, 'Gender, family, and sexuality, 1800–2000', in Liam Kennedy and Philip Ollerenshaw (Eds), *Ulster since 1600: politics, economy and society* (Oxford, 2013), 245–59, 247–8.
[148] Gray, 'Social history of illegitimacy', 296.
[149] Blaikie and Gray, 'Archives of abuse', 83; Luddy and O'Dowd, *Marriage in Ireland*, 147.
[150] PRONI, CR4/12/B/1, Templepatrick Kirk Session minute book, 1646–1743.
[151] PRONI, T1447/1, First Dromara Kirk Session minute book, 1780–1805.
[152] *OSMI*, Rashee, vol. 32, 139.
[153] Calvert, '"From a woman's point of view"', 307.
[154] Luddy and O'Dowd, *Marriage in Ireland*, 147.
[155] Calvert, '"From a woman's point of view"', 309; Luddy and O'Dowd, *Marriage in Ireland*, 147.
[156] Luddy and O'Dowd, *Marriage in Ireland*, 148.
[157] Elaine Farrell, *'A most diabolical deed': infanticide and Irish society, 1850–1900* (Manchester, 2009); James Kelly, 'Infanticide in eighteenth-century Ireland', *Irish Economic and Social History* 19 (1992), 5–26.
[158] Myrtle Hill, 'Religion, gender, and sexuality in Ireland, 1800–1922', in Gladys Ganiel and Andrew R. Holmes (eds), *The Oxford handbook of religion in modern Ireland* (Oxford, 2024), 124–44: 130.

Chapter One

[1] PRONI, CR4/18/1, Ballycarry Kirk Session minutes, 9 January 1723.
[2] Leanne Calvert, '"A more careful tender nurse cannot be than my dear husband": reassessing the role of men in pregnancy and childbirth in Ulster, 1780–1838', *Journal of Family History* 42 (1) (2017), 22–36.
[3] James Wolveridge, *Speculum matricis hybernicum, or, The Irish midwives handmaid* (London, 1670). See also Jo Murphy-Lawless, 'Images of "poor" women in the writing of Irish men midwives', in Margaret MacCurtain and Mary O'Dowd (eds), *Women in early modern Ireland* (Edinburgh, 1991), 291–303.
[4] Wolveridge, *Speculum matricis*, 97.
[5] J.R.R. Adams, *The Printed word & the common man. Popular culture in Ulster, 1700–1900* (Belfast, 1987), 20–1.
[6] Adams, *Printed word*, 29–31.
[7] Adams, *Printed word*, 81. Adams notes that both of these works were available in Ulster.
[8] See Roy Porter and Lesley Hall, *The facts of life. The creation of sexual knowledge in Britain, 1650–1950* (New Haven and London, 1995), 33–64.
[9] Adams, *Printed word*, 81.

[10] Nicholas Culpeper, *A directory for midwives: or, a guide for women, in their conception, bearing, and suckling their children…* (London, 1701), 86.
[11] Calvert, '"A more careful tender nurse"', 25–6.
[12] Wolveridge, *Speculum matricis*, 95.
[13] Wolveridge, *Speculum matricis*, 81.
[14] Wolveridge, *Speculum matricis*, 81.
[15] Union Theological College (hereafter UTC), Burt Kirk Session minutes, 22 May 1701.
[16] UTC, Burt Kirk Session minutes, 29 March 1702.
[17] UTC, Burt Kirk Session minutes, 29 March 1702.
[18] UTC, Burt Kirk Session minutes, 29 March 1702.
[19] UTC, Burt Kirk Session minutes, 13 April 1702; 3 May 1702.
[20] PRONI, CR4/12/B/1, Templepatrick Kirk Session minutes, 28 April 1702.
[21] PRONI, CR4/12/B/1, Templepatrick Kirk Session minutes, 28 April 1702.
[22] PRONI, CR4/12/B/1, Templepatrick Kirk Session minutes, 14 August 1702.
[23] PRONI, CR4/12/B/1, Templepatrick Kirk Session minutes, 14 August 1702.
[24] PRONI, CR4/12/B/1, Templepatrick Kirk Session minutes, 6 September 1702.
[25] PRONI, CR4/12/B/1, Templepatrick Kirk Session minutes, 12 June 1705.
[26] PRONI, CR4/12/B/1, Templepatrick Kirk Session minutes, 12 June 1705.
[27] PRONI, CR4/12/B/1, Templepatrick Kirk Session minutes, 26 October 1705.
[28] PRONI, CR4/12/B/1, Templepatrick Kirk Session minutes, 24 September 1706.
[29] PRONI, CR4/12/B/1, Templepatrick Kirk Session minutes, 8 July 1727; 28 July 1727; 3 August 1727.
[30] PRONI, CR4/12/B/1, Templepatrick Kirk Session minutes, 23 June 1702.
[31] PRONI, CR4/12/B/1, Templepatrick Kirk Session minutes, 30 June 1702.
[32] Laura Gowing, 'Secret births and infanticide in seventeenth-century England', *Past and Present* 156 (1997), 87–115: 90–1; Joanne McEwen, '"At my mother's house": community and household spaces in early eighteenth century Scottish infanticide narratives', in Susan Broomhall (ed.), *Spaces for feeling: emotions and sociabilities in Britain, 1650–1850* (London, 2015), 12–24:18–21.
[33] PRONI, CR4/12/B/1, Templepatrick Kirk Session minutes, 5 July 1702.
[34] PRONI, MIC1P/37/4/9, Carnmoney Kirk Session minutes, 9 November 1705.
[35] PRONI, MIC1P/37/4/9, Carnmoney Kirk Session minutes, 9 November 1705; 5 February 1706.
[36] PRONI, MIC1P/37/4/9, Carnmoney Kirk Session minutes, 5 February 1706.
[37] PRONI, MIC1P/37/4/9, Carnmoney Kirk Session minutes, 9 November 1705.
[38] PRONI, MIC1P/37/4/9, Carnmoney Kirk Session minutes, 15 December 1706.
[39] Leanne McCormick, '"No sense of wrongdoing": abortion in Belfast, 1917–1967', *Journal of Social History* 49(1) (2015), 125–48: 138.
[40] Jennifer Evans and Sara Read, '"Before midnight she had miscarried": women, men and miscarriage in early modern England', *Journal of Family History* 40:1 (2015), 3–23.
[41] Wolveridge, *Speculum matricis*, 104.
[42] Wolveridge, *Speculum matricis*, 105.
[43] Wolveridge, *Speculum matricis*, 104–5.
[44] Wolveridge, *Speculum matricis*, 106–7.
[45] R. Sauer, 'Infanticide and abortion in nineteenth-century Britain', *Population Studies* 32:1 (1978), 81–93: 83–4.
[46] Sauer, 'Infanticide and abortion', 83–4.
[47] Sauer, 'Infanticide and abortion', 83–4.
[48] 'An Act for the further Prevention of malicious shooting and attempting to discharge loaded fire arms, stabbing, cutting, wounding, poisoning, and the malicious using of means to procure the miscarriage of women, and also the malicious setting fire to buildings; and also for repealing a certain Act, made in the twenty-first year of the late King James the First, intituled, *An Act to prevent the destroying and murthering of Bastard Children*, and for substituting other provisions in lieu of the same'. 43 Geo. iii, c. 58.

[49] The terms of the 1829 Act were based on the English Act that was passed in 1828. See 9 Geo. iv, c. 31. The law also made the inducement of miscarriage by means of an 'instrument' in a quickened foetus an offence. This closed a 'loophole' in the 1803 Act. See Sauer, 'Infanticide and abortion', 84, fn. 27.
[50] 9 Geo. iv, c. 31.
[51] 'An Act to amend the Laws relating to Offences against the Person'. 7 Will. 4 and 1 Vic., c. 85. K.W. Masterson, 'The law of abortion in England and Northern Ireland', *Police Journal* 50(1) (1977), 50–61: 50–1.
[52] Offences Against the Person Act (1861). Full text can be found at: https://www.irishstatutebook.ie/eli/1861/act/100/enacted/en/print.html (accessed 21 March 2025).
[53] Lindsey Earner-Byrne and Diane Urquhart, *The Irish abortion journey, 1920–2018* (Cham, Switzerland, 2019), 3.
[54] Cara Delay, 'Pills, potions, and purgatives: women and abortion methods in Ireland, 1900–1950', *Women's History Review* 28(3) (2019), 479–99; McCormick, '"No sense of wrongdoing"', 124–48.
[55] K.H. Connell, *Irish peasant society: four historical essays* (Oxford, 1968), 62–3.
[56] Delay, 'Pills, potions', 484.
[57] Eileen M. Murphy, 'The child that is born of one's far body': maternal and infant death in medieval Ireland', *Childhood in the Past* 14(1) (2021), 13–37.
[58] John K'Eogh, *Botanalogia Universalis Hibernica, Or, A general Irish herbal calculated for this kingdom, giving an account of the herbs, shrubs and trees, naturally produced therein, in English, Irish, and Latin; with a true description of them, and their medicinal virtues and qualities* (Cork,1735), 108.
[59] K'Eogh, *Botanalogia*, 108.
[60] K'Eogh, *Botanalogia*, 82.
[61] K'Eogh, *Botanalogia*, 82.
[62] K'Eogh, *Botanalogia*, 83.
[63] K'Eogh, *Botanalogia*, 17.
[64] PRONI, MIC1P/37/4/9, Carnmoney Kirk Session minutes, 5 October 1706.
[65] PRONI, MIC1P/37/4/9, Carnmoney Kirk Session minutes, 1 October1710.
[66] PRONI, MIC1P/37/4/9, Carnmoney Kirk Session minutes, 1 October 1710.
[67] PRONI, MIC1P/37/4/9, Carnmoney Kirk Session minutes, 1 October 1710. 'March', also known as 'March Violet' or 'Purple Violet', was used in a variety of remedies, including the treatment of inflammation, swellings and colds.
[68] K'Eogh, *Botanalogica*, 126; Ronan Foley, 'Indigenous narratives of health: (re)placing folk-medicine with Irish health histories', *Journal of Medical Humanities* 36:1 (2015), 5–18: 12.
[69] Nicholas Culpeper, *Culpeper's complete herbal, to which is now added, upwards of one hundred additional herbs, with a display of their medicinal and occult properties* (London, 1816), 188.
[70] PRONI, MIC1P/37/4/9, Carnmoney Kirk Session minutes, November 1710.
[71] PRONI, MIC1P/37/4/9, Carnmoney Kirk Session minutes, November 1710.
[72] Elaine Farrell, '"The fellow said it was not harm and only tricks": the role of the father in suspected cases of infanticide in Ireland, 1850–1900', *Journal of Social History* 45(4) (2012), 990–1004: 995.
[73] UTC, Burt Kirk Session minutes, 26 May 1710.
[74] UTC, Burt Kirk Session minutes, 26 May 1710.
[75] UTC, Burt Kirk Session minutes, 26 May 1710.
[76] UTC, Burt Kirk Session minutes, 26 May 1710.
[77] UTC, Burt Kirk Session minutes, 26 May 1710.
[78] URC, Burt Kirk Session minutes, 2 June 1710.
[79] UTC, Burt Kirk Session minutes, 26 July 1710; 24 July 1712.
[80] Elaine Farrell, *'A most diabolical deed': infanticide and Irish society, 1850–1900* (Manchester, 2013); James Kelly, '"An unnatural crime": infanticide in early nineteenth-century Ireland',

Irish Economic and Social History 46(1) (2019), 66–110; James Kelly, 'Infanticide in eighteenth-century Ireland', *Irish Economic and Social History* 19(1) (1992), 5–26.
[81] Farrell, 'A most diabolical deed', 2.
[82] Farrell, 'A most diabolical deed', 2.
[83] Kelly, 'Infanticide', 23.
[84] PRONI, CR4/12/B/1, Templepatrick Kirk Session minutes, 2 January 1701.
[85] A similar case was recorded in St Cuthbert's, Scotland in July 1756. Rabina Gemils claimed to have miscarried after four months of pregnancy. The father was reputed to be her master William Wallace and it was 'known' that his wife had buried the child's body. The Session arranged for the body to be dug up and brought to the Kirk, where it was inspected by two midwives. See Leneman and Mitchison, *Sin in the city*, 59.
[86] PRONI, CR4/12/B/1, Templepatrick Kirk Session minutes, 2 March 1701.
[87] PRONI, CR4/12/B/1, Templepatrick Kirk Session minutes, 14 September 1701.
[88] PRONI, CR4/12/B/1, Templepatrick Kirk Session minutes, 14 September 1701.
[89] PRONI, CR4/12/B/1, Templepatrick Kirk Session minutes, 14 September 1701.
[90] PRONI, CR4/18/1, Ballycarry Kirk Session minutes, 3 November 1738.
[91] PRONI, CR4/18/1, Ballycarry Kirk Session minutes, 3 November 1738.
[92] Calvert, '"From a woman's point of view", 301–18: 316; Farrell, 'A most diabolical deed', 28; Virginia Crossman, *The Poor Law in Ireland, 1838–1948* (Dublin, 2006), 4.
[93] Church of Scotland, *Form of process*.
[94] Presbyterian Church in Ireland, *Code*.
[95] Church of Scotland, *Form of process*, 11.
[96] Presbyterian Church in Ireland, *Code*, 68.
[97] PRONI, CR4/18/1, Ballycarry Kirk Session minutes, July 1710.
[98] Rosalind Mitchison and Leah Leneman, *Sexuality and social control: Scotland, 1660–1780* (Oxford, 1989), 208.
[99] PRONI, CR3/25/B/1, Cahans Kirk Session minutes, 14 June 1753.
[100] PRONI, CR4/12/B/1, Templepatrick Kirk Session minutes, 5 January 1704.
[101] Church of Scotland, *Form of process*, 13.
[102] Church of Scotland, *Form of process*, 13.
[103] PRONI, CR3/25/B/1, Cahans Kirk Session minutes, 25 July 1755.
[104] PRONI, CR3/25/B/1, Cahans Kirk Session minutes, 25 July 1755.
[105] PRONI, CR3/25/B/1, Cahans Kirk Session minutes, 22 June 1755.
[106] PRONI, CR3/25/B/1, Cahans Kirk Session minutes, 22 June 1755.
[107] PRONI, CR3/25/B/1, Cahans Kirk Session minutes, 22 June 1755.
[108] PRONI, CR3/25/B/1, Cahans Kirk Session minutes, 22 June 1755.
[109] PRONI, CR3/25/B/1, Cahans Kirk Session minutes, 22 June 1755.
[110] Church of Scotland, *Form of process*, 11.
[111] Church of Scotland, *Form of process*, 11.
[112] PRONI, CR4/18/1, Ballycarry Kirk Session minutes, 29 February 1723.
[113] PRONI, CR4/12/B/1, Templepatrick Kirk Session minutes, 16 November 1701.
[114] PRONI, CR4/12/B/1, Templepatrick Kirk Session minutes, 23 November 1701.
[115] Mitchison and Leneman, *Sexuality and social control*, 207; Cathy McClive, *Menstruation and procreation in early modern France* (Farnham, 2015), 178–80.
[116] PRONI, CR4/12/B/1, Templepatrick Kirk Session minutes, 2 April 1704.
[117] PRONI, CR4/12/B/1, Templepatrick Kirk Session minutes, 30 May 1704.
[118] PRONI, CR4/12/B/1, Templepatrick Kirk Session minutes, 30 May 1704.
[119] PRONI, CR4/12/B/1, Templepatrick Kirk Session minutes, 25 April 1705.
[120] PRONI, CR4/12/B/1, Templepatrick Kirk Session minutes, 26 October 1705; 8 May 1706.
[121] PRONI, CR4/12/B/1, Templepatrick Kirk Session minutes, 6 August 1707.
[122] PRONI, CR4/12/B/1, Templepatrick Kirk Session minutes, 6 August 1707.
[123] PRONI, CR4/12/B/1, Templepatrick Kirk Session minutes, 20 June 1704.
[124] PRONI, CR4/12/B/1, Templepatrick Kirk Session minutes, 16 May 1710.

[125] PRONI, MIC1P/37/4/9, Carnmoney Kirk Session minutes, 6 March 1811.
[126] PRONI, MIC1P/37/4/9, Carnmoney Kirk Session minutes, 3 April 1811.
[127] PRONI, MIC1P/37/4/9, Carnmoney Kirk Session minutes, 3 April 1811; 1 April 1812.
[128] PRONI, MIC1P/37/4/9, Carnmoney Kirk Session minutes, 4 July 1703.
[129] PRONI, MIC1P/37/4/9, Carnmoney Kirk Session minutes, 4 July 1703. In Scotland, men's behaviour following the birth of children was sometimes closely watched and used as evidence in paternity claims. See Leah Leneman and Rosalind Mitchison, *Sin the city: sexuality and social control in urban Scotland, 1660-1780* (Edinburgh, 1998), 106–8.
[130] PRONI, CR4/12/B/1, Templepatrick Kirk Session minutes, 19 January 1701; 22 January 1701.
[131] PRONI, CR4/12/B/1, Templepatrick Kirk Session minutes, 22 January 1701.
[132] PRONI, MIC1P/37/4/9, Carnmoney Kirk Session minutes, 25 December 1720.
[133] PRONI, MIC1P/37/4/9, Carnmoney Kirk Session minutes, 29 March 1721.
[134] PRONI, MIC1P/37/4/9, Carnmoney Kirk Session minutes, 11 April 1721.
[135] See Cara Delay, 'Women, childbirth customs and authority in Ireland, 1850–1930', *Lilith: a feminist history journal* 21 (2015), 6–18; Ciara Breathnach, 'Handywomen and birthing in rural Ireland, 1851–1955', *Gender and History* 28(1) (2016), 34–56.
[136] Presbyterian Historical Society of Ireland, Belfast (hereafter PHSI), Monaghan Presbytery minutes, May 1811.
[137] PHSI, Monaghan Presbytery minutes, 11 June 1811.
[138] PHSI, Monaghan Presbytery minutes, 31 March 1812.
[139] PRONI, CR4/18/1, Ballycarry Kirk Session minutes, 27 April 1726.
[140] PRONI, CR4/18/1, Ballycarry Kirk Session minutes, 28 April 1726.
[141] PRONI, MIC1P/37/4/9, Carnmoney Kirk Session minutes, 11 January 1721.
[142] PRONI, MIC1P/37/4/9, Carnmoney Kirk Session minutes, 11 January 1721.
[143] Church of Scotland, *Form of Process*, 12.
[144] Church of Scotland, *Form of Process*, 13.
[145] Church of Scotland, *Form of Process*, 13.
[146] PRONI, CR4/12/B/1, Templepatrick Kirk Session minutes, 25 January 1704.
[147] PRONI, CR4/12/B/1, Templepatrick Kirk Session minutes, 2 February 1704.
[148] PRONI, CR4/12/B/1, Templepatrick Kirk Session minutes, 4 June 1704; 25 June 1704; 23 July 1704; 6 February 1705.
[149] PRONI, CR4/12/B/1, Templepatrick Kirk Session minutes, 25 July 1704.
[150] PRONI, CR4/12/B/1, Templepatrick Kirk Session minutes, 24 September 1706.
[151] PRONI, CR4/12/B/1, Templepatrick Kirk Session minutes, 29 June 1712.
[152] PRONI, CR4/12/B/1, Templepatrick Kirk Session minutes, 29 June 1712.
[153] PRONI, CR4/12/B/1, Templepatrick Kirk Session minutes, 21 September 1712.
[154] Calvert, '"From a woman's point of view"', 316–17.
[155] PRONI, MIC1P/37/4/9, Carnmoney Kirk Session minutes, 6 March 1816; 2 May 1816.
[156] PRONI, CR4/12/B/1, Templepatrick Kirk Session minutes, 30 September 1704.

Chapter Two

[1] *The Drennan–McTier letters, 1794–1801*, ed. Jean Agnew (3 vols, Dublin, 1998–9), vol. 2, 612.
[2] *Drennan–McTier letters*, vol. 2, 612.
[3] *Drennan–McTier letters*, vol. 2, 612.
[4] *Drennan–McTier letters*, vol. 2, 616.
[5] Jean Agnew, 'Martha McTier', *Dictionary of Irish Biography* (Dublin), online edition: https://www.dib.ie/biography/mctier-martha-a5762 (accessed February 2024).
[6] *Drennan–McTier letters*, vol. 2, 621.
[7] *Drennan–McTier letters*, vol. 2, 673, 679, 683–4.
[8] *Drennan–McTier letters*, vol. 2, 681, 684.

[9] *Drennan–McTier letters*, vol. 2, 685.
[10] *Drennan–McTier letters*, vol. 2, 685–6.
[11] *Drennan–McTier letters*, vol. 2, 685–6.
[12] Presbyterian Church in Ireland, *Code*, 93.
[13] For a discussion of these differences see Holmes, *Shaping of Ulster Presbyterian belief and practice*, 202–3.
[14] Church of Scotland, *Confession*, 143.
[15] Church of Scotland, *Confession*, 145.
[16] Presbyterian Church in Ireland, *Code*, 93.
[17] Holmes, *Shaping of Ulster Presbyterian belief and practice*, 201–2.
[18] Church of Scotland, *Confession*, 144.
[19] Holmes, *Shaping of Ulster Presbyterian*, 488; Presbyterian Church in Ireland, *Code*, 93.
[20] Presbyterian Church in Ireland, *Code*, 93.
[21] Church of Scotland, *Confession*, 144–5.
[22] Holmes, *Shaping of Ulster Presbyterian belief and practice*, 203.
[23] Holmes, *Shaping of Ulster Presbyterian belief and practice*, 209–10.
[24] Presbyterian Church in Ireland, *Code*, 93.
[25] Presbyterian Church in Ireland, *Code*, 93.
[26] Presbyterian Church in Ireland, *Code*, 93.
[27] Presbyterian Church in Ireland, *Code*, 93.
[28] See Calvert, '"From a woman's point of view", 301–18, 316–17.
[29] PHSI, Ballykelly Kirk Session minutes, 1 November 1803; 1 January 1804.
[30] PRONI, CR3/8/1, Loughaghery Kirk Session minutes, March 1835.
[31] PRONI, CR3/8/1, Loughaghery Kirk Session minutes, c. 1808.
[32] PRONI, CR3/8/1, Loughaghery Kirk Session minutes, c. 1808.
[33] Holmes, *Shaping of Ulster Presbyterian belief and practice*, 206.
[34] PHSI, Ballykelly Kirk Session minutes, 8 May 1808.
[35] PRONI, CR3/8/1, Loughaghery Kirk Session minutes, 11 September 1831.
[36] Andrew Holmes, 'Community and discipline in Ulster Presbyterianism, c. 1770–1840', in Kate Copper and Jeremy Gregory (eds), *Retribution, repentance and reconciliation: studies in church history* (Woodbridge, 2004), 266–77: 273; Holmes, *Shaping of Ulster Presbyterian belief and practice*, 206–7; Andrew Blaikie and Paul Gray, 'Archives of abuse and discontent? Presbyterianism and sexual behaviour during the eighteenth and nineteenth centuries', in R.J. Morris and Liam Kennedy (eds), *Ireland and Scotland: order and disorder, 1600–2000* (Edinburgh, 2005), 61–84: 67–9; Paul Gray, 'A social history of illegitimacy in Ireland from the late eighteenth to the early twentieth century' (unpublished PhD thesis, Queen's University Belfast, 2000), 112–16; Roisin Browne, 'Kirk and community: Ulster Presbyterian society, 1640–1740' (unpublished M.Phil. thesis, Queen's University Belfast, 1999), 99.
[37] Presbyterian Church in Ireland, *Code*, 43.
[38] J.G. Kenny (ed.), *As the crow flies over rough terrain: incorporating the Diary 1827–1828 and More of a divine* (Newtownabbey, 1988), 300.
[39] Kenny, *As the crow flies*, 316.
[40] Clodagh Tait, 'Spiritual bonds, social bonds: baptism and godparenthood in Ireland, 1530–1690', *Cultural and Social History* 2 (2005), 301–27: 305.
[41] Presbyterian Church in Ireland, *Code*, 43.
[42] PRONI, MIC1P/181A/2, Loughbrickland baptism register, 1841–1844; PRONI, MIC-1B/6A/3, Baptism register of Larne and Kilwaugher non-subscribing church, 1826–1929; PRONI, CR4/2/A/1, Baptism register of Rademon non-subscribing church, 1830–92.
[43] *OSMI*, Killead, vol. 35, 23.
[44] *OSMI*, Ballycor, vol. 32, 6; *OSMI*, Donegore, vol. 29, 113.
[45] PRONI, D2930/9/6, Diary of Reverend Robert Magill (1821), 27 February 1821; 21 September 1821.
[46] PRONI, CR3/8/1, Loughaghery Kirk Session minutes, 2 January 1818; 17 July 1834; 28 September 1835; 26 June 1836; 14 April 1843.

[47] PRONI, CR3/8/1, Loughaghery Kirk Session minutes, 2 January 1818.
[48] PRONI, CR3/8/1, Loughaghery Kirk Session minutes, 17 July 1834; 28 September 1835.
[49] PRONI, CR3/8/1, Loughaghery Kirk Session minutes, 23 June 1836.
[50] PRONI, D2003/A/2/16/9, Reverend Alexander Crawford to anonymous, n.d.
[51] PRONI, CR3/1/B/4, Ballymoney Kirk Session minutes, 12 May 1839.
[52] *Drennan–McTier letters*, vol. 2, 696–7.
[53] PRONI, D2003/A/2/14/4, Reverend Alexander Crawford to Helen Gardner, 10 April 1835.
[54] William Buchan, *Domestic medicine; or, a treatise on the prevention and cure of diseases by regimen and simple medicines* (Dublin, 1781), 25–6.
[55] Buchan, *Domestic medicine*, 26.
[56] Hugh Smythson, *The compleat family physician; or, universal medical repository* (London, 1781), 9.
[57] PRONI, MIC1P/37/4/9, Carnmoney Kirk Session minutes, 19 September 1711.
[58] PRONI, T3541/5/3, Typescript copy of the reminiscences of John Caldwell Junior, entitled 'Particulars of a north county Irish family'.
[59] PRONI, T3541/5/3, John Caldwell Junior, 'Particulars of a north county Irish family'.
[60] PRONI, T3541/5/3, John Caldwell Junior, 'Particulars of a north county Irish family'.
[61] PRONI, D1748/G/804/1A&1B, Robert James Tennent, 'Reminiscences of my childhood, 1824'.
[62] PRONI, D1748/G/804/1A&1B, Robert James Tennent, 'Reminiscences of my childhood, 1824'.
[63] *Drennan–McTier letters*, vol. 2, 655.
[64] *Drennan–McTier letters*, vol. 2, 656, 659–60, 667–9.
[65] *Drennan–McTier letters*, vol. 2, 667–9.
[66] *Drennan–McTier letters*, vol. 2, 667–9.
[67] *Drennan–McTier letters*, vol. 2, 667–9.
[68] *Drennan–McTier letters*, vol. 2, 667–9.
[69] *Drennan–McTier letters*, vol. 2, 667–9.
[70] *Drennan–McTier letters*, vol. 2, 668, 680, 685.
[71] *Drennan–McTier letters*, vol. 2, 668.
[72] *Drennan–McTier letters*, vol. 2, 671–2.
[73] *Drennan–McTier letters*, vol. 2, 671–2.
[74] *Drennan–McTier letters*, vol. 2, 671–2.
[75] *Drennan–McTier letters*, vol. 2, 671–2.
[76] *Drennan–McTier letters*, vol. 2, 697–8. Betty, however, turned out to be a difficult servant and her behaviour was the subject of letters between Sarah and Martha. See *Drennan-McTier letters*, vol. 1, xxxii–xxxiii.
[77] Ralph Houlbrooke, *The English family, 1450–1700* (Oxford and New York, 2013), 139.
[78] *Drennan–McTier letters*, vol. 2, 649.
[79] *Drennan–McTier letters*, vol. 2, 649.
[80] Claudia Kinmonth, *Irish rural interiors in art* (London, 2006), 145.
[81] *Drennan–McTier letters*, vol. 2, 697–8.
[82] Daniel Defoe, *The complete family instructor: in five parts …* (Liverpool, 1800), 5–6.
[83] PRONI, D2930/9/11, Diary of Reverend Robert Magill (1832) and Kenny, *As the crow flies*, 302–3.
[84] Kenny, *As the crow flies*, 302–3 (*Emphasis author's own*).
[85] Kenny, *As the crow flies*, 341.
[86] PRONI, D2003/A/2/5/6, Anna Crawford to John Gardner, 5 December 1825.
[87] *Drennan–McTier letters*, vol. 3, 202, 206.
[88] PRONI, D2003/A/2/7/11, Anna Crawford to Helen Gardner, 31 August 1827.
[89] Mary Hatfield, *Growing up in nineteenth-century Ireland. A cultural history of middle-class childhood and gender* (Oxford, 2019), 50.
[90] *Drennan–McTier letters*, vol. 3, 168.

[91] *Drennan–McTier letters*, vol. 3, 167.
[92] Other editions of Mrs. Barbauld's works for children printed in Belfast included, John Aikin and Anna Laetitia Aikin, *Miscellaneous pieces, in prose* (Belfast, 1774); Mrs. Barbauld, *Poems, by Anna Laetitia Aikin* (Belfast, 1774).
[93] *Drennan–McTier letters*, vol. 3, 171. This book was advertised in a list of publications sold by G. Bonham, at no. 37 William Street, Dublin. See *The Brother's gift; or, the naughty girl reformed. Published for the advantage of the rising generation* (Dublin, 1775), 27–8.
[94] Calvert, 'Journal of John Tennent', 69–128: 87–9.
[95] James Morgan, *Recollections of my life and times: an autobiography by the Reverend James Morgan, D.D., late minister of Fisherwick Place Church, Belfast, with selections from his journal, edited by his son* (Belfast, 1874), 2–3.
[96] Holmes, *Shaping of Ulster Presbyterian belief and practice*, 270.
[97] J.R.R. Adams, *The printed word and the common man. Popular culture in Ulster, 1700–1900* (Belfast, 1987), 15.
[98] A.B. Boylan, 'Sunday Schools and changing Evangelical views of children in the 1820s', *Church History* 48(3) (1979), 320–33: 320–2.
[99] PRONI, MIC1P/460/G/1, Sunday School attendance book of Third Cookstown Presbyterian congregation, 1837.
[100] PRONI, MIC1P/181/A/2, Reports of Sabbath School of Loughbrickland Presbyterian church, 1845–46.
[101] PRONI, MIC1P/181/A/2, Reports of Sabbath School of Loughbrickland Presbyterian church, 1845–46; PRONI, MIC1P/460/G/1, Sunday School attendance book of Third Cookstown Presbyterian congregation.
[102] PRONI, D2930/9/15, Life of Reverend Robert Magill. Other books published by Manson included, *An accurate pronouncing and spelling dictionary, and complete English depositor* (Belfast, 1774); *Directions to play the literary cards...* (Belfast, 1764); *A new pocket dictionary ...* (Belfast, 1762). See also Thomas Hamilton, 'Manson, David (1726–1792)', in *Oxford Dictionary of National Biography* (Oxford, 2004) and Linde Lunney, 'David Manson', in James McGuire and James Quinn (eds), *Dictionary of Irish Biography* (9 vols, Cambridge, 2009).
[103] John Willison, *An example of plain catechising upon the Assembly's shorter catechism: humbly offered as an help for instructing the young ... with a preface* (Belfast, 1784), xvii.
[104] PRONI, D2930/9/6, Diary of Reverend Robert Magill (1821), 1 January 1821.
[105] PRONI, D2930/9/6, Diary of Reverend Robert Magill (1821), 1 January 1821.
[106] Toby Barnard, 'Educating eighteenth-century Ulster', in D.W. Hayton and Andrew R. Holmes (eds), *Ourselves alone? Religion, society and politics in eighteenth- and nineteenth-century Ireland* (Dublin, 2016), 104–25: 118.
[107] Barnard, 'Educating eighteenth-century Ulster', 105.
[108] Calvert, 'Journal of John Tennent', 88.
[109] Calvert, 'Journal of John Tennent', 88–9.
[110] PRONI, D3215/4/44, Robert Kennedy to Reverend William Kennedy, 3 March 1788.
[111] Clodagh Tait, 'Some sources for the study of infant and maternal mortality in later seventeenth-century Ireland', in Elaine Farrell (ed.), '*She said she was in the family way*': *pregnancy and infancy in modern Ireland* (London, 2012), 55–74: 71.
[112] Valerie Morgan, 'Mortality in Magherafelt, County Derry, in the early eighteenth century', *Irish Historical Studies* 19(74) (1974), 125–35: 130, 134; William Macafee and Valerie Morgan, 'Mortality in Magherafelt, County Derry, in the early eighteenth century reappraised', *Irish Historical Studies* 23(89) (1982), 50–60.
[113] PRONI, D2930/9/11, Diary of Reverend Robert Magill, 8 September 1832.
[114] PRONI, D2930/9/11, Diary of Reverend Robert Magill, 17 September 1832.
[115] PRONI, D2003/A/2/9/3, Medical certificate discharging Reverend Alexander Crawford, 30 April 1829.
[116] See Calvert, 'A more careful tender nurse', 22–36.
[117] PRONI, D2003/A/2/9/8, Anna Crawford to John Gardner, 8 October 1829.

[118] PRONI, D2003/A/2/9/8, Anna Crawford to John Gardner, 8 October 1829.
[119] PRONI, D2003/A/2/9/8, Anna Crawford to John Gardner, 8 October 1829.
[120] PHSI, Diary of Reverend James Morell, 30 July 1815.
[121] PHSI, Diary of Reverend James Morell, 30 July 1815.
[122] For a discussion of this event in the context of ideas of 'assurance of salvation', see Holmes, *Shaping of Ulster Presbyterian belief and practice*, 230–50. See also Pat Jalland, *Death in the Victorian family* (Oxford, 1996), ch. 6; Julie Rugg, 'From reason to regulation, 1760–1850', in P.C. Jupp and Clare Gittings (eds), *Death in England: an illustrated history* (Manchester, 1999), 202–29; Ralph Houlbrooke, 'The age of decency, 1660–1760', in Jupp and Gittings (eds), *Death in England*, 174–201.
[123] PHSI, Diary of Reverend James Morell, 31 July 1816.
[124] PHSI, Diary of Reverend James Morell, 30 July 1815; 6 August 1815.
[125] PHSI, Diary of Reverend James Morell, 6 August 1815.
[126] PHSI, Diary of Reverend James Morell, 6 August 1815.
[127] PHSI, Diary of Reverend James Morell, 18 September 1815.
[128] *Drennan–McTier letters*, vol. 3, 710.
[129] Mary McNeill, *Little Tom Drennan: portrait of a Georgian childhood* (Dublin, 1962), 119.
[130] McNeill, *Little Tom Drennan*, 120.

Chapter Three

[1] Calvert, 'Journal of John Tennent', 69–128: 81.
[2] Calvert, '"What a wonderful change have I undergone"', 70–89: 74–6.
[3] Calvert, 'Journal of John Tennent', 71, 76.
[4] Calvert, 'Journal of John Tennent', 84.
[5] Calvert, 'Journal of John Tennent', 117.
[6] Calvert, 'Journal of John Tennent', 117–18.
[7] Calvert, 'Journal of John Tennent', 90.
[8] Calvert, 'Journal of John Tennent', 109.
[9] Calvert, 'Journal of John Tennent', 109.
[10] Calvert, 'Journal of John Tennent', 109.
[11] Calvert, 'Journal of John Tennent', 109.
[12] Illana Krausman Ben-Amos, *Adolescence and youth in early modern England* (New Haven and London, 1994), 9.
[13] Samuel Pomfret, *A directory for youth: Or, a discourse of youthful lusts* (London, 1722), 6.
[14] Pomfret, *A directory for youth*, 7–8. M.J. Mercer, 'Pomfret, Samuel (1650–1722), Presbyterian minister',in *Oxford dictionary of national biography*; available online: https://www.oxforddnb.com/view/10.1093/ref:odnb/9780198614128.001.0001/odnb-9780198614128-e-22486 (accessed 19 August 2024).
[15] Elizabeth Bonhote, *The parental monitor. In two volumes*, vol. ii (Dublin, 1788), 167.
[16] Bonhote, *Parental monitor*, vol. ii, 168.
[17] Bonhote, *Parental monitor*, vol. ii, 167–8.
[18] John Willison, *The young communicant's catechism: or, a help both short and plain, for instructing and preparing the young to make a right approach unto the Lord's Table. With a proposal, for public renewing of the baptismal covenant* (Belfast, ninth edn, 1754), iii–iv.
[19] Examples of these works that were published in Belfast and Dublin include, F.L. Esq., *The virgin's nosegay; or, The duties of Christian virgins, digested into succinct chapters, and stated under three principal heads ...* (London and Belfast: reprinted 1744); John Hamilton Moore, *The young gentleman and ladies monitor, being a collection of select pieces from our best modern writers: particularly calculated to form the mind and manners of the youth of both sexes, adapted to the*

use of schools and academies (Belfast, 1788); William Enfield, *Sermons for the use of families, volume one* (Belfast, 1776); Anon, *The moral miscellany: or, a collection of select pieces, in prose and verse, for the instruction and entertainment of youth* (Dublin, 1774); Hall Hartson, *Youth. A poem* (Dublin, 1773); John Huddlestone Wynne, *Tales for youth; in thirty poems. To which are annexed, historical remarks and moral applications in prose* (Dublin, 1795); Mary Leadbeater, *Extracts and original anecdotes; for the improvement of youth* (Dublin, 1794).

[20] PRONI, CR3/25/B/1, Cahans Kirk Session minutes, 1 May 1785.

[21] PRONI, CR3/25/B/1, Cahans Kirk Session minutes, 1 May 1785.

[22] PRONI, CR3/25/B/1, Cahans Kirk Session minutes, 1 May 1785.

[23] PRONI, CR3/25/B/1, Cahans Kirk Session minutes, 1 May 1785.

[24] PRONI, CR3/25/B/1, Cahans Kirk Session minutes, 1 May 1785.

[25] Katie Barclay, 'Making the bed, making the lower-order home in eighteenth-century Scotland', in Stephen G. Hague and Karen Lipsedge (eds), *At home in the eighteenth century. Interrogating domestic space* (New York, 2021), 266–82: 271–4.

[26] Calvert, '"From a woman's point of view"', 312–14.

[27] PRONI, MIC1P/37/4/9, Carnmoney Kirk Session minutes, 10 June 1700; 26 June 1700; 3 July 1700.

[28] PRONI, MIC1P/37/4/9, Carnmoney Kirk Session minutes, 16 September 1700; 18 October 1700.

[29] PRONI, CR4/12/B/1, Templepatrick Kirk Session minutes, 8 June 1701; 9 June 1701.

[30] PRONI, CR4/12/B/1, Templepatrick Kirk Session minutes, 10 August 1701; 5 November 1701.

[31] See for example, T. C Smout, 'Aspects of sexual behaviour in nineteenth-century Scotland', in A. Allan McLaren (ed.), *Social class in Scotland: past and present* (Edinburgh, 1981), 55–85: 76–8; Katie Barclay, 'Intimacy, community and power: bedding rituals in eighteenth-century Scotland', in Merridee Bailey and Katie Barclay (eds), *Emotion, ritual and power in Europe, 1200–1920. Family, state and church* (Basingstoke, 2017), 43–61; Rosalind Mitchison and Leah Leneman, *Sexuality and social control: Scotland, 1660–1780* (Oxford, 1989), 182–3; Richard Adair, *Courtship, illegitimacy and marriage in early modern England* (Manchester, 1996), 6; Angela Joy Muir, 'Courtship, sex and poverty: illegitimacy in eighteenth century Wales', *Social History* 43(1) (2017), 56–80: 67.

[32] Calvert, '"He came to her bed pretending courtship"', 256–7; Linda May Ballard, *Forgetting frolic. Marriage traditions in Ireland* (Belfast, 1998), 41–2.

[33] PRONI, MIC1P/37/4/9, Carnmoney Kirk Session minutes, 27 December 1704.

[34] PRONI, MIC1P/37/4/9, Carnmoney Kirk Session minutes, 27 December 1704.

[35] PRONI, MIC1P/37/4/9, Carnmoney Kirk Session minutes, 27 December 1704.

[36] PRONI, MIC1P/37/4/9, Carnmoney Kirk Session minutes, 27 December 1704.

[37] Barclay, 'Making the bed', 272.

[38] PRONI, CR3/25/B/1, Cahans Kirk Session minutes, 25 June 1758.

[39] PRONI, CR3/25/B/1, Cahans Kirk Session minutes, 10 August 1758.

[40] PRONI, CR3/25/B/1, Cahans Kirk Session minutes, 10 August 1758.

[41] PRONI, MIC1P/37/4/9, Carnmoney Kirk Session minutes, 19 September 1711.

[42] PRONI, MIC1P/37/4/9, Carnmoney Kirk Session minutes, 19 September 1711.

[43] PRONI, MIC1P/37/4/9, Carnmoney Kirk Session minutes, 19 September 1711.

[44] PRONI, MIC1P/37/4/9, Carnmoney Kirk Session minutes, 30 September 1711.

[45] PRONI, MIC1P/37/4/9, Carnmoney Kirk Session minutes, 30 September 1711.

[46] PRONI, MIC1P/37/4/9, Carnmoney Kirk Session minutes, 17 October 1711.

[47] Leanne Calvert, '"To recover his reputation among the people of God": sex, religion and the double standard in Presbyterian Ireland, *c.* 1700–1838', *Gender and History* 35(3) (2023), 898–915: 904–5.

[48] UTC, Burt Kirk Session minutes, 2 May 1710.

[49] UTC, Burt Kirk Session minutes, 2 May 1710.

[50] UTC, Burt Kirk Session minutes, 2 May 1710.

[51] UTC, Burt Kirk Session minutes, 2 May 1710.
[52] UTC, Burt Kirk Session minutes, 2 May 1710.
[53] UTC, Burt Kirk Session minutes, 9 May 1710.
[54] UTC, Burt Kirk Session minutes, 9 May 1710.
[55] UTC, Burt Kirk Session minutes, 26 July 1710.
[56] UTC, Burt Kirk Session minutes, 29 March 1712; 9 August 1712.
[57] Michael Stolberg, 'Self-pollution, moral reform, and the venereal trade: notes on the sources and historical context of *Onania* (1716)', *Journal of the History of Sexuality* 9 (2000), 37–61: 45–6.
[58] *Onania, or the heinous sin of self-pollution, and all its frightful consequences in both sexes, considered. With spiritual and physical advice to those who have already imjur'd themselves by this abominable practice* (London, 1716). See Michael Stolberg, 'An unmanly vice: self-pollution, anxiety, and the body in the eighteenth century', *Society for the Social History of Medicine* 13(1) (2000), 1–21: 1.
[59] Thomas W. Laqueur, *Solitary sex. A cultural history of masturbation* (New York, 2003), 37–9.
[60] Stolberg, 'Self-pollution', 37–61.
[61] Stolberg, 'An unmanly vice', 4.
[62] Sameul Tissot, *Three essays: first, on the disorders of people of fashion. Second on diseases incidental to literary and sedentary persons, with proper rules for preventing their fatal consequences, and instructions for their cure. Third, on onanism: Or, a Treatise upon the disorders produced by masturbation: or, the effects of secret and excessive venery* (Dublin, 1772), 40.
[63] Tissot, *Three essays*, 40.
[64] Samuel Tissot, *Onanism: or, a treatise upon the disorders produced by masturbation: or, the dangerous effects of secret and excessive venery* (London, 1766), 41.
[65] Tissot, *Onanism*, 42.
[66] *Onania*, 49.
[67] Brian D. Carroll, '"I indulged my desire too freely": sexuality, spirituality and the sin of self-pollution in the diary of Joseph Moody, 1720–1724', *William and Mary Quarterly* 60(1) (2003), 155–70: 160; Stolberg, 'An unmanly vice', 10.
[68] UTC, Burt Kirk Session minutes, 10 June 1712. This case has been discussed in work by other historians, but the masturbation angle of the incident has received less attention. See Patrick Griffin, *The people with no name. Ireland's Ulster Scots, America's Scots Irish, and the creation of a British Atlantic world, 1689–1764* (New Jersey, 2001), 42; Ian McBride, 'Protestant dissenters, c. 1690–1800', in James Kelly (ed.), *The Cambridge History of Ireland*, vol. III. *1730–1880* (Cambridge, 2018), 305–30: 310.
[69] UTC, Burt Kirk Session minutes, 10 June 1712.
[70] UTC, Burt Kirk Session minutes, 16 June 1712.
[71] UTC, Burt Kirk Session minutes, 16 June 1712.
[72] UTC, Burt Kirk Session minutes, 16 June 1712.
[73] UTC, Burt Kirk Session minutes, 10 June 1712; 16 June 1712.
[74] *Onania*, 55.
[75] *Onania*, 55.
[76] *Onania*, 55.
[77] *Onania*, 55
[78] *Onania*, 52–3.
[79] *Onania*, 50.
[80] *Onania*, 50–3.
[81] UTC, Burt Kirk Session minutes, 16 June 1712.
[82] UTC, Burt Kirk Session minutes, 16 June 1712; 3 October 1712.
[83] UTC, Burt Kirk Session minutes, 3 October 1712.
[84] Anne Yarbrough, 'Apprentices as adolescents in sixteenth-century Bristol', *Journal of Social History* 13(1) (1979), 67–81: 68–9; E.D. Spindler, 'Youth and old age in late medieval London', *London Journal*, 36(1) (2011), 1–22: 3; Peter Fleming, *Family and household in medieval England* (New York, 2001), 73–4.

[85] See for example, Laura Gowing, *Ingenious trade. Women and work in seventeenth-century London* (Cambridge, 2022).
[86] Philip Ollerenshaw, 'Business and finance, 1780–1945', in Liam Kennedy and Philip Ollerenshaw (eds), *Ulster since 1600: politics, economy and society* (Oxford, 2013), 177–81.
[87] Hincks's engravings are reprinted in W.H. Crawford, *The impact of the domestic linen industry in Ulster* (Belfast, 2005), see especially chs 5 and 9, for a discussion of the role of women.
[88] Margaret Hunt, *The middling sort: commerce, gender and the family in England, 1680–1780* (London, 1996), 81.
[89] PRONI, D1748/A/1/5/13, Robert Tennent to Reverend John Tennent, 2 June 1801.
[90] PRONI, D1748/A/1/5/13, Robert Tennent to Reverend John Tennent, 16 June 1801.
[91] J.J. Wright, 'Frustrated ambition in the eighteenth-century Atlantic: Robert Tennent in Jamaica, *c.* 1784–95', in Toby Barnard and Alison Fitzgerald (eds), *Speculative minds in Georgian Ireland: novelty, experiment and widening horizons* (Dublin, 2023), 229–55: 233.
[92] PRONI, D1748/D/1/5/12, Reverend John Tennent to John Tennent, 5 September 1791. See also PRONI, D1748/D/1/5/24, Reverend John Tennent to John Tennent, 21 February 1793.
[93] Hunt, *The middling sort*, 80–2.
[94] See PRONI, D1748/D/1/5/8; 12; 24; 35; 44; 47–9; 59; 61, Letters between Reverend John Tennent and John Tennent, and PRONI, D1748/B/1/317/15;17, Letters from Reverend John Tennent to William Tennent, 5 November 1798; 20 March 1798.
[95] Christopher Brooks, 'Apprenticeship, social mobility and the middling sort, 1550–1800', in Jonathan Barry and Christopher Brooks (eds), *The middling sort of people: culture, society and politics in England, 1550–1800* (London, 1994), 52–83: 60.
[96] PRONI, D1748/D/2/1/B, Agreement relating to John Tennent's indenture, 9 August 1786; Calvert, 'Journal of John Tennent', 76.
[97] Calvert, 'Journal of John Tennent', p. 128.
[98] PRONI, T3541/5/3, John Caldwell Junior, 'Particulars of a North county Irish family', 51.
[99] Brooks, 'Apprenticeship, social mobility and the middling sort', 68.
[100] Jonathan Bardon, *An interesting and honourable history: the Belfast Charitable Society. The first 250 years, 1752–2002* (Belfast, 2003), 12, 18–19. See also Lauren Smyth, 'Child welfare and education in the industrialising town', in Olwen Purdue (ed.), *The first great charity of this town. The Belfast Charitable Society and its role in the developing city* (Kildare, 2022), 80–91.
[101] *Belfast Newsletter*, 14 November 1817.
[102] Clifton House (hereafter CH), MS1/2015/004/0010, Belfast Charitable Society Committee minute book (hereafter BCSC), 7 November 1813.
[103] CH, MS1/2015/004/0010, BCSC minute book, 7 March 1818.
[104] CH, MSS/2015/010/0170, Reports of the Belfast Charitable Society, 1828–43. Returns for the years 1831, 1839 and 1844 are missing.
[105] See Barnard, 'Educating eighteenth-century Ulster', in Hayton and Holmes (eds), *Ourselves alone?*, 104–25: 111–12.
[106] PRONI, D433/5, Roll book of the Vaughan Charitable Charter School, 1787–1934.
[107] PRONI, D433/5, Roll book of the Vaughan Charitable Charter School, 1787–1934.
[108] R.A. Coffey, 'The foundation and early history of the Southwell schools, Downpatrick, 1733–1800', *Lecale Miscellany* 8 (1990), 53–64: 57.
[109] Cited in R.M. Strain, *Belfast and its charitable society: a story of urban social development* (London, 1961), 110 (*Emphasis author's own*).
[110] Smyth, 'Child welfare', 86.
[111] PRONI, D433/5, Roll book of the Vaughan Charitable Charter School, 1787–1934.
[112] PRONI, D2961/1/3, Apprenticeship indentures relating to girls educated at the Blue Coat School, 1850–1890 and PRONI, D2961/1/4, Apprenticeship indentures relating to boys educated at the Blue Coat School, 1859–1893.
[113] PRONI, D433/5, Roll book of the Vaughan Charitable Charter School, 1787–1934.
[114] Barbara Hanawalt, '"The childe of Bristowe" and the making of middle-class adolescence', in Barbara Hanawalt (ed.), *'Of good and ill repute': gender and social control in medieval England*

(Oxford, 1998), 178–202: 159; Brooks, 'Apprenticeship, social mobility and the middling sort', 53.

[115] Ralph Houlbrooke, *The English family, 1450–1700* (London, 1984), 175.

[116] Matthew Dutton, *The law of masters and servants in Ireland* (Dublin, 1723), 80.

[117] Richard Burton, *The apprentices' companion, containing plain and useful directions for servants, especially apprentices, how to perform their particular dutys to their masters, so as to please God…* (London, 1681), 9.

[118] Burton, *The apprentices' companion*, 10.

[119] PRONI, D3874/4/81, Reverend David Young to Thomas Reed, 6 September 1802.

[120] PRONI, D848/1A, Petition for admission of Michael Crossin as freeman of the City of Londonderry, *c.* 1821; PRONI, D848/1B, Indenture of apprenticeship from Michael Crossin to Andrew McLaughlin, bricklayer, 26 July 1822.

[121] PRONI, D848/1A, Petition for admission of Michael Crossin as freeman of the City of Londonderry, *c.* 1821; PRONI, D848/1B, Indenture of apprenticeship from Michael Crossin to Andrew McLaughlin, bricklayer, 26 July 1822.

[122] PRONI, D848/1A, Petition for admission of Michael Crossin as freeman of the City of Londonderry, *c.* 1821; PRONI, D848/1B, Indenture of apprenticeship from Michael Crossin to Andrew McLaughlin, bricklayer, 26 July 1822.

[123] Hanawalt, '"The childe of Bristowe"', 183; Brooks, 'Apprenticeship, social mobility and the middling sort', 74.

[124] Spindler, 'Youth and old age', 9; Peter Rushton, 'The matter in variance: adolescents and domestic conflict in the pre-industrial economy of northeast England, 1600–1800', *Journal of Social History* 25(1) (1991), 89–107.

[125] Rushton, 'The matter in variance', 94–6.

[126] PRONI, D1748/B/1/317/294/2, Ann Jane Stuart to John Stuart, n.d.

[127] PRONI, D1748/B/1/317/294/2, Ann Jane Stuart to John Stuart, n.d.

[128] PRONI, D1748/B/1/294/1, John Stuart to William Tennent, 14 May 1819. See also PRONI, D1748/B/1/251/1, William Patton to William Tennent, 18–19 May 1819.

[129] PRONI, D1748/B/1/293/2, Ann Jane Stuart to William Tennent, 21 November n.d.

[130] PRONI, D1748/B/1/297/1, Margaretta Stuart to William Tennent, 7 December 1830.

[131] PRONI, D433/5, Roll book of the Vaughan Charitable Charter School, 1787–1934.

[132] PRONI, D433/5, Roll book of the Vaughan Charitable Charter School, 1787–1934.

[133] CH, MS1/2015/004/0010, BCSC minute book 1811–18, 18 January 1812.

[134] CH, MS1/2015/004/0010, BCSC minute book 1811–18, 18 January 1812.

[135] CH, MS1/2015/004/0010, BCSC minute book 1811–18, 18 January 1812.

[136] CH, MS1/2015/004/0010, BCSC minute book 1811–18, 18 January 1812.

[137] CH, MS1/2015/004/0010, BCSC minute book 1811–18, 18 January 1812.

[138] CH, MS1/2015/004/0010, BCSC minute book 1811–18, 18 January 1812.

[139] *Belfast Newsletter* 18 September 1767.

[140] *Belfast Newsletter*, 22 September 1769.

[141] *Belfast Newsletter*, 13 June 1769.

[142] *Belfast Newsletter*, 9 June 1769.

[143] CH, MS1/2015/004/0010, BCSC minute book 1811–18, 25 April 1812.

[144] CH, MS1/2015/004/0010, BCSC minute book 1811–18, 25 April 1812.

[145] CH, MS1/2015/004/0010, BCSC minute book 1811–18, 25 April 1812.

[146] CH, MS1/2015/004/0010, BCSC minute book 1811–18, 25 April 1812.

[147] CH, MS1/2015/004/0010, BCSC minute book 1811–18, 25 April 1812.

[148] CH, MS1/2015/004/0010, BCSC minute book 1811–18, 25 April 1812.

[149] Calvert, 'Journal of John Tennent', 128.

[150] Calvert, 'Journal of John Tennent', 128.

[151] Calvert, 'Journal of John Tennent', 128.

[152] Calvert, 'Journal of John Tennent', 128.

[153] Calvert, 'Journal of John Tennent', 128.

[154] PRONI, D1748/D/1/5/6;8, Reverend John Tennent to John Tennent, 17 January 1791; 18 March 1791.
[155] W.A. Maguire, 'Tennent, John', *Dictionary of Irish Biography*; available online: https://www.dib.ie/biography/tennent-john-a8503 (accessed 22 March 2025).

Chapter Four

[1] PRONI, T/2884/1, William Drennan to Sarah Swanwick, 23 August 1793.
[2] PRONI, T/2884/1, William Drennan to Sarah Swanwick, 23 August 1793.
[3] PRONI, T/2884/2, William Drennan to Sarah Swanwick, 31 August 1793.
[4] PRONI, T/2884/3, William Drennan to Sarah Swanwick, 14 September 1793.
[5] PRONI, T/2884/3, William Drennan to Sarah Swanwick, 14 September 1793.
[6] PRONI, T/2884/4, William Drennan to Sarah Swanwick, 26 September 1793.
[7] PRONI, T/2884/7, William Drennan to Sarah Swanwick, 7 November 1793.
[8] PRONI, T/2884/4, William Drennan to Sarah Swanwick, 26 September 1793.
[9] Luddy, *Matters of deceit*, 22–3.
[10] David Cressy, *Birth, marriage and death: ritual, religion and the life-cycle in Tudor and Stuart England* (Oxford, 1997), 234; R.E.L. Debutts., 'Lee in love: courtship and correspondence in Antebellum Virginia', *Virginia Magazine of History and Biography* 115(4) (2007), 486–575: 496–7.
[11] See Katie Barclay, 'Doing the paperwork: the emotional world of wedding certificates', *Cultural and Social History* 17(3) (2019), 315–32; Sally Holloway, 'Love, custom and consumption: Valentine's Day in England c. 1660–1830', *Cultural and Social History* 17(3) (2019), 295–314.
[12] Maria Luddy and Mary O'Dowd, *Marriage in Ireland, 1660–1925* (Cambridge, 2020), 101–5.
[13] Luddy and O'Dowd, *Marriage in Ireland*, 101.
[14] Presbyterian Church in Ireland, *Code*, 42.
[15] See PRONI, MIC1P/28/1, Marriage register of Carland Presbyterian congregation, 1770–1802; PRONI, MIC1B/9/1, Marriage register of Greyabbey Presbyterian congregation, 1835–43; PRONI, MIC1B/6A/3, Marriage register of Larne and Kilwaughter Presbyterian congregation, 1826–32; 1834–44; PRONI, MIC1P/460/B/7, Marriage register of various congregations belonging to Tyrone Presbytery, 1819–28; PRONI, CR3/8/1, Marriage register of Loughaghery Presbyterian congregation, 1801–1917; PRONI, T/1539/2, Marriage register of Rathfriland Presbyterian congregation, 1805–42.
[16] PRONI, CR3/8/1, Marriage register of Loughaghery Presbyterian congregation, 1801–1917; PRONI, MIC1B/9/1, Marriage register of Greyabbey Presbyterian congregation, 1835–43; PRONI, MIC1B/6A/3, Marriage register of Larne and Kilwaughter Presbyterian congregation, 1826–32; 1834–44.
[17] Diana O'Hara, *Courtship and constraint: rethinking the making of marriage in Tudor England* (Manchester and New York, 2000), 139–45; Alan MacFarlane, *Marriage and love in England: modes of reproduction, 1300–1840* (Oxford, 1986), 296; Maria Luddy, *Matters of deceit: breach of promise to marry cases in nineteenth- and twentieth-century Limerick* (Dublin, 2011), 21.
[18] PRONI, CR3/25/B/1, Cahans Kirk Session minutes, 31 July 1754.
[19] PRONI, T3541/5/3, John Caldwell Junior, 'Particulars of a North County Irish family', 1850.
[20] PRONI, T3541/5/3, John Caldwell Junior, 'Particulars of a North County Irish family', 1850.
[21] Calvert, 'Journal of John Tennent', 91, 117.
[22] *OSMI*, Ballymoney, vol. 16, 6.
[23] *OSMI*, Ballymoney, vol. 16, 6.
[24] *OSMI*, Ballymoney, vol. 16, 18.

[25] *OSMI*, Antrim, vol. 29, 16–17.
[26] *OSMI*, Antrim, vol. 29, 16–17.
[27] *OSMI*, Ballycor vol. 32, 6.
[28] PRONI, CR4/18/1, Ballycarry Kirk Session minutes, 27 October 1729.
[29] See *OSMI*, Ballycor, vol. 32, 6; *OSMI*, Ballylinny, vol. 32, 20; *OSMI*, Ballynure, vol. 32, 37; *OSMI*, Island-magee, vol. 10, 40; *OSMI*, Killead, vol. 35, 23; *OSMI*, Kilwaugher, vol. 10, 115; *OSMI*, Rashee, vol. 32, 140.
[30] *OSMI*, Doagh, vol. 29, 77, 87.
[31] *OSMI*, Island-magee, vol. 10, 40.
[32] PRONI, CR3/8/1, Loughaghery Kirk Session minutes, 18 June 1802.
[33] PRONI, CR3/25/B/2, Cahans Kirk Session minutes, 16 October 1796.
[34] PRONI, CR3/25/B/2, Cahans Kirk Session minutes, 16 October 1796.
[35] PRONI, CR3/25/B/2, Cahans Kirk Session minutes, 16 October 1796.
[36] Calvert, 'Journal of John Tennent', 99–100.
[37] Holmes, *Shaping of Ulster Presbyterian belief and practice*, 73–4.
[38] Holmes, *Shaping of Ulster Presbyterian belief and practice*, 74.
[39] Luddy and O'Dowd, *Marriage in Ireland*, 140.
[40] Linda M. Ballard, *Forgetting frolic: marriage traditions in Ireland* (Belfast, 1998), 14–18, 36–8.
[41] National Folklore Collection, 'The Schools' Collection', vol. 1016, 195; by Dúchas © National Folklore Collection, UCD; licensed under CC BY-NC 4.0.
[42] Ballard, *Forgetting frolic*, 15–16; Jennifer Evans, *Aphrodisiacs, fertility and medicine in early modern England* (Woodbridge, 2014), 1111–12.
[43] National Folklore Collection, 'The Schools' Collection', vol. 1116, 216; by Dúchas © National Folklore Collection, UCD; licensed under CC BY-NC 4.0.
[44] National Folklore Collection, 'The Schools' Collection', vol. 0942, 97–8; by Dúchas © National Folklore Collection, UCD; licensed under CC BY-NC 4.0.
[45] Sally Holloway, *The game of love in Georgian England: courtship, emotions and material culture* (Oxford, 2018), 69.
[46] O'Hara, *Courtship*, 57–98; Cressy, *Birth, marriage and death*, 263.
[47] Holloway, *Game of love*, 79.
[48] PRONI, CR4/12/B/1, Templepatrick Kirk Session minutes, 7 November 1704.
[49] PRONI, CR4/12/B/1, Templepatrick Kirk Session minutes, 7 November 1704.
[50] PRONI, CR4/12/B/1, Templepatrick Kirk Session minutes, 7 November 1704.
[51] PRONI, CR3/25/B/2, Cahans Kirk Session minutes, 7 July 1767.
[52] PRONI, CR3/25/B/2, Cahans Kirk Session minutes, 7 July 1767.
[53] PRONI, CR3/25/B/2, Cahans Kirk Session minutes, 7 July 1767.
[54] PRONI, CR3/25/B/2, Cahans Kirk Session minutes, 7 July 1767.
[55] PRONI, CR3/2B/2, Cahans Kirk Session minutes, 7 July 1767.
[56] Bridget Hourican, 'Magill, Robert', *Dictionary of Irish Biography*, available online: https://www.dib.ie/biography/magill-robert-a5343 (accessed 12 June 2024).
[57] PRONI, D2930/9/5, Diary extracts of Reverend Robert Magill (1821–8).
[58] PRONI, D2930/9/5, Diary extracts of Reverend Robert Magill, 5 April 1821–24 July 1821.
[59] PRONI, D2930/9/6, Diary of Reverend Robert Magill (1821), 26 Janurary 1821.
[60] PRONI, D2930/9/5, Diary extracts of Reverend Robert Magill (1821–8), 23 May 1822.
[61] PRONI, D2930/9/5, Diary extracts of Reverend Robert Magill (1821–8), 6 June 1822.
[62] PRONI, D2930/9/5, Diary extracts of Reverend Robert Magill (1821–8), 12 July 1822; 29 September 1822.
[63] PRONI, D2930/9/5, Diary extracts of Reverend Robert Magill (1821–8), 16 July 1822; 8 October 1822; 28 October 1822.
[64] PRONI, D2930/9/5, Diary extracts of Reverend Robert Magill (1821–8), 5 November 1822.
[65] PRONI, D2930/9/8, Diary of Reverend Robert Magill (1823), 27 January 1823.
[66] PRONI, D2930/9/8, Diary of Reverend Robert Magill (1823), 18 November 1823; 20 November 1823; 11 December 1823; PRONI, D2930/9/5, Diary extracts of Reverend Robert Magill (1821–8), 18 November 1823.

[67] PRONI, D2930/9/5, Diary extracts of Reverend Robert Magill (1821–8), 5 January 1821; 31 January 1821; 14 March 1821; 11 October 1822; 23 October 1822; 26 October 1822.
[68] Robert recorded in his diary how he paid Mr Skelton £1 15s. 0d for groceries; see PRONI, D2930/8/5, Diary extracts of Reverend Robert Magill (1821–28), 25 February 1822.
[69] PRONI, D2930/9/7, Diary of Reverend Robert Magill (1822), 11 October 1822 (*Emphasis author's own*).
[70] PRONI, D2930/9/5, Diary extracts of Reverend Robert Magill (1821–8), 20 December 1823.
[71] PRONI, D2930/9/5, Diary extracts of Reverend Robert Magill (1821–8), 25 December 1823.
[72] PRONI, D2930/9/5, Diary extracts of Reverend Robert Magill (1821–8), 2 August 1821; 17 October 1821; 2 November 1822; 15 February 1823; 25 November 1823.
[73] Holloway, *Game of love*, 81.
[74] These ages have been estimated from the earliest dated courtship memento given to Robert by Hannah on 1 May 1818. It is possible to estimate Hannah's age from a hand-written note referring to her twentieth birthday, which was recorded as being 18 May 1821, making her almost seventeen years of age in 1818. Robert, we know, was born in 1803, and he would have been 15 years old in 1818. See PRONI, D1748/G/407/3, Hannah McGee to Robert James Tennent, 18 May 1821.
[75] PRONI, D1748/G/802/6;11, Hair of Hannah McGee, 1 May 1818; 3 September 1820. These are part of a larger collection of women's hair, fourteen locks in total, which Robert received from his love interests. See PRONI, D1748/G/802/1–17, Locks of hair of numerous young ladies, 1818–27. The collection has been written about by the author, see Leanne Calvert, 'Objects of affection? Materialising courtship, love and sex in Ireland, c. 1800–1830', *Cultural and Social History* (19)3 (2022), 247–63.
[76] PRONI, D1748/G/407/1, Hannah McGee to Robert James Tennent, 2 April 1821; PRONI, D1748/G/407/5, Robert James Tennent to Hannah McGee, May–June 1821.
[77] PRONI, D1748/G/650/1, Katherine Templeton to Hannah McGee, 7 January 1821.
[78] PRONI, D1748/G/407/6, Hannah McGee to Robert James Tennent, 12 July 1821.
[79] PRONI, D1748/G/802/16, Half a broken ring, c. 12 July 1821.
[80] PRONI, D1748/G/407/5, Robert James Tennent to Hannah McGee, May–June 1821.
[81] PRONI, D1748/G/407/6, Hannah McGee to Robert James Tennent, 12 July 1821.
[82] PRONI, D1748/G/407/6, Hannah McGee to Robert James Tennent, 12 July 1821.
[83] See also J.J. Wright, 'Robert Hyndman's toe: Romanticism, schoolboy politics and the affective revolution in late Georgian Belfast', in Catherine Cox and Susannah Riordan (eds), *Adolescence and youth in modern Irish history* (Basingstoke, 2015), 15–41.
[84] These locks included those belonging to Catharine Louisa Lawless, dated 10–11 November 1820, Maria Owens dated 30 June 1821, Eliza Blow dated June 1818, and an envelope labelled 'Hair' with the date 2 May 1818 that likely once contained a lock of hair. See PRONI, D1748/G/802/1–17, Locks of hair belonging to numerous young ladies
[85] Calvert, 'Objects of affection', 252.
[86] *Drennan–McTier letters, 1794–1801*, vol. 2, 380–1.
[87] *Drennan–McTier letters*, vol. 2, 374, 380–1.
[88] *Drennan–McTier letters*, vol. 2, 374, 381.
[89] Karen Lystra, *Searching the heart: women, men and romantic love in nineteenth-century America* (New York and Oxford, 1989), 10; Martyn Lyons, 'Love letters and writing practices: on *écritures intimes* in the nineteenth century', *Journal of Family History* 24 (1999), 232–9: 237–8.
[90] Nicole Eustace, '"The cornerstone of a copious work": love and power in eighteenth-century courtship', *Journal of Social History* 39(3) (Spring, 2001), 517–46: 518.
[91] Kevin O'Neill, '"Pale & dejected exhausted by the waste of sorrow": courtship and the expression of emotion, Mary Shackleton, 1783–1791', in Willemijn Ruberg and Kristine Steenbergh (eds), *Sexed sentiments: interdisciplinary perspectives on gender and emotion* (Amsterdam and New York, 2011), 47–70: 53–7.
[92] Lystra, *Searching the heart*, chapter six.
[93] Wright, 'Love, loss and learning in late Georgian Belfast: the case of Eliza McCracken', in Hayton and Holmes (eds), *Ourselves alone?*, 169–91.

[94] *Drennan–McTier letters*, vol. 1, 563.
[95] PRONI, T/2884/1, William Drennan to Sarah Swanwick, 23 August 1793.
[96] Debutts, 'Lee in love', 496–8.
[97] PRONI, T/2884/1, William Drennan to Sarah Swanwick, 23 August 1793.
[98] PRONI, T/2884/1, William Drennan to Sarah Swanwick, 23 August 1793 (*Emphasis author's own*).
[99] PRONI, T/2884/3-4, William Drennan to Sarah Swanwick, 14 September 1793; 26 September 1793.
[100] PRONI, T/2884/4, William Drennan to Sarah Swanwick, 26 September 1793.
[101] For an innovative exploration of the relationship between letters and the body, see Sarah Goldsmith, Sheryllynne Haggerty and Karen Harvey (eds), *Letters and the body, 1700–1830. Writing and embodiment* (New York, 2023).
[102] PRONI, T/2884/4-5, William Drennan to Sarah Swanwick, 26 September. 1793; 10 October 1793.
[103] PRONI, D1748/C/1/205/11, Eliza Macrone to Robert Tennent, 10 April 1800.
[104] PRONI, D1748/C/1/205/11, Eliza Macrone to Robert Tennent, 10 April 1800.
[105] PRONI, D1748/C/1/205/11, Eliza Macrone to Robert Tennent, 10 April 1800.
[106] Eustace, '"The cornerstone of a copious work"', 530; O'Neill, '"Pale & dejected exhausted by the waste of sorrow"', 53–4.
[107] PRONI, D2930/9/7, Diary of Reverend Robert Magill (1822); and Glennis Byron, 'Landon, Letitia Elizabeth (1802–38)', in H.C.G. Matthew and Brian Harrison (eds), *Oxford dictionary of national biography* (Oxford, 2004).
[108] Eustace, '"Cornerstone of a copious work"', 524.
[109] Eustace, '"Cornerstone of a copious work"', 520, 523; O'Neill, '"Pale & dejected"', 51, 58–60.
[110] Eustace, '"Cornerstone of a copious work"', 522–31.
[111] See PRONI, T/2884/1, William Drennan to Sarah Swanwick, 23 August 1793 and *Drennan–McTier letters*, vol. 1, 579; *Drennan–McTier letters*, vol. 2, 503, 529–30.
[112] PRONI, T/2884/1, William Drennan to Sarah Swanwick, 23 August 1793.
[113] PRONI, T/2884/1, William Drennan to Sarah Swanwick, 23 August 1793.
[114] PRONI, T/2884/3, 14 September 1793.
[115] PRONI, T/2884/3, 14 September 1793.
[116] *Drennan–McTier letters*, vol. 2, 503.
[117] *Drennan–McTier letters*, vol. 2, 503.
[118] PRONI, T/2884/3, William Drennan to Sarah Swanwick, 14 September 1793.
[119] *Drennan–McTier letters*, vol. 1, 563.
[120] PRONI, T/2884/10, William Drennan to Sarah Swanwick, 23 December 1793.
[121] PRONI, T/2884/9-10, William Drennan to Sarah Swanwick, December 1793; 23 December 1793.
[122] *Drennan–McTier letters*, vol. 2, 417.
[123] *Drennan–McTier letters*, vol. 1, 579.
[124] Holloway, *Game of love*.
[125] PRONI, T/2884/11, William Drennan to Sarah Swanwick, 6–8 August 1799.
[126] See for example, *Drennan–McTier letters*, vol. 2, 369–70.
[127] *Drennan–McTier letters*, vol. 2, 502.

Chapter Five

[1] PRONI, D1748/B/1/317/16, Reverend John Tennent to William Tennent, 22 October 1798.
[2] PRONI, D1748/B/1/317/16, Reverend John Tennent to William Tennent, 22 October 1798.
[3] PRONI, D1748/B/1/317/16, Reverend John Tennent to William Tennent, 22 October 1798.
[4] PRONI, D1748/B/1/317/16, Reverend John Tennent to William Tennent, 22 October 1798.

[5] PRONI, D1748/B/1/317/17, Reverend John Tennent to William Tennent, 5 November 1798.
[6] PRONI, D1748/B/1/317/16, Reverend John Tennent to William Tennent, 22 October 1798.
[7] PRONI, D1748/B/1/317/16, Reverend John Tennent to William Tennent, 22 October 1798.
[8] J.J. Wright writes that Ann was a 'woman whose will was as strong as her tongue was sharp'; see Wright, 'Frustrated ambition in the eighteenth-century Atlantic', 233.
[9] PRONI, D1748/B/1/317/16, Reverend John Tennent to William Tennent, 22 October 1798.
[10] Presbyterian Church in Ireland, *Code*.
[11] Church of Scotland, *Confession*, 54.
[12] Church of Scotland, *Confession*, 54–5, 269; Presbyterian Church in Ireland, *Code*, 98.
[13] Church of Scotland, *Confession*, 269; Presbyterian Church in Ireland, *Code*, 98.
[14] Church of Scotland, *Confession*, 269; Presbyterian Church in Ireland, *Code*, 98.
[15] Church of Scotland, *Confession*, 269–70; Presbyterian Church in Ireland, *Code*, 98.
[16] Church of Scotland, *Confession*, 270.
[17] Church of Scotland, *Confession*, 269.
[18] See Holmes, *Shaping of Ulster Presbyterian belief and practice*, 214–16.
[19] Luddy and O'Dowd, *Marriage in Ireland, 1660–1925*, 38–9.
[20] Rosalind Mitchison and Leah Leneman, *Sexuality and social control: Scotland, 1660–1780* (Oxford, 1989), 130; Holmes, *Shaping of Ulster Presbyterian belief and practice*, 217.
[21] PRONI, CR3/8/1, Marriage register of Loughaghery Presbyterian church, 1801–44.
[22] PRONI, D2930/9/5, Diary extracts of the Reverend Robert Magill (1821–1828), 11 December 1823.
[23] Whereas the General Synod of Ulster voted in 1803 to reduce the number of proclamations to one, the Secession Burgher Synod voted in July 1812 to enable couples to marry after just two proclamations; see PRONI, CR3/46/1/1, Minutes of the Burgher Secession Synod, July 1812. This was reaffirmed in July 1816, see PRONI, CR3/46/1/2A, Minutes of the Secession Burgher Synod and of the United Secession Synod, July 1816. In June 1804 ministers attending the Synod of Ulster agreed that proclamation should be made optional. See *Records of the General Synod of Ulster, 1691–1820* (3 vols; Belfast,1898), vol. 3, 278; Holmes, *Shaping of Ulster Presbyterian belief and practice*, 215; Luddy and O'Dowd, *Marriage in Ireland*, 39.
[24] PRONI, MIC1P/412/A/1, First Dunboe Kirk Session minutes, 13 April 1802; PRONI, MIC1P/37/4/9, Carnmoney Kirk Session minutes, 11 April 1821; PRONI, T1539/2, Rathfriland Kirk Session minutes, 4 December 1831.
[25] Holmes, *Shaping of Ulster Presbyterian belief and practice*, 215.
[26] Luddy and O'Dowd, *Marriage in Ireland*, 24–7; Patrick Corish, 'Catholic marriage under the Penal code', in Art Cosgrove (ed), *Marriage in Ireland* (Dublin, 1985), 67–77: 67–71.
[27] J.C. Beckett, *Protestant dissent in Ireland, 1687–1780* (London, 1948), 116. For discussions of the issues Presbyterians faced more generally, see D.W. Hayton, 'Presbyterians and the confessional state: the sacramental test as an issue in Irish politics, 1704–1780', *Bulletin of the Presbyterian Historical Society* 26 (1997), 11–31: 11; I.R. McBride, 'Presbyterians in the Penal era', *Bullan* 1 (1994), 73–86; I.R. McBride, 'Ulster Presbyterians and the confessional state, *c.* 1688–1733', in D.G. Boyce, Robert Eccleshall and Vince Geoghegan (eds), *Political discourse in seventeenth- and eighteenth-century Ireland* (Basingstoke, 2001), 169–92 and S.J. Connolly, *Religion, law and power: the making of Protestant Ireland, 1660–1760* (Oxford, 1992).
[28] Luddy and O'Dowd, *Marriage in Ireland*, 28; Corish, 'Catholic marriage', 70.
[29] Holmes, *Shaping of Ulster Presbyterian belief and practice*, 213; Phil Kilroy, *Protestant dissent and controversy in Ireland, 1660–1714* (Cork, 1994), 197.
[30] J.M. Barkley, 'Marriage and the Presbyterian tradition', *Ulster Folklife* 39 (1993), 29–40: 30–1.
[31] Luddy and O'Dowd, *Marriage in Ireland*, 62–88.
[32] UTC, Burt Kirk Session minutes, 26 April 1708.
[33] UTC, Burt Kirk Session minutes, 26 April 1708.
[34] UTC, Burt Kirk Session minutes, 22 May 1708.

[35] UTC Burt Kirk Session minutes, 20 December 1708.
[36] PRONI, CR3/25/B/2, Cahans Kirk Session minutes, 17 October 1824.
[37] Holmes, *Shaping of Ulster Presbyterian belief and practice*, 218–22.
[38] PRONI, T1447/1, First Dromara (GSU) session book, 1762–99.
[39] See Calvert, '"He came to her bed pretending courtship"', 244–64.
[40] PRONI, CR3/25/B/1, Cahans Kirk Session minutes, 11 March 1753 (*Emphasis author's own*).
[41] PRONI, CR3/25/B/2, Cahans Kirk Session minutes, 7 January 1777.
[42] PRONI, MIC1P/179/1, Coronary Kirk Session minutes, 10 May 1786.
[43] PRONI, MIC1P/179/1, Coronary Kirk Session minutes, 15 May 1786.
[44] PRONI, MIC1P/179/1, Coronary Kirk Session minutes, 15 May 1786.
[45] PRONI, MIC1P/179/1, Coronary Kirk Session minutes, 15 May 1786.
[46] PRONI, MIC1P/179/1, Coronary Kirk Session minutes, 15 May 1786.
[47] PRONI, MIC1P/179/1, Coronary Kirk Session minutes, 15 May 1786.
[48] PRONI, MIC1P/179/1, Coronary Kirk Session minutes, 15 May 1786.
[49] PRONI, MIC1P/179/1, Coronary Kirk Session minutes, 15 May 1786.
[50] PRONI, MIC1P/179/1, Coronary Kirk Session minutes, 15 May 1786.
[51] PRONI, MIC1P/179/1, Coronary Kirk Session minutes, 1 April 1787.
[52] PRONI, MIC1P/179/1, Coronary Kirk Session minutes, 27 May 1787.
[53] UTC, Burt Kirk Session minutes, 25 December 1699.
[54] UTC, Burt Kirk Session minutes, 25 December 1699.
[55] UTC, Burt Kirk Session minutes, 25 December 1699.
[56] UTC, Burt Kirk Session minutes, 25 December 1699.
[57] UTC, Burt Kirk Session minutes, 25 December 1699.
[58] UTC, Burt Kirk Session minutes, 25 December 1699.
[59] UTC, Burt Kirk Session minutes, 25 December 1699.
[60] UTC, Burt Kirk Session minutes, 25 December 1699.
[61] UTC, Burt Kirk Session minutes, 25 December 1699.
[62] UTC, Burt Kirk Session minutes, 25 December 1699.
[63] UTC, Burt Kirk Session minutes, 25 December 1699.
[64] UTC, Burt Kirk Session minutes, 24 November 1700.
[65] PHSI, Down Presbytery minutes, 23 January 1788.
[66] PHSI, Down Presbytery minutes, 23 January 1788.
[67] PHSI, Down Presbytery minutes, 23 January 1788.
[68] PHSI, Down Presbytery minutes, 23 January 1788.
[69] PHSI, Down Presbytery minutes, 23 January 1788.
[70] PHSI, Down Presbytery minutes, 16 April 1788.
[71] PHSI, Down Presbytery minutes, 10 December 1788.
[72] PRONI, CR3/25/B/1, Cahans Kirk Session minutes, 1 December 1754.
[73] PRONI, CR3/25/B/1, Cahans Kirk Session minutes, 1 December 1754.
[74] PRONI, CR3/25/B/2, Cahans Kirk Session minutes, 17 May 1772.
[75] PRONI, CR3/25/B/2, Cahans Kirk Session minutes, 17 May 1772.
[76] PRONI, CR3/25/B/2, Cahans Kirk Session minutes, 17 May 1772.
[77] PRONI, CR3/25/B/2, Cahans Kirk Session minutes, 17 May 1772.
[78] PRONI, CR3/25/B/2, Cahans Kirk Session minutes, 17 May 1772.
[79] PRONI, CR3/25/B/2, Cahans Kirk Session minutes, 17 May 1772.
[80] PRONI, MIC1P/37/4/9, Carnmoney Kirk Session minutes, December 1719.
[81] PRONI, CR3/25/B/2, Cahans Kirk Session minutes, 13 September 1829.
[82] PRONI, CR4/12/B/1, Templepatrick Kirk Session minutes, 20 September 1713.
[83] PRONI, CR4/12/B/1, Templepatrick Kirk Session minutes, 18 October 1713.
[84] PRONI, CR4/12/B/1, Templepatrick Kirk Session minutes, 12 September 1715.
[85] S.J. Connolly, *Priests and people in pre-Famine Ireland, 1780–1845* (Dublin, 1982), 207.
[86] Ballard, *Forgetting frolic*, 24.
[87] PRONI, MIC1P/179/1, Coronary Kirk Session minutes, *c.* 1783.

[88] PRONI, CR3/25/B/2, Cahans Kirk Session minutes, 16 March 1785.
[89] PRONI, CR3/25/B/2, Cahans Kirk Session minutes, 16 March 1785.
[90] PRONI, D1749/A/1/5/3, Robert Tennent to Reverend John Tennent, 12 August 1799.
[91] PRONI, D1749/A/1/5/3, Robert Tennent to Reverend John Tennent, 12 August 1799.
[92] PRONI, D1748/A/1/5/14, Robert Tennent to Reverend John Tennent, 24 June 1801.
[93] PRONI, D1748/A/1/5/13, Robert Tennent to Reverend John Tennent, 2 June 1801.
[94] PRONI, D1748/A/1/5/13, Robert Tennent to Reverend John Tennent, 2 June 1801.
[95] PRONI, D1748/A/1/5/13, Robert Tennent to Reverend John Tennent, 2 June 1801.
[96] PRONI, MIC1P/37/4/9, Carnmoney Kirk Session minutes, 19 December 1713.
[97] PRONI, MIC1P/37/4/9, Carnmoney Kirk Session minutes, 19 December 1713.
[98] PRONI, MIC1P/37/4/9, Carnmoney Kirk Session minutes, 19 December 1713.
[99] PRONI, MIC1P/37/4/9, Carnmoney Kirk Session minutes, 19 December 1713.
[100] PRONI, MIC1P/37/4/9, Carnmoney Kirk Session minutes, 16 March 1715.
[101] Luddy and O'Dowd, *Marriage in Ireland*, 40; Harding, 'The comeback', 29–32.
[102] PHSI, Down Presbytery minutes, 1707–1715.
[103] PHSI, Glascar Kirk Session minutes, 1760–1818.
[104] Church of Scotland, *Confession*, 131–2.
[105] Church of Scotland, *Confession*, 131–2.
[106] PRONI, MIC1P/37/4/9, Carnmoney Kirk Session minutes, 29 March 1721.
[107] PRONI, MIC1P/37/4/9, Carnmoney Kirk Session minutes, 29 March 1721.
[108] PRONI, MIC1P/37/4/9, Carnmoney Kirk Session minutes, 29 March 1721.
[109] PRONI, MIC1P/37/4/9, Carnmoney Kirk Session minutes, 29 March 1721.
[110] PRONI, CR3/25/B/2, Cahans Kirk Session minutes, 18 January 1776.
[111] PRONI, CR3/25/B/2, Cahans Kirk Session minutes, 18 January 1776.
[112] PRONI, CR3/25/B/2, Cahans Kirk Session minutes, 8 January 1776; 4 February 1776.
[113] Elisabeth Bell was sentenced to public rebuke for her marriage with John McCourt 'a Papish' in March 1781 and William Bell was sentenced to the same in July 1787 for his irregular marriage with Mary O'Neale 'a papish'. See PHSI, Carland Kirk Session minutes, 11 March 1781; 15 July 1787.
[114] PHSI, Aghadowey Kirk Session minutes, 29 November 1703; 28 December 1703; PRONI, CR3/31/1, Ballycarry Kirk Session minutes, 12 March 1738.
[115] Marianne Elliott, *The Catholics of Ulster. A History* (London, 2000), 340. See also Luddy and O'Dowd, *Marriage in Ireland*, 40–8.
[116] Elliott, *Catholics of Ulster*, 341.
[117] Holmes, *Shaping of Ulster Presbyterian belief and practice*, 221.
[118] Holmes, *Shaping of Ulster Presbyterian belief and practice*, 222.
[119] There are several excellent studies of abduction in an Irish context; see Toby Barnard, *The abduction of a Limerick heiress. Social and political relations in mid-eighteenth century Ireland* (Dublin, 1998); Michael Durey, 'Abduction and rape in Ireland in the era of the 1798 rebellion', *Eighteenth-Century Ireland / Iris an dá chultúr* 21 (2006), 27–41; James Kelly, 'The abduction of women of fortune in eighteenth century Ireland', *Eighteenth-Century Ireland / Iris an dá chultúr* 9 (1994), 7–43; Keira Lindsey, '"The absolute distress of females": Irish abduction and the British newspapers, 1800 to 1850', *Journal of Imperial and Commonwealth History* 42(4) (2014), 625–44; Maria Luddy, 'Abductions in nineteenth century Ireland', *New Hibernia Review* 17(2) (2013), 17–44; Luddy and O'Dowd, *Marriage in Ireland*, 181–218; Thomas P. Power, *Forcibly without her consent: abductions in Ireland, 1700–1850* (Indiana, 2010).
[120] Luddy, 'Abductions in nineteenth century Ireland', 18.
[121] Luddy and O'Dowd, *Marriage in Ireland*, 187 fn. 23; Luddy, 'Abductions in nineteenth century Ireland", 21.
[122] Luddy, 'Abductions in nineteenth century Ireland", 21; Kelly, 'Abduction of women', 16.
[123] Luddy and O'Dowd, *Marriage in Ireland*, 182.
[124] Kelly, 'Abduction of women in nineteenth century Ireland", 25–6.

[125] Power, *Forcibly without her consent*, 19.
[126] Power, *Forcibly without her consent*, 19–20.
[127] See Luddy and O'Dowd, *Marriage in Ireland*, 210–16.
[128] Kelly, 'Abduction of women in nineteenth century Ireland", 18.
[129] Kelly, 'Abduction of women in nineteenth century Ireland", 18–19.
[130] Luddy and O'Dowd, *Marriage in Ireland*, 184–5.
[131] Luddy and O'Dowd, *Marriage in Ireland*, 184–5.
[132] Luddy and O'Dowd, *Marriage in Ireland*, 184–5.
[133] Luddy and O'Dowd, *Marriage in Ireland*, 185.
[134] UTC, Burt Kirk Session minutes, 20 November 1704; 26 December 1704.
[135] UTC, Burt Kirk Session minutes, 26 December 1704.
[136] UTC, Burt Kirk Session minutes, 26 December 1704.
[137] UTC, Burt Kirk Session minutes, 22 February 1708; 24 February 1708.
[138] UTC, Burt Kirk Session minutes, 24 February 1708.
[139] UTC, Burt Kirk Session minutes, 24 February 1708.
[140] UTC, Burt Kirk Session minutes, 24 February 1708.
[141] UTC, Burt Kirk Session minutes, 24 February 1708; 9 March 1708; 26 April 1708.
[142] UTC, Burt Kirk Session minutes, 26 April 1708.
[143] UTC, Burt Kirk Session minutes, 30 December 1708.
[144] Luddy and O'Dowd, *Marriage in Ireland*, 202–3. Collusive abductions are also discussed by A.P.W. Malcomson in relation to elopements, see Malcomson, *The pursuit of the heiress*, 155–85.
[145] UTC, Burt Kirk Session minutes, 29 December 1707.
[146] UTC, Burt Kirk Session minutes, 29 December 1707.
[147] UTC, Burt Kirk Session minutes, 29 December 1707.
[148] UTC, Burt Kirk Session minutes, 29 December 1707.
[149] UTC, Burt Kirk Session minutes, 26 April 1708.
[150] Calvert, "'Your marage will make a change with them all'", 1144–73: 1150–1.
[151] Calvert, "'Your marage'", 1150–1.
[152] PRONI, D1748/B/1/317/28, Reverend John Tennent to William Tennent, 25 March 1802.
[153] PRONI, D1748/B/1/317/28, Reverend John Tennent to William Tennent, 25 March 1802.
[154] Luddy and O'Dowd, *Marriage in Ireland*, 278–89.
[155] PRONI, D1748/B/1/317/55, Reverend John Tennent to William Tennent, 27 February 1805.
[156] PRONI, D1748/B/1/317/55, Reverend John Tennent to William Tennent, 27 February 1805.
[157] PRONI, D1748/B/1/317/55, Reverend John Tennent to William Tennent, 27 February 1805.
[158] PRONI, D1748/B/1/317/55, Reverend John Tennent to William Tennent, 27 February 1805.

Chapter Six

[1] PRONI, MIC1P/37/4/9, Carnmoney Kirk Session minutes, 12 April 1703.
[2] PRONI, MIC1P/37/4/9, Carnmoney Kirk Session minutes, 30 May 1703.
[3] PRONI, MIC1P/37/4/9, Carnmoney Kirk Session minutes, 8 June 1703.
[4] PRONI, MIC1P/37/4/9, Carnmoney Kirk Session minutes, 8 June 1703.
[5] PRONI, MIC1P/37/4/9, Carnmoney Kirk Session minutes, 10 August 1703, 24 August 1703, 4 September 1703, 21 September 1703.
[6] PRONI, MIC1P/37/4/9, Carnmoney Kirk Session minutes, 11 July 1703, 18 August 1703, 24 August 1703.
[7] PRONI, MIC1P/37/4/9, Carnmoney Kirk Session minutes, 11 October 1703, 20 October 1703.
[8] Luddy and O'Dowd, *Marriage in Ireland*, 377–8.

[9] Luddy and O'Dowd, *Marriage in Ireland*, 384.
[10] Luddy and O'Dowd, *Marriage in Ireland*, 384.
[11] Diane Urquhart, '"Divorce Irish style": marriage dissolution in Ireland, 1850–1950', in Kevin Costello and Niamh Howlin (eds), *Law and the family in Ireland, 1800–1950* (London, 2017), 107–24: 108–10; Luddy and O'Dowd, *Marriage in Ireland*, 383.
[12] Diane Urquhart, *Irish divorce. A history* (Cambridge, 2020), 10.
[13] Niamh Howlin, 'Adultery in the courts: damages for criminal conversation in Ireland', in Niamh Howlin and Kevin Costello (eds), *Law and the family in Ireland, 1800–1950* (London, 2017), 87–106: 88.
[14] Howlin, 'Adultery in the courts', 88.
[15] Howlin, 'Adultery in the courts', 92–3; Urquhart, *Irish divorce*, 11.
[16] Diane Urquhart, 'Irish divorce and domestic violence, 1857–1922', *Women's History Review*, 22(5) (2013), 820–37, 821; Urquhart, *Irish divorce*, 10–13; Urquhart, '"Divorce Irish style"', 108; Luddy and O'Dowd, *Marriage in Ireland*, 394.
[17] Luddy, 'Marriage, sexuality and the law', 349; Luddy and O'Dowd, *Marriage in Ireland*, 394–5.
[18] Urquhart, *Irish divorce*, 18.
[19] Urquhart, *Irish divorce*, 18.
[20] Urquhart, '"Divorce Irish style"', 110.
[21] Church of Scotland, *Confession*, 55.
[22] Church of Scotland, *Confession*, 55
[23] Church of Scotland, *Confession*, 56.
[24] See PRONI, D1759/1/B/2, Armagh Burgher Presbytery minutes, 1810–40; PHSI, Armagh Presbytery minutes, 1797–1816; 1825–32; PHSI, Bangor Presbytery minutes, 1739–93; PHSI, Down Presbytery minutes, 1707–15; PRONI, D1759/1/D/17, Down Presbytery minutes, 1785–1800; PRONI, D1759/1/D/10, Presbytery of Killyleagh, 1725–32; PHSI, Minutes of the Presbytery of Moira and Lisburn, 1774–86; PHSI, Tyrone Upper Presbytery minutes, 1802–7;1810–30; PHSI, Tyrone Lower Presbytery minutes, 1806–9; PHSI, Route Presbytery minutes, 1701–6; Route Presbytery minutes, 1811–34; PRONI, CR5/5/A/1/2, Minutes of the Reformed Presbytery, 1803–11; PHSI, Monaghan Presbytery minutes, 1702–8; PHSI Monaghan Presbytery minutes, 1800–17; PRONI, CR3/26/2/1, Strabane Presbytery minutes, 1717–40.
[25] Luddy and O'Dowd, *Marriage in Ireland*, 381.
[26] Luddy and O'Dowd, *Marriage in Ireland*, 385.
[27] Luddy and O'Dowd, *Marriage in Ireland*, 385.
[28] Luddy and O'Dowd, *Marriage in Ireland*, 360–4.
[29] PHSI, Route Presbytery minutes, 26 July 1814.
[30] PHSI, Route Presbytery minutes, 26 July 1814.
[31] PHSI, Route Presbytery minutes, 26 July 1814.
[32] PHSI, Route Presbytery minutes, 26 July 1814.
[33] PHSI, Route Presbytery minutes, 26 July 1814.
[34] PHSI, Route Presbytery minutes, 26 July 1814.
[35] O'Dowd, 'Marriage breakdown', 14–21.
[36] O'Dowd, 'Marriage breakdown', 14; Luddy and O'Dowd, *Marriage in Ireland*, 351.
[37] O'Dowd, 'Marriage breakdown', 14.
[38] Luddy and O'Dowd, *Marriage in Ireland*, 352–3.
[39] *Belfast Newsletter*, 27 November 1761.
[40] *Belfast Newsletter*, 27 November 1761.
[41] O'Dowd, 'Marriage breakdown', 19.
[42] *Belfast Newsletter*, 4 June 1799.
[43] *Belfast Newsletter*, 8 January 1754.
[44] Luddy and O'Dowd, *Marriage in Ireland*, 354–5.
[45] *Belfast Newsletter*, 4 November 1755.

[46] *Belfast Newsletter*, 4 November 1755.
[47] *Belfast Newsletter*, 31 March 1769
[48] *Belfast Newsletter*, 31 March 1769.
[49] *Belfast Newsletter*, 31 March 1769.
[50] *Belfast Newsletter*, 31 March 1769.
[51] *Belfast Newsletter*, 31 March 1769.
[52] *Belfast Newsletter*, 31 March 1769.
[53] *Belfast Newsletter*, 31 March 1769.
[54] *Belfast Newsletter*, 31 March 1769.
[55] *Belfast Newsletter*, 31 March 1769.
[56] *Belfast Newsletter*, 31 March 1769.
[57] *Belfast Newsletter*, 31 March 1769.
[58] *Belfast Newsletter*, 31 March 1769.
[59] *Belfast Newsletter*, 31 March 1769.
[60] Luddy and O'Dowd, *Marriage in Ireland*, 287–8.
[61] PHSI, Monaghan Presbytery minutes, 6 October 1807.
[62] PHSI, Monaghan Presbytery minutes, 6 October 1807.
[63] PHSI, Monaghan Presbytery minutes, 6 October 1807.
[64] PHSI, Monaghan Presbytery minutes, 6 October 1807.
[65] PHSI, Down Presbytery minutes, 18 February 1823.
[66] PHSI, Down Presbytery minutes, 18 February 1823.
[67] PHSI, Down Presbytery minutes, 18 February 1823.
[68] PHSI, Down Presbytery minutes, 18 February 1823.
[69] PHSI, Down Presbytery minutes, 18 February 1823.
[70] PHSI, Down Presbytery minutes, 18 February 1823.
[71] Luddy and O'Dowd, *Marriage in Ireland*, 381.
[72] PHSI, Down Presbytery minutes, 18 February 1823.
[73] John McBride, *A vindication of marriage, as solemnised by Presbyterians in the north of Ireland, by a minister of the Gospel* (Belfast, 1702), 13.
[74] McBride, *Vindication*, 13.
[75] Luddy and O'Dowd, *Marriage in Ireland*, 261.
[76] Niamh Howlin, 'Adultery in the courts: damages for criminal conversation in Ireland', in Niamh Howlin and Kevin Costello (eds), *Law and the family in Ireland, 1800–1950* (London, 2017), 87–106: 97.
[77] Howlin, 'Adultery in the courts', 100.
[78] Urquhart, *Irish divorce*, 13.
[79] See PHSI, Aghadowey Kirk Session minutes, 1702–65; PRONI, CR3/31/1, Ballycarry Kirk Session minutes, 1700–80; PHSI, Ballykelly Kirk Session minutes, 1803–19; PRONI, MIC1P/72/1-2, Boardmills Kirk Session minutes, 1784–1815; 1824–42; PRONI, CR3/12/B/1-2, Cahans Kirk Session minutes, 1751–66; 1767–1836; PHSI, Carland Kirk Session minutes, 1780–1802; PRONI, MIC1P/37/4/9, Carnmoney Kirk Session minutes, 1700–1821; PRONI, MIC1P/179/1A&1B, Coronary Kirk Session minutes, 1764–87; PRONI, MIC1P/450C/1, Dawson's Bridge Kirk Session minutes, 1703–10; PRONI, T1447/1, First Dromara Kirk Session minutes, 1780–1805; PHSI, Glascar Kirk Session minutes, 1760–1818; PRONI, MIC1B/6/1, Larne and Kilwaughter Kirk Session minutes, 1720–69; PRONI, CR3/8/1, Loughaghery Kirk Session minutes, 1801–44; PRONI, T1537/1, Rathfriland Kirk Session minutes, 1805–37; PRONI, CR4/12/B/1, Templepatrick Kirk Session minutes, 1700–44; Clontarf and Scots Presbyterian church (private possession), Usher's Quay Kirk Session minute book, 1726–66.
[80] PRONI, CR3/25/B/1, Cahans Kirk Session minutes, 16 November 1755.
[81] PRONI, CR3/25/B/1, Cahans Kirk Session minutes, 16 November 1755
[82] PRONI, CR3/25/B/1, Cahans Kirk Session minutes, 16 November 1755.
[83] PRONI, CR3/25/B/1, Cahans Kirk Session minutes, 16 November 1755.
[84] PRONI, CR3/25/B/1, Cahans Kirk Session minutes, 23 November 1755.

[85] PRONI, CR3/25/B/1, Cahans Kirk Session minutes, 15 March 1756.
[86] PRONI, CR3/25/B/1, Cahans Kirk Session minutes, 15 March 1756,
[87] PRONI, CR3/25/B/1, Cahans Kirk Session minutes, 15 March 1756.
[88] PRONI, CR3/25/B/1, Cahans Kirk Session minutes, 15 March 1756,
[89] PRONI, CR3/25/B/1, Cahans Kirk Session minutes, 15 March 1756.
[90] PRONI, CR3/25/B/1, Cahans Kirk Session minutes, 15 April 1756.
[91] PRONI, CR3/25/B/1, Cahans Kirk Session minutes, 15 April 1756.
[92] PRONI, CR3/25/B/1, Cahans Kirk Session minutes, 15 April 1756.
[93] PRONI, CR3/25/B/1, Cahans Kirk Session minutes, 15 April 1756.
[94] PRONI, CR3/25/B/1, Cahans Kirk Session minutes, 20 June 1756.
[95] PRONI, CR3/25/B/1, Cahans Kirk Session minutes, 20 June 1756.
[96] PRONI, CR3/25/B/1, Cahans Kirk Session minutes, 25 July 1756.
[97] PRONI, CR3/25/B/1, Cahans Kirk Session minutes, 15 August 1757.
[98] PRONI, CR3/25/B/1, Cahans Kirk Session minutes, 16 October 1757.
[99] See Chapter 1.
[100] PRONI, CR3/31/1, Ballycarry Kirk Session minutes, 13 March 1726.
[101] PRONI, CR3/31/1, Ballycarry Kirk Session minutes, 13 March 1726.
[102] PRONI, CR3/31/1, Ballycarry Kirk Session minutes, 13 March 1726.
[103] PRONI, CR3/31/1, Ballycarry Kirk Session minutes, 13 March 1726.
[104] PRONI, CR3/31/1, Ballycarry Kirk Session minutes, 13 March 1726.
[105] 'Mule' is a Scots word meaning 'made of earth or soil'; see Dictionaries of the Scots Language, available online: https://dsl.ac.uk/entry/dost/mule_n_5 (accessed 8 February 2025). My thanks to Allie Nickell for responding to my query about this word and pointing me to the online resource.
[106] PRONI, CR3/31/1, Ballycarry Kirk Session minutes, 13 March 1726.
[107] PRONI, CR3/25/B/2, Cahans Kirk Session minutes, 29 June 1768.
[108] PRONI, CR3/25/B/2, Cahans Kirk Session minutes, 29 June 1768.
[109] PRONI, CR3/25/B/2, Cahans Kirk Session minutes, 29 June 1768.
[110] PRONI, CR3/25/B/2, Cahans Kirk Session minutes, 29 June 1768.
[111] PRONI, CR3/25/B/2, Cahans Kirk Session minutes, 29 June 1768.
[112] PRONI, CR3/25/B/2, Cahans Kirk Session minutes, 29 June 1768.
[113] PRONI, CR3/25/B/2, Cahans Kirk Session minutes, 29 June 1768.
[114] PRONI, CR3/25/B/2, Cahans Kirk Session minutes, August 1768.
[115] PRONI, CR3/25/B/2, Cahans Kirk Session minutes, August 1768.
[116] PRONI, CR3/25/B/2, Cahans Kirk Session minutes, August 1768.
[117] PRONI, MIC1P/37/4/9, Carnmoney Kirk Session minutes, 9 November 1705.
[118] PRONI, MIC1P/37/4/9, Carnmoney Kirk Session minutes, 15 December 1705.
[119] PRONI, MIC1P/37/4/9, Carnmoney Kirk Session minutes, 15 December 1705.
[120] PRONI, MIC1P/37/4/9, Carnmoney Kirk Session minutes, 15 December 1705.
[121] PRONI, MIC1P/37/4/9, Carnmoney Kirk Session minutes, 15 December 1705.
[122] PRONI, MIC1P/37/4/9, 1 January 1706.
[123] Calvert, "'I am friends wt you & do Entertain no malice'", 185–209.
[124] PHSI, Route Presbytery minutes, 5 April 1703.
[125] PHSI, Route Presbytery minutes, 5 April 1703; 30 December 1701; 3 February 1702.
[126] PHSI, Route Presbytery minutes, 3 February 1802.
[127] PHSI, Route Presbytery minutes, 5 April 1703.
[128] PHSI, Route Presbytery minutes, 5 April 1703.
[129] Leanne Calvert, "'To recover his reputation among the people of God'", 906.
[130] PHSI, Route Presbytery minutes, 5 April 1703.
[131] See Leanne Calvert, "'Her husband went away some time agoe'": marriage breakdown in Presbyterian Ulster, c. 1690–1830', *Women's History* 2(15) (2020), 6–13: 9.
[132] Luddy and O'Dowd, *Marriage in Ireland*, 313. See also Elizabeth Steiner-Scott, "'To bounce a boot off her now and then…'": domestic violence in post-Famine Ireland', in Maryann

Gialanella Valiulis and Mary O'Dowd (eds), *Women in Irish history: essays in honour of Margaret MacCurtain* (Dublin, 1997), 125–43.
[133] Luddy and O'Dowd, *Marriage in Ireland*, 315.
[134] PHSI, Presbytery of Monaghan minutes, 21 August 1711.
[135] PHSI, Presbytery of Monaghan minutes, 21 August 1711. Crossle genealogical abstracts, Parcel 1A-32-19 v. E – F; available online: www.findmypast.com, Register of Deeds 5-452-2469, registered 14 November 1711; deed dated 19 April 1709. Ann had died before the execution of the deed.
[136] PHSI, Presbytery of Monaghan minutes, 21 August 1711.
[137] PHSI, Presbytery of Monaghan minutes, February 1712.
[138] PHSI, Presbytery of Monaghan minutes, February 1712.
[139] PHSI, Presbytery of Monaghan minutes, February 1712.
[140] PHSI, Presbytery of Monaghan minutes, February 1712.
[141] Joanne Bailey, '"I dye [sic] by Inches": locating wife beating in the concept of privatization of marriage and violence in eighteenth century England', *Social History* 31(3) (2006), 273–94: 285.
[142] Bailey, '"I dye [sic] by Inches"', 285.
[143] Bailey, '"I dye [sic] by Inches"', 285.
[144] Janay Nugent, '"None must meddle betueene man and wife": assessing family and fluidity of public and private in early modern Scotland', *Journal of Family History* 35(3) (2010), 219–31: 226.
[145] Nugent, '"None must meddle"', 226.
[146] *Records of the General Synod of Ulster, from 1691 to 1820* (3 vols; Belfast, 1890), vol. 1, 224; PHSI, Monaghan Presbytery minutes, 8 August 1710.
[147] PHSI, Monaghan Presbytery minutes, 21 August 1711.
[148] PHSI, Monaghan Presbytery minutes, 27 May 1712.
[149] PHSI, Monaghan Presbytery minutes, 27 May 1712.
[150] PHSI, Monaghan Presbytery minutes, 5 February 1712.
[151] PHSI, Monaghan Presbytery minutes, 5 February 1712.
[152] PHSI, Monaghan Presbytery minutes, 5 February 1712.
[153] PHSI, Monaghan Presbytery minutes, 5 February 1712.
[154] PHSI, Monaghan Presbytery minutes, 5 February 1712.
[155] PHSI, Monaghan Presbytery minutes, 5 February 1712.
[156] *Records of the General Synod of Ulster*, vol. 1, 262.
[157] True to form, Darragh continued to obstruct church authority and refused to cede his ministerial authority. He continued to preach. Darragh unsuccessfully appealed his sentence in the Synod. See James Seaton Reid, *History of the Presbyterian church in Ireland* (3 vols; Belfast, 1867), vol. iii, 34–5.
[158] Crossle genealogical abstracts, Parcel 1A-32-19 v. E – F, Register of Deeds 5-452-2469.
[159] PRONI, MIC1P/37/4/9, Carnmoney Kirk Session minutes, 21 September 1703.
[160] PRONI, MIC1P/37/4/9, Carnmoney Kirk Session minutes, 21 September 1703.
[161] PRONI, MIC1P/37/4/9, Carnmoney Kirk Session minutes, 21 September 1703.
[162] PRONI, MIC1P/37/4/9, Carnmoney Kirk Session minutes, 21 September 1703.
[163] PRONI, MIC1P/37/4/9, Carnmoney Kirk Session minutes, 21 September 1703.
[164] Calvert, '"From a woman's point of view"', 316–17.

Chapter Seven

[1] PRONI, D2930/9/11, Diary of Reverend Robert Magill (19 July 1832–April 1833), 14 September 1832.
[2] PRONI, D2930/9/11, Diary of Reverend Robert Magill (19 July 1832–April 1833), 14 September 1832.

3 PRONI, D2930/9/11, Diary of Reverend Robert Magill (19 July 1832–April 1833), 14 September 1832.
4 PRONI, D2930/9/11, Diary of Reverend Robert Magill (19 July 1832–April 1833), 14 September 1832.
5 See Fióna Gallagher, 'Mapping the miasma; the geographies of a forgotten Irish epidemic', *Irish Geography* 55(2) (2022), 69–98.
6 PRONI, D2930/9/11, Diary of Reverend Robert Magill (19 July 1832–April 1833), 14 September 1832.
7 PRONI, D2930/9/11, Diary of Reverend Robert Magill (19 July 1832–April 1833), 14 September 1832.
8 PRONI, D2930/9/11, Diary of Reverend Robert Magill (19 July 1832–April 1833), 14 September 1832.
9 In a diary entry dated 7 September 1832, Robert marked his own birthday as follows: 'My Birth day – I was born 7th Sept[embe]r 1788 – I am therefore 44 years of age. I am in excellent health – thanks be to the Giver of all good – never was bled or blistered – Never was unwell except from cold or fatigue – never was intoxicated but have uniformly enjoyed excellent health'; PRONI, D2930/9/11, Diary of Reverend Robert Magill (19 July 1823–April 1833), 7 September 1832.
10 Department of Health, 'Life expectancy in Northern Ireland, 2020–2. Published 6 December 2023', available online: https://www.health-ni.gov.uk/news/life-expectancy-northern-ireland-2020-22 (accessed May 2024).
11 Liam Kennedy and L.A. Clarkson, 'Birth, death and exile: Irish population history, 1700–1921', in B.J. Graham and L.J. Proudfoot (eds), *An historical geography of Ireland* (London, 1993), 158–78: 169.
12 L.A. Clarkson, 'The demography of Carrick-on-Suir, 1799', *Proceedings of the Royal Irish Academy*, 87C (1987), 13–36: 31.
13 Fíona Gallagher, 'Mapping the miasma', 69–98.
14 Chris Gilleard, *Old age in nineteenth-century Ireland. Ageing under the union* (London, 2017), 22–3.
15 Gilleard, *Old age in nineteenth century Ireland*, 23.
16 J.E. Smith, 'Widowhood and ageing in traditional English society', *Ageing and Society* 4(4) (1984),429–49: 433; M.E. Wiesner, *Women and gender in early modern Europe* (Cambridge, 1993), 73–81; Lisa Wilson, *Life after death: widows in Pennsylvania, 1750–1850* (Philadelphia, 1992), 1–2; Sylvia Hahn, 'Women in older ages–"old" women?', *History of the Family* 7(1) (2002), 33–58: 36–8.
17 L.A. Clarkson and M.E. Crawford, 'Life after death: widows in Carrick-on-Suir, 1799', in Margaret MacCurtain and Mary O'Dowd (eds), *Women in early modern Ireland* (Edinburgh, 1991), 236–54: 237.
18 Frans von Poppel, 'Widows, widowers and remarriage in nineteenth-century Netherlands', *Population Studies* 49(3) (1995), 421–1: 421.
19 Smith, 'Widowhood and ageing', 433.
20 L.A. Clarkson, 'Love, labour and life: women in Carrick-on-Suir in the late eighteenth century', *Irish Economic and Social History* 20 (1992), 18–24: 29.
21 Clarkson, 'Love, labour and life', 29.
22 Poppel, 'Widows, widowers and remarriage', 423; S.J. Wright, 'The elderly and the bereaved in eighteenth-century Ludlow', in Margaret Pelling and R.M. Smith (eds), *Life, death and the elderly: historical perspectives* (London, 1991), 102–33: 126.
23 Ida Blom, 'The history of widowhood: a bibliographic review', *Journal of Family History* 16(2) (1991), 191–210: 195.
24 Pamela Sharpe, 'Survival strategies and stories: poor widows and widowers in early industrial England', in Sandra Cavallo and Lyndan Warner (eds), *Widowhood in medieval and early modern Europe* (Harlow, 1999), 220–39: 221–2, 229.
25 PRONI, T1447/1, Poor money list of First Dromara congregation, 1769–99.

26 PRONI, D2930/9/6, Diary of Reverend Robert Magill (1821), 29 November 1821.
27 PRONI, D2930/9/6, Diary of Reverend Robert Magill (1821), 29 November 1821; 10 December 1821; 15 December1821.
28 PRONI, D2930/9/6, Diary of Reverend Robert Magill, from 1 January 1821 to 31 December, 21 December 1821.
29 The poor lists of First Dromara congregation also refer to monies distributed to 'poor woman', 'the poor at the door'; see PRONI, T1447/1, Poor money list of First Dromara congregation, 1769–99.
30 These figures are drawn from the poor lists of the following communities: PRONI, T1447/1, First Dromara poor fund, 1769–99; PRONI, MIC1P/412/C, First Dunboe poor list, April 1830; PRONI, MIC1P/302/1, Ballynahinch poor householders, 1840; PRONI, MIC1P/342/C, Donacloney poor list, 1831; PRONI, T1342/1, Minutes and accounts of Killinchy Presbyterian poor relief committee, 1800–1901; PRONI, D2930/9/6, Millrow poor relief, in Diary of Reverend Robert Magill (1821), December 1821.
31 PRONI, T1447/1, First Dromara poor fund, 1769–99.
32 PRONI, T1447/1, First Dromara poor fund, 1769–99.
33 PRONI, T1342/1, Minutes and accounts of Killinchy Presbyterian poor relief committee, 2.
34 PRONI, T1342/1, Minutes and accounts of Killinchy Presbyterian poor relief committee, 3–4.
35 PRONI, T1342/1, Minutes and accounts of Killinchy Presbyterian poor relief committee, 3–4, 9.
36 PRONI, T1342/1, Minutes and accounts of Killinchy Presbyterian poor relief committee. 4. Unlike the other poor relief registers in our sample, poor monies collected by the Killinchy Presbyterian committee made support available to persons of other religious persuasions. Indeed, eight recipients were Roman Catholic, and two belonged to the Church of Ireland.
37 PRONI, T1342/1, Minutes and accounts of Killinchy Presbyterian poor relief committee, 10.
38 PRONI, T1342/1, Minutes and accounts of Killinchy Presbyterian poor relief committee, 10.
39 PRONI, T1342/1, Minutes and accounts of Killinchy Presbyterian poor relief committee, 5.
40 PRONI, T1342/1, Minutes and accounts of Killinchy Presbyterian poor relief committee.
41 PRONI, T1342/1, Minutes and accounts of Killinchy Presbyterian poor relief committee, 48.
42 PRONI, T1342/1, Minutes and accounts of Killinchy Presbyterian poor relief committee, 48.
43 PRONI, T1342/1, Minutes and accounts of Killinchy Presbyterian poor relief committee, 48.
44 Clarkson and Crawford, 'Life after death', 241.
45 Dagmar Freist, 'Religious difference and the experience of widowhood in seventeenth- and eighteenth-century Germany', in Cavallo and Warner (eds), *Widowhood in medieval and early modern Europe*, 164–77: 168.
46 Barbara J. Todd, 'The remarrying widow: a stereotype reconsidered', in Mary Prior (ed.), *Women in English society, 1500–1800* (London, 1985), 549–71.
47 Cynthia Curran, 'Private women, public needs: middle-class widows in Victorian England', *Albion: A Quarterly Journal concerned with British Studies* 25(2) (1993), 217–36: 219–20. Curran notes that contemporary estimates suggested that the 'absolute minimum that a respectable lady and gentlemen' needed to get by on was £200 per annum; see Curran, 219, fn. 11.
48 Kevin P. Conway, 'The Presbyterian ministry of Ulster in the eighteenth and nineteenth centuries: a prosopographical study' (unpublished PhD thesis, Queen's University, Belfast, 1996), 218.
49 PHSI, Diary of Reverend James Morell, 9 June 1822; 14 July 1822.
50 James Morgan, *Recollections of my life and times: an autobiography by the Reverend James Morgan, D.D. late minister of Fisherwick Place, Church, Belfast, with selections from his journal* (Belfast, 1874), 213–14.
51 Morgan, *Recollections of my life and times*, 111–12.
52 Ministers who belonged to the Synod of Ulster received £33 per annum and those who were Seceders received £27 per annum. An augmentation of the *regium donum* in 1803 divided congregations into three classes. In the Synod of Ulster, the largest congregations received £100, those of middling size received £75, and the smallest congregations received £50. Seceding

53 *Records of the General Synod of Ulster, from 1691 to 1820* (3 vols; Belfast, 1890), vol. 1, 445.
54 *Records of the General Synod*, vol. 2, 339.
55 James Seaton Reid, *History of the Presbyterian Church in Ireland* (London, 1853), 322–3.
56 Reid, *History of the Presbyterian church*, 364. It was unclear, however, whether a remarrying widow who was childless would receive this annuity after she remarried.
57 *Records of the General Synod*, vol. 2, 347.
58 Reid, *History of the Presbyterian Church*, p. 325.
59 *Records of the General Synod*, vol. 2, 346–7.
60 *Records of the General Synod*, vol. 2, 347.
61 *Records of the General Synod*, vol. 2,14, 23, 30, 38.
62 *Records of the General Synod*, vol. 2, 372, 417, 430.
63 *Records of the General Synod*, vol. 2, 349.
64 *Records of the General Synod*, vol. 2, 287, 347.
65 *Records of the General Synod*, vol. 2, 347.
66 Reid, *History of the Presbyterian church*, 326. The Secession Synod had its own scheme for the benefits of widows, established in 1783. See PRONI, CR3/46/1/1, Minutes of the Secession Burgher Synod, 1779–1814, and PRONI, CR3/46/1/2A, Minutes of the Secession (Burgher) Synod, 1815–18 and of the United Secession Synod, 1818–23.
67 *Records of the General Synod*, vol. 2, 146.
68 *Records of the General Synod*, vol. 2, 429.
69 *Records of the General Synod*, vol. 2, 36.
70 *Records of the General Synod*, vol. 2, 42. See also the cases of Mrs Sprat, Mrs Whiteside, the family of Mr Moorhead, and Mr Ker in *Records of the General Synod*, vol. 2, 132, 284, 345, 358, 386.
71 *Records of the General Synod*, vol. 2, 345, 358.
72 Myrtle Hill, 'Expressions of faith: Protestantism in nineteenth century Tyrone', in Charles Dillon and H.A. Jefferies (eds), *Tyrone: history and society* (Dublin, 2000), 637–63, 641–3.
73 *Records of the General Synod*, iii, 300–1. Calculated using National Archives, 'Currency converter', http://www.nationalarchives.gov.ac.uk/currency.
74 *Records of the General Synod*, vol. 3, 93, 273.
75 *Records of the General Synod*, vol. 3 161.
76 *Records of the General Synod*, vol. 3 53, 61, 80, 226, 240, 306, 458.
77 *Records of the General Synod*, vol. 3, 217, 253. Others included Mrs Hay, widow of Mr Joseph Hay, minister of Donoughmore (d. 1803), removed to Co. Donegal; Mrs Smyth, widow of Mr John Smyth, minister of Loughbrickland (d. 1804), removed to Dublin; Mrs Isabella Little, widow of Mr Joseph Little, minister of Killyleagh (d. 1813), removed to Banbridge; Mrs Rogers, widow of Mr Robert Rogers, minister of Longford congregation (d. 1791), removed to Dublin. See *Records of the General Synod*, vol. 3, 294, 524–5, 526.
78 *Records of the General Synod*, vol. 3, 62.
79 *Records of the General Synod*, vol. 3, 170.
80 *Records of the General Synod*, vol. 3, 191.
81 PRONI, D2930/9/11, Diary of Reverend Robert Magill (1832–3), 10 January 1833.
82 Robert recorded in his diary on 26 January 1833 that Sarah had gone to stay with her grandparents again, having not been there for almost a fortnight, see PRONI, D2930/9/11, Diary of Reverend Robert Magill (1832–3), 26 January 1833.
83 PRONI, D2930/9/11, Diary of Reverend Robert Magill (1832–3), 20 November 1832.
84 PRONI, D2930/9/15, Life of Reverend Robert Magill (1831), 31 March 1828; 6 March 1829.
85 PRONI, D1748/B/3/3/5, Diary of William Tennent, 1805–8.
86 See PRONI, D1748/G/667/1–7, Letters between Robert James Tennent and Robert Tennent.

[87] PRONI, D1748/B/1/317/41, Reverend John Tennent to William Tennent, 10 October 1803.
[88] PRONI, D1748/B/1/317/63, Reverend John Tennent to William Tennent, 27 January 1807.
[89] PRONI, D2930/9/17, Manuscript music book belonging to Ann Jane Skelton.
[90] PRONI, D2930/9/11, Diary of Reverend Robert Magill (1832–3), 31 October 1832.
[91] PRONI, D2930/9/11, Diary of Reverend Robert Magill (1832–3), 11 December 1832.
[92] PRONI, D2930/9/11, Diary of Reverend Robert Magill (1832–3), 11 December 1832; 6 October 1832.
[93] There is no date on this entry, but the list he titled 'Articles of apparel belonging to my Dear wife at her death', see PRONI, D2930/9/11, Diary of Reverend Robert Magill (1832–3).
[94] PRONI, D2930/9/11, Diary of Reverend Robert Magill (1832–3), 18 September 1832; 27 September 1832.
[95] PRONI, D2930/9/11, Diary of Reverend Robert Magill (1832–3), 18 September 1832; 25 September 1832.
[96] PRONI, D2930/9/11, Diary of Reverend Robert Magill (1832–3), 27 September 1832.
[97] PRONI, D2930/9/11, Diary of Reverend Robert Magill (1832–3), 18 November 1832.
[98] PRONI, D2315/4/15, Reverend William Kennedy to Robert Kennedy, 8 February 1782; PRONI, D2315/4/17, Family letter to Robert Kennedy, 9 April 1782.
[99] J. Carmichael-Ferrall, 'Note on the Kennedy and Bailie pedigrees', *Journal of the Royal Historical and Archaeological Association of Ireland* 7(61) (1885), 30–6: 32.
[100] PRONI, D2315/4/19, Reverend William Kennedy to Robert Kennedy, 23 August 1783; PRONI, D2315/4/16, Reverend William Kennedy to Robert Kennedy, 20 September 1782.
[101] PRONI, D2315/4/16, Reverend William Kennedy to Robert Kennedy, 20 September 1782.
[102] PRONI, D2315/4/10–1; 16, Reverend William Kennedy to Robert Kennedy, n.d.; 9 April 1782; 20 September 1782.
[103] The first mention of this living arrangement is in a letter dated *c.* 1782, just after Elizabeth Bailie's death. The last reference to their residence is a letter dated February 1788. See PRONI, D2315/4/10; 43, Reverend William Kennedy to Robert Kennedy, *c.* 1782; 18 February 1788.
[104] In a letter to his son Robert, in which he reported that he was experiencing financial difficulties caused by the distress of Carland congregation, William Kennedy admitted that were, 'it not for my two worthy Lodgers your [Aunt] & Cousin I shou'd be exceeding ill', see PRONI, D2315/4/43, Reverend William Kennedy to Robert Kennedy, 18 February 1788.
[105] PRONI, D2315/4/11, Reverend William Kennedy to Robert Kennedy, 9 April 1782.
[106] PRONI, D2315/4/11, Reverend William Kennedy to Robert Kennedy, 9 April 1782.
[107] PRONI, D2315/4/11, Reverend William Kennedy to Robert Kennedy, 9 April 1782. See also PRONI, D2315/4/14, Reverend William Kennedy to Robert Kennedy, 12 April 1782.
[108] PRONI, D2315/4/11, Reverend William Kennedy to Robert Kennedy, 9 April 1782.
[109] PRONI, D2315/4/24, Reverend William Kennedy to Robert Kennedy, 28 November 1783.
[110] PRONI, D1748/C/1/211/50, Reverend John Tennent to Robert Tennent, 2 August 1805.
[111] PRONI, D1748/B/1/317/63, Reverend John Tennent to William Tennent, 27 January 1807.
[112] PRONI, D1748/B/1/317/56, Reverend John Tennent to William Tennent, 9 August 1805.
[113] PRONI, D1748/B/1/317/56, Reverend John Tennent to William Tennent, 9 August 1805.
[114] PRONI, D1748/B/1/317/56, Reverend John Tennent to William Tennent, 9 August 1805.
[115] See Helen Berry and Elizabeth Foyster, 'Ageing and loneliness in England, 1500–1800', in Katie Barclay, Elaine Chalus and Deborah Simonton (eds), *The Routledge history of loneliness* (Abingdon and New York, 2023), 207–24.
[116] PRONI, D1748/B/1/317/56, Reverend John Tennent to William Tennent, 9 August 1805.
[117] PRONI, D1748/B/1/317/57, Reverend John Tennent to William Tennent, 12 February.
[118] PRONI, D1748/B/1/317/57, Reverend John Tennent to William Tennent, 12 February.
[119] PRONI, D1748/B/1/317/57, Reverend John Tennent to William Tennent, 12 February.
[120] PRONI, D1748/B/1/317/57, Reverend John Tennent to William Tennent, 12 February.
[121] PRONI, D1748/B/1/317/58, Reverend John Tennent to Willam Tennent, 25 February 1806.
[122] PRONI, D1748/B/1/317/62, Reverend John Tennent to William Tennent, 23 May 1806.
[123] PRONI, D1748/B/1/317/31–2; 39, Reverend John Tennent to William Tennent, 11 March 1803; 14 March 1803; 21 March 1803; PRONI, D1748/C/1/211/30B, Reverend

John Tennent to Robert Tennent, 2 April 1802; PRONI, D1748/A/1/5/21, Robert Tennent to Reverend John Tennent, 30 March 1802.
[124] PRONI, D1748/B/1/317/56, Reverend John Tennent to William Tennent, 9 August 1805.
[125] PRONI, D1748/B/1/317/56, Reverend John Tennent to William Tennent, 9 August 1805.
[126] PRONI, CR3/2/C/1, Register book of Reverend Robert Magill (1838), 11 June 1838.
[127] PRONI, CR3/2/C/1, Register book of Reverend Robert Magill (1838), 2 February 1838; 23 February 1838; 6 March 1838.
[128] PRONI, CR3/2/C/1, Register book of Reverend Robert Magill (1838), 27 March 1838; 30 March 1838.
[129] PRONI, CR3/2/C/1, Register book of Reverend Robert Magill (1838), 2 January 1838.
[130] W.S. Smith, *Historical gleanings in Antrim and neighbourhood* (Belfast, 1888), 53.
[131] Bridget Hourican, 'Robert Magill (1788–1839)', *Dictionary of Irish Biography*, online edition at: https://doi.org/10.3318/dib.005343.v1 (accessed 31 March 2024).

Conclusion

[1] James's surname is spelled differently in the minutes, with variations such as Hoey, Hooey and Hovy; see PHSI, Minutes of the Presbytery of Monaghan, 29 May 1804.
[2] PHSI, Minutes of the Presbytery of Monaghan, 29 May 1804.
[3] PHSI, Minutes of the Presbytery of Monaghan, 29 May 1804.
[4] PHSI, Minutes of the Presbytery of Monaghan, 8 September 1804.
[5] PHSI, Minutes of the Presbytery of Monaghan, 8 September 1804.
[6] PHSI, Minutes of the Presbytery of Monaghan, 4 September 1810.
[7] PHSI, Minutes of the Presbytery of Monaghan, 4 September 1810.
[8] PHSI, Minutes of the Presbytery of Monaghan, 4 September 1810.
[9] For example, in 2016 Toby Barnard opened his essay on education in eighteenth-century Ulster by drawing attention to the perceived irrelevance of his conclusions for Ireland as a whole. As he noted, 'Immediately, it can be objected that Ulster, owing to its confessional and socio-economic demography, is unlikely to be representative of all Ireland. True enough, but a start has to be made'; see Barnard, 'Educating eighteenth-century Ulster', in David Hayton and Andrew R. Holmes (eds), *Ourselves alone? Religion, society and politics in eighteenth- and nineteenth-century Ireland* (Dublin, 2016), 104–25: 105.
[10] Patrick Fitzgerald, 'Scottish migration to Ireland in the seventeenth century', in Alexia Grosjean and Steve Murdock (eds), *Scottish communities abroad in the early modern period* (Leiden and Boston, 2005), 27–52: 33.
[11] Andrew R. Holmes, *The shaping of Ulster Presbyterian belief and practice, 1770–1840* (Oxford, 2006), 306.
[12] See the Bibliography for a full list of my other published work.
[13] Mary O'Dowd, 'Men, women and children in Ireland, 1500–1730', in Jane Ohlmeyer (ed.), *The Cambridge history of Ireland*, volume 2, *1550–1730* (Cambridge, 2018), 298–320: 298; Mary O'Dowd, 'Marriage breakdown in Ireland, c.1660–1857', in Howlin and Costello (eds), *Law and the family in Ireland, 1800–1950*, 7–23: 7–8.
[14] Leanne Calvert and Maeve O'Riordan, 'RIFNET. A new agenda for the Irish family: messy realities and messier lives', *History of the Family* 29(1) (2024), 1–14.
[15] Calvert and O'Riordan, 'RIFNET', 1, 8.

A note on the Bibliography

[1] See for example, I.R. McBride, *Scripture politics. Ulster Presbyterians and Irish Radicalism in the late eighteenth century* (Oxford, 1998); Peter Brooke, *Ulster Presbyterianism: the historical perspective, 1610–1970* (Belfast, 1994); Phil Kilroy, *Protestant dissent and controversy in Ireland,*

1660–1714 (Cork, 1994); J.C. Beckett, *Protestant dissent in Ireland, 1687–1780* (London, 1948); W.G. Brown, 'A theological interpretation of the first Subscription Controversy (1719–1728)', in J.L.M. Haire *et al.* (eds), *Challenge and conflict: essays in Irish Presbyterian history and doctrine* (Antrim, 1981), 28–45.

[2] See J.M. Barkley, *A short history of the Presbyterian church in Ireland* (Belfast, 1959); J.M. Barkley, 'History of the ruling eldership in Irish Presbyterianism' (unpublished M.A. thesis, Queen's University, Belfast, 1952); J.M. Barkley, 'Marriage and the Presbyterian tradition', *Ulster Folklife* 39 (1993), 29–40; J.M. Barkley, 'The Presbyterian minister in eighteenth-century Ireland', in J.L.M. Haire (ed.), *Challenge and conflict: essays in Irish Presbyterian history and doctrine* (Antrim, 1981), 46–71; J.M. Barkley, 'The evidence of old Irish session books on the sacrament of the Lord's Supper', *Church Service Society Annual* 32 (1952), 24–34; J.M. Barkley and W.J. Philbin, 'Baptism: Eucharist: Marriage', *The Furrow* 25(1) (1974), 34–43; Andrew R. Holmes, *The shaping of Ulster Presbyterian belief and practice, 1770–1840* (Oxford, 2006); Andrew R. Holmes, 'Community and discipline in Ulster Presbyterianism, *c.* 1770–1840', *Studies in Church History* 40 (2004), 266–77; Andrew R. Holmes, 'Ulster Presbyterianism as a popular religious culture, 1750–1860', *Studies in Church History* 42, 315–26.

[3] Robert Whan, *Presbyterians of Ulster, 1680–1730* (Woodbridge, 2013).

[4] Whan, *Presbyterians of Ulster,* 201.

[5] I have written extensively on family life using Presbyterian sources. See the Bibliography for a full list.

[6] Jonathan Jeffrey Wright, *The 'natural leaders' and their world: politics, culture and society in Belfast, c. 1801–1832* (Liverpool, 2012); Jonathan Jeffrey Wright, 'Love, loss and learning in late Georgian Belfast: the case of Eliza McCracken', in David Hayton and Andrew R. Holmes (eds), *Ourselves alone? Religion, society and politics in eighteenth- and nineteenth-century Ireland* (Dublin, 2016), 169–91; Jonathan Jeffrey Wright, 'Robert Hyndman's toe: romanticism, schoolboy politics and the affective revolution in late Georgian Belfast', in Catherine Cox and Susannah Riordan (eds), *Adolescence in modern Irish history: innocence and experience* (Basingstoke, Hampshire, 2015), 15–41.

[7] Alice Johnson, *Middle-class life in Victorian Belfast* (Liverpool, 2020); Shannon Devlin, *Siblinghood and sociability in nineteenth-century Ulster* (Liverpool, 2025).

[8] Maria Luddy and Mary O'Dowd, *Marriage in Ireland, 1660–1925* (Cambridge, 2020); Maria Luddy, 'Marriage, sexuality and the law', in Eugenio F. Biagini and Mary E. Daly (eds), *The Cambridge social history of modern Ireland* (Cambridge, 2017), 344–62; Mary O'Dowd, 'Marriage breakdown in Ireland, *c.* 1660–1857', in Niamh Howlin and Kevin Costello (eds), *Law and the family in Ireland, 1800–1950* (London, 2017), 7–23.

[9] See for example, Leanne Calvert, '"Came to her dressed in mans cloaths": transgender histories and queer approaches to the family in eighteenth-century Ireland', *History of the Family* 29(1) (2024), 109–30; Leanne Calvert, '"From a woman's point of view": the Presbyterian archive as a source for women's and gender history in eighteenth- and nineteenth-century Ireland', *Irish Historical Studies* 46(170) (2022), 301–18; Leanne Calvert, '"To recover his reputation among the people of God": sex, religion and the double standard in Presbyterian Ireland, *c.* 1700–1838', *Gender and History* 35(3) (2023), 898–915.

[10] Roisin Browne, 'Kirk and community: Ulster Presbyterian society, 1640–1740' (unpublished MPhil. thesis, Queen's University, Belfast, 1999); Frances Norman, '"She committed that abominable act of uncleanness": locating female sexual agency in Presbyterian Ireland, *c.* 1690–1750', *Women's History Today* 3(3) (2022), 4–11.

[11] Holmes, *Shaping of Ulster Presbyterian belief and practice,* 23.

[12] See Myrtle Hill, '"Women's work for women": the Irish Presbyterian Zenana Mission, 1874–1914', in Rosemary Raughter (ed.), *Religious women and their history: breaking the silence* (Dublin, 2005), 82–97; Myrtle Hill, 'Ulster reawakened: the '59 Revival reconsidered', *Journal of Ecclesiastical History,* 41(3) (1990), 443–62; Janice Holmes, 'The world "turned upside down": women in the Ulster Revival of 1859', in Janice Holmes and Diane Urquhart (eds), *Coming into the light: the work, politics and religion of women in Ulster, 1840–1940* (Belfast,

1994), 126–53; Andrea Ebel Brozyna, '"The cursed cup hath cast her down": constructions of female piety in Ulster evangelical temperance literature, 1863–1914', in Janice Holmes and Diane Urquhart (eds), *Coming into the light: the work, politics and religion of women in Ulster, 1840-1940* (Belfast, 1994),154–78; David Hempton and Myrtle Hill, *Evangelical Protestantism in Ulster society, 1740–1890* (London, 1992).

[13] Leah Leneman and Rosalind Mitchison, *Sin in the city. Sexuality and social control in urban Scotland, 1660–1780* (Edinburgh, 1998) and Rosalind Mitchison and Leah Leneman, *Sexuality and social control: Scotland, 1660–1780* (Oxford, 1989).

[14] See Calvert, '"From a woman's point of view"'.

BIBLIOGRAPHY

Archival sources

Belfast Charitable Society
Belfast Charitable Society Committee minute book, 1811–18
Reports of the Belfast Charitable Society, 1828–43

Presbyterian Historical Society of Ireland, Belfast
Sub-Synod records
Minutes of the Sub-Synod of Derry, 1744–1802

Presbytery records
Armagh Presbytery minutes, 1797–1816; 1825–32
Ballymena Presbytery minutes, 1808–19
Bangor Presbytery minutes, 1739–93
Down Presbytery minutes, 1707–15
Moira and Lisburn Presbytery minutes, 1774–86
Monaghan Presbytery minutes, 1702–8; 1800–17
Route Presbytery minutes, 1701–6; 1811–34
Tyrone Lower Presbytery minutes, 1806–9
Tyrone Upper Presbytery minutes, 1802–7; 1810–30

Congregational records
Aghadowey Session minutes, 1702–65
Ballybay Session minutes, 1811–34
Ballykelly Session minutes, 1803–19

Carland Session minutes, 1754–1801
Glascar Session minutes, 1780–1818

Private papers
Diary of the Reverend James Morell, 1814–22

Plunkett Street Presbyterian Church
Usher's Quay Kirk Session minute book, 1726–66

Public Record Office of Northern Ireland
Synod records
Minutes of the Reformed Presbyterian Synod, 1811–25
Minutes of the Secession Burgher Synod, 1779–1814 and the United Secession Synod, 1818–23
Minutes of the Secession Synod, 1818–40
Typescript copy of minutes of the Secession Burgher Synod, 1779–1814

Presbytery records
Antrim Presbytery minutes, 1783–1834
Armagh Burgher Presbytery minutes, 1810–40
Down Presbytery minutes, 1785–1800
Killyleagh Presbytery minutes, 1725–32
Reformed Presbytery minutes, 1803–11
Strabane Presbytery minutes, 1717–40
Templepatrick Presbytery minutes, 1795–1817

Congregational records
Ballycarry Session book, 1704–80
Ballynahinch list of poor householders, 1840
Cahans Session book, 1751–8; 1767–1836
Carland marriage register, 1770–1802
Carnmoney marriage register, 1708–1807
Carnmoney Session book, 1686–1842
Coronary Session book, 1764–87
Dawson's Bridge Session book, 1703–82
Donacloney poor list, 1831
Drumbolg Session book, 1809–59
First Ballymoney Session book, 1827–66
First Boardmills Session book, 1784–1816; 1824–42
First Dunboe poor list, 1830
First Dunboe Session book, 1802
First Dromara poor money fund, 1769–99

First Dromara Session book, 1762–99
Greyabbey marriage register, 1835–43
Larne and Kilwaughter baptism register, 1834–44
Larne and Kilwaughter marriage register, 1826–32; 1834–45
Larne and Kilwaughter Session minutes, 1720–69
Magherafelt Session book, 1832–81
Marriage register of various congregations belonging to Tyrone Presbytery, 1819–28
Minutes and accounts of Killinchy Presbyterian poor relief committee, 1800–1901
Loanends Session book, 1832–1921
Loughaghery marriage register, 1801–1917
Loughaghery Session book, 1801–63
Loughbrickland baptism register, 1841–4
Loughbrickland Sabbath school reports, 1845–6
Rademon baptism register, 1830–92
Rathfriland marriage register, 1805–42
Rathfriland Session minute book, 1804–60
Templepatrick Session minute book, 1646–1743
Third Cookstown Session minute book, 1834–1966
Third Cookstown Sunday School attendance register, 1837

Private papers
Crawford Papers
Papers of the Gaussen, Kennedy, Bailie and Magill families
Papers of the Reverend Robert Magill
Papers of the Vaughan Charity, 1776–1934
Petitions, leases and addresses relating to the City of Londonderry, 1793–1863
Register book of the Reverend Robert Magill, 1838
Reverend Samuel Elder 'Population of Ballyeaston congregation', 1813
Parks and Caldwell Papers
Southwell Charity Papers, 1722–1924
Tennent Papers
William Drennan Papers
Young family Papers

Special Collections, Queen's University, Belfast
The constitution and discipline of the Presbyterian church; with a directory for the celebration of ordinances, and the performance of ministerial duties. Published by authority of the General Synod of Ulster (Belfast, 1825).

Union Theological College
Presbytery records
Belfast Presbytery minutes, 1774–1800
Derry Presbytery minutes, 1764–96

Congregational records
Burt Session minute book, 1676–1719

Newspapers
Belfast Newsletter

Printed sources

Agnew, Jean (ed.), 1998–9 *The Drennan–McTier letters, 1794–1801* (3 vols), vols 1–3. Dublin. Irish Manuscripts Commission.

Anon, 1716 *Onania, or the heinous sin of self-pollution, and all its frightful consequences in both sexes, considered. With spiritual and physical advice to those who have already injur'd themselves by this abominable practice.* London. Printed for and sold by P. Varenne.

Anon, 1775 *The Brother's gift; or, the naughty girl reformed. Published for the advantage of the rising generation.* Dublin. Printed by George Bonham.

Anon, 1774 *The moral miscellany: or, a collection of select pieces, in prose and verse, for the instruction and entertainment of youth.* Dublin. Printed for J. Williams, no. 5 Skinner-Row.

Barbauld, Mrs (Anna Laetitia), 1774 *Miscellaneous pieces, in prose, by J. and A.L. Aikin.* Belfast. Printed by James Magee.

Barbauld, Mrs (Anna Laetitita Akin) 1774 *Poems, by Anna Laetitia Aikin.* Belfast. Printed by James Magee.

Bonhote, Elizabeth 1788 *The parental monitor. In two volumes,* vol. ii. Dublin. Printed by William Porter.

Brooks, Thomas, 1693 *Apples of gold for young men and women, and a crown of glory for old men and women: or, the happiness of being good betimes: and the honour of being an Old disciple.* London. John Hancock.

Buchan, William, 1781 *Domestic medicine; or, a treatise on the prevention and cure of diseases by regimen and simple medicines.* Dublin. Printed by D. Graisberry, for Messrs. Sleater, Whitestone, Chamberlaine, Williams, and Moncrieffe.

Burton, Richard, 1681 *The apprentices' companion, containing plain and useful directions for servants, especially apprentices, how to perform their particular dutys to their masters, so as to please God.* London. Thomas Mercer.

Church of Scotland, 1744 *The confession of faith: and the larger and shorter catechisms. First agreed upon by the Assembly of Divines at Westminster, and now appointed by the General Assembly of the Kirk of Scotland, to be a part of uniformity in religion between the Kirks of Christ in the three kingdoms. Together with the directions of the General Assembly concerning secret and private worship: and the sum of saving knowledge, with the practical use thereof.* Edinburgh. Printed by T. Lumisden and J. Robertson, and sold at their printing-house, and by Mrs. Brown.

Church of Scotland, 1763 *The form of process in the Judicatories of the Church of Scotland; with relation to scandals and censures: to which is subjoined, several acts and overtures of the General Assemblies.* Glasgow. Printed by John Bryce and sold at his shop.

Culpeper, Nicholas, 1701 *A directory for midwives: or, a guide for women, in their conception, bearing, and suckling their children. The first part contains, 1. The anatomy of the vessels of generation. 2. The formation of the child in the womb. 3. What hinders conception, and its remedies. 4. What furthers conception. 5. A guide for women in conception. 6. Of miscarriage in women. 7. A guide for women in their labour. 8. A guide for women in their lying-in. 9. Of nursing children. To cure all diseases in women, read the second part of this book.* London. Printed for J. and A. Churchill, at the Black Swan in Pater-Noster-Row.

Culpeper, Nicholas, 1816 *Culpeper's complete herbal, to which is now added, upwards of one hundred additional herbs, with a display of their medicinal and occult properties.* London. Richard Evans, No. 8 White's Row, Spitalfields.

Defoe, Daniel, 1800 *The complete family instructor: in five parts.* Liverpool. Printed and sold by H. Forshaw.

Enfield, William, 1776 *Sermons for the use of families, volume one.* Belfast. Printed by James Magee, at the Bible and Crown in Bridge-Street.

Hartson, Hall, 1773 *Youth. A poem.* Dublin. Printed for G. Faulkner, in Parliament Street and R. Moncrieffe, in Capel-Street.

K'Eogh, John, 1735 *Botanalogia Universalis Hibernica, or, A general Irish herbal calculated for this kingdom, giving an account of the herbs, shrubs and trees, naturally produced therein, in English, Irish, and Latin; with a true description of them, and their medicinal virtues and qualities.* Cork. Printed and sold by George Harrison at the corner of Meeting house Lane.

L.F., 1744 *The virgin's nosegay; or, The duties of Christian virgins, digested into succinct chapters, and stated under three principal heads ....* London and Belfast. Reprinted by Fr. Joy, at the Peaccock in Bridge-Street.

Leadbeater, Mary, 1794 *Extracts and original anecdotes; for the improvement of youth.* Dublin. Printed by R.M. Jackson, no. 20 Meath Street.

McBride, John, 1702 *A Vindication of marriage, as solemnised by Presbyterians in the north of Ireland, by a minister of the Gospel.* Belfast.

Manson, David, 1762 *A new pocket dictionary; or, English expositor.* Belfast. Daniel Blow.

Manson, David, 1774 *An accurate pronouncing and spelling dictionary, and complete English depositor. Particularly calculated for the use of schools: being also an excellent pocket companion for young people, tradesmen and others.* Belfast.

Manson, David, 1764 *Directions to play the literary cards: invented for the improvement of children in learning and morals, from their beginning to learn the letters, till they become proficient in spelling, reading, parsing, and arithmetick.* Belfast. Printed for the author.

Moore, Hamilton John, 1788 *The young gentleman and ladies monitor, being a collection of select pieces from our best modern writers: particularly calculated to form the mind and manners of the youth of both sexes, adapted to the use of schools and academies.* Belfast. Printed by James Magee, No. 9 Bridge Street.

Morgan, James, 1874 *Recollections of my life and times: an autobiography by the Reverend James Morgan, D.D., late minister of Fisherwick Place Church, Belfast, with selections from his journal, edited by his son.* Belfast. William Mullan.

Pomfret, Samuel, 1722 *A directory for youth: or, a discourse of youthful lusts.* London. Printed for and sold by Joseph Marshal.

Presbyterian Church in Ireland, 1890–8 *Records of the General Synod of Ulster, 1691–1820* (3 vols). Belfast.

Smythson, Hugh, 1781 *The compleat family physician; or, universal medical repository.* London. Printed for Harrison and Co.

Tissot, Samuel, 1772 *Three essays: first, on the disorders of people of fashion. Second on diseases incidental to literary and sedentary persons, with proper rules for preventing their fatal consequences, and instructions for their cure. Third, on onanism: or, a treatise upon the disorders produced by masturbation: or, the effects of secret and excessive venery.* Dublin. Printed for James Williams, at no. 5 Skinner-Row.

Tissot, Samuel, 1766 *Onanism: or, a treatise upon the disorders produced by masturbation: or, the dangerous effects of secret and excessive venery. By M. Tissot, M.D. Fellow of the Royal Society of London. Member of the*

Medico-Physical Society of Basle, and of the Oeconomical Society of Berne. Translated from the last Paris edition by A. Hume, M.D. London. Printed for the translator; and sold by J. Pridden, in Fleet-Street.

Willison, John, 1784 *An example of plain catechising upon the Assembly's shorter catechism: humbly offered as an help for instructing the young ... with a preface.* Belfast. Printed by James Magee.

Willison, John, 1754 *The young communicant's catechism: or, a help both short and plain, for instructing and preparing the young to make a right approach unto the Lord's Table. With a proposal, for public renewing of the Baptismal Covenant.* Belfast. Printed by and for James Magee.

Wolveridge, James, 1670 *Speculum matricis hybernicum, or, The Irish midwives handmaid.* London. E. Okes, and are to be sold by Rowland Reynolds.

Wynne, John Huddlestone, 1795 *Tales for youth; in thirty poems. To which are annexed, historical remarks and moral applications in prose.* Dublin. Printed by N. Kelly, for T. Jackson, 23 Parliament Street.

Secondary sources

Adams, J.R.R., 1987 *The printed word & the common man. Popular culture in Ulster, 1700–1900.* Belfast. Institute of Irish Studies.

Adair, Richard, 1996 *Courtship, illegitimacy and marriage in early modern England.* Manchester. Manchester University Press.

Akenson, Donald H., 1979 *Between two revolutions: Islandmagee, County Antrim, 1798–1920.* Ontario. Academy Press.

Akenson, Donald H., 1991 *Small differences: Irish Catholics and Irish Protestants, 1815–1922: an international perspective.* Montreal and London. McGill-Queen's University Press.

Bailey, Joanne, 2006 '"I dye [sic] by Inches": locating wife beating in the concept of privatization of marriage and violence in eighteenth century England', *Social History* 31(3), 273–94.

Ballard, Linda, 1998 *Forgetting frolic: marriage traditions in Ireland.* Belfast. Institute of Irish Studies.

Bankhurst, Benjamin, 2013 *Ulster Presbyterians and the Scots Irish diaspora, 1750–1764.* Basingstoke. Palgrave Macmillan.

Barclay, Katie, 2011 *Love, intimacy and power. Marriage and patriarchy in Scotland, 1650–1850.* Manchester. Manchester University Press.

Barclay, Katie, 2015 'Illicit intimacies: the imagined "homes" of Gilbert Innes of Stow and his mistresses (1751–1832)', in *Gender and History* 27(3), 576–90.

Barclay, Katie, 2017 'Intimacy, community and power: bedding rituals in eighteenth-century Scotland', in Merridee L. Bailey and Katie Barclay (eds), *Emotion, ritual and power in Europe, 1200–1920: family, state and church,* 43–61. Basingstoke. Palgrave Macmillan.

Barclay, Katie, 2019 'Doing the paperwork: the emotional world of wedding certificates', *Cultural and Social History* 17(3), 315–32.

Barclay, Katie, 2021 'Making the bed, making the lower-order home in eighteenth-century Scotland', in Stephen G. Hague and Karen Lipsedge (eds), *At home in the eighteenth century. Interrogating domestic space,* 266–82. New York. Routledge.

Bardon, Jonathan, 2003 *An interesting and honourable history: the Belfast Charitable Society. The first 250 years, 1752–2002.* Belfast. Belfast Charitable Society.

Barker, Hannah, 2008 'Soul, purse and family: middling and lower-class masculinity in eighteenth-century Manchester', *Social History* 33(1), 12–35.

Barkley, J.M., 1952 'History of the ruling eldership in Irish Presbyterianism'. Unpublished M.A. Thesis. Queen's University, Belfast.

Barkley, J.M., 1952 'The evidence of old Irish session books on the sacrament of the Lord's Supper', *Church Service Society Annual* 32 (1952), 24–34.

Barkley, J.M., 1959 *A short history of the Presbyterian church in Ireland.* Belfast. Publications Committee of the Presbyterian Church in Ireland.

Barkley, J.M., 1963 *The eldership in Irish Presbyterianism.* Belfast. J.M. Barkley.

Barkley, J.M., 1981 'The Presbyterian minister in eighteenth-century Ireland', in J.L.M. Haire (ed.), *Challenge and conflict: essays in Irish Presbyterian history and doctrine,* 46–71. Antrim. Greystones Press.

Barkley, J.M., 1993 'Marriage and the Presbyterian tradition', *Ulster Folklife* 39, 29–40.

Barkley, J.M. and Philbin, W.J., 1974 'Baptism: Eucharist: Marriage', *The Furrow,* 25(1), 34–43.

Barnard, Toby, 1998 *The abduction of a Limerick heiress. Social and political relations in mid-eighteenth century Ireland.* Dublin. Irish Academic Press.

Barnard, Toby, 2016 'Educating eighteenth-century Ulster', in D.W. Hayton and Andrew R. Holmes (eds), *Ourselves alone? Religion, society and politics in eighteenth- and nineteenth-century Ireland,* 104–25. Dublin. Four Courts.

Beckett, J.C., 1948 *Protestant dissent in Ireland, 1687–1780.* London. Faber and Faber.

Ben-Amos, Illana Krausman, 1994 *Adolescence and youth in early modern England*. New Haven and London. Yale University Press.

Berry, Helen and Foyster, Elizabeth, 2023 'Ageing and loneliness in England, 1500–1800', in Katie Barclay, Elaine Chalus and Deborah Simonton (eds), *The Routledge history of loneliness*, 207–24. Abingdon and New York. Routledge.

Blaikie, Andrew and Gray, Paul, 2005 'Archives of abuse and discontent? Presbyterianism and sexual behaviour during the eighteenth and nineteenth centuries', in R.J. Morris and Liam Kennedy (eds), *Ireland and Scotland: order and disorder, 1600–2000*, 61–84. Edinburgh. John Donald.

Blom, Ida, 1991 'The history of widowhood: a bibliographic review', *Journal of Family History* 16(2), 191–210.

Boylan, A.B., 1979 'Sunday schools and changing Evangelical views of children in the 1820s', *Church History* 48(3), 320–33.

Breathnach, Ciara, 2016 'Handywomen and birthing in rural Ireland, 1851–1955', *Gender and History* 28(1), 34–56.

Brooke, Peter, 1994 *Ulster Presbyterianism: the historical perspective, 1610–1970*. Belfast. Athol.

Brooks, Christopher, 1994 'Apprenticeship, social mobility and the middling sort, 1550-1800', in Jonathan Barry and Christopher Brooks (eds), *The middling sort of people: culture, society and politics in England, 1550–1800*, 52–83. Basingstoke. Macmillan.

Brown, W.G., 1981 'A theological interpretation of the First Subscription Controversy (1719–1728)', in J.L.M. Haire *et al.* (eds), *Challenge and conflict: essays in Irish Presbyterian history and doctrine*, 28–45. Antrim. Greystones Press.

Browne, Roisin M., 1999 'Kirk and community: Ulster Presbyterian society, 1640–1740'. Unpublished MPhil. thesis. Queen's University Belfast.

Brozyna, Andrea Ebel, 1994 '"The cursed cup hath cast her down": constructions of female piety in Ulster evangelical temperance literature, 1863-1914', in Janice Holmes and Diane Urquhart (eds), *Coming into the light: the work, politics and religion of women in Ulster, 1840-1940*, 154–78. Belfast. Institute of Irish Studies.

Calvert, Leanne, 2012 'The journal of John Tennent, 1789–90', *Analecta Hibernica* 43, 69–128.

Calvert, Leanne, 2017 '"A more careful tender nurse cannot be than my dear husband": reassessing the role of men in pregnancy and childbirth in Ulster, 1780–1838', *Journal of Family History* 42(1), 22–36.

Calvert, Leanne, 2017 '"Do not forget your bit wife": love, marriage and the negotiation of patriarchy in Irish Presbyterian marriages, *c.* 1780–1850', *Women's History Review* 26(3), 433–54.

Calvert, Leanne, 2018 '"He came to her bed pretending courtship": sex, courtship and the making of marriage in Ulster, 1750–1844', *Irish Historical Studies* 42(162), 244–64.

Calvert, Leanne, 2019 '"What a wonderful change have I undergone … So altered in stature, knowledge & ideas!": apprenticeship, adolescence and growing up in eighteenth- and nineteenth-century Ulster', *Irish Economic and Social History* 45(1), 70–89.

Calvert, Leanne, 2020 '"Her husband went away some time agoe": marriage breakdown in Presbyterian Ulster, *c.* 1690–1830', *Women's History* 2(15), 6–13.

Calvert, Leanne, 2021 '"I am friends wt you & do Entertain no malice": discord, disputes and defamation in Ulster Presbyterian church courts, *c.* 1700–1838', in Niamh Howlin and Kevin Costello (eds), *Law and religion in Ireland, 1700–1970,* 185–209. Cham, Switzerland. Springer International Publishing.

Calvert, Leanne, 2022 '"From a woman's point of view": the Presbyterian archive as a source for women's and gender history in eighteenth- and nineteenth-century Ireland', *Irish Historical Studies* 46(170), 301–18.

Calvert, Leanne, 2022 'Objects of affection? Materialising courtship, love and sex in Ireland, *c.* 1800–1830', *Cultural and Social History* 19(3), 247–63.

Calvert, Leanne, 2022 '"Your marage will make a change with them all … when you get another famely": illegitimate children, parenthood, and siblinghood in Ireland, *c.* 1759-1832', *English Historical Review* 136(587), 1144–73.

Calvert, Leanne, 2023 '"To recover his reputation among the people of God": sex, religion and the double standard in Presbyterian Ireland, *c.* 1700–1838', *Gender and History* 35(3), 898–915.

Calvert, Leanne, 2024 '"Came to her dressed in mans cloaths": transgender histories and queer approaches to the family in eighteenth-century Ireland', *History of the Family* 29(1), 109–30.

Calvert, Leanne and O'Riordan, Maeve, 2024 'RIFNET. A new agenda for the Irish family: messy realities and messier lives', *History of the Family* 29(1), 1–14.

Carmichael-Ferrall, J., 1885 'Note on the Kennedy and Bailie pedigrees', *Journal of the Royal Historical and Archaeological Association of Ireland* 7(61), 30–6.

Carroll, Brian D., 2003 '"I indulged my desire too freely": sexuality, spirituality and the sin of self-pollution in the diary of Joseph Moody, 1720–1724', *William and Mary Quarterly* 60(1), 155–70.

Carter, Kathryn, 1997 'The cultural work of diaries in mid-century Victorian Britain', *Victorian Review* 23(2), 251–67.

Clarkson, L.A., 1987 'The demography of Carrick-on-Suir, 1799', *Proceedings of the Royal Irish Academy* 87C, 13–36.

Clarkson, L.A., 1992 'Love, labour and life: women in Carrick-on-Suir in the late eighteenth century', *Irish Economic and Social History* 20, 18–24.

Clarkson, L.A. and Crawford, M.E., 1991 'Life after death: widows in Carrick-on-Suir, 1799', in Margaret MacCurtain and Mary O'Dowd (eds), *Women in early modern Ireland*, 236–54. Edinburgh. Edinburgh University Press.

Coffey, R.A., 1990 'The foundation and early history of the Southwell schools, Downpatrick, 1733–1800', *Lecale Miscellany* 8, 53–64.

Collins, Brenda, 1982 'Proto-industrialization and pre-famine emigration', *Social History* 7(2), 127–46.

Connell, K.H., 1968 *Irish peasant society: four historical essays*. Oxford. Clarendon Press.

Connolly, S.J., 1979 'Illegitimacy and pre-nuptial pregnancy in Ireland before 1864: the evidence of some Catholic parish registers', *Irish Economic and Social History* 6, 5–23.

Connolly, S.J., 1982 *Priests and the people in pre-Famine Ireland, 1780–1845*. Dublin. Gill and Macmillan.

Connolly, S.J., 1985 *Religion and society in nineteenth-century Ireland*. Dundalk. Economic and Social History Society of Ireland.

Connolly, S.J., 1992 *Religion, law and power: the making of Protestant Ireland, 1660–1760*. Oxford. Clarendon Press.

Connolly, S.J., 1997 'Ulster Presbyterians: religion, culture, and politics, 1660–1850', in Tyler Blethen (ed.), *Ulster and North America: transatlantic perspectives on the Scotch-Irish,* 24–40. Tuscaloosa. University of Alabama Press.

Connolly, S.J., 2008 *Divided kingdom: Ireland, 1630–1800*. Oxford. Oxford University Press.

Conway, Kevin, 1997 'The Presbyterian ministry of Ulster in the eighteenth and nineteenth centuries: a prosopographical study'. Unpublished PhD thesis. Queen's University Belfast.

Corish, Patrick, 1985 'Catholic marriage under the Penal code', in Art Cosgrove (ed.), *Marriage in Ireland,* 67–77. Dublin. College Press.

Crawford, W.H., 1988 'The evolution of the linen trade in Ulster before industrialization', *Irish Economic and Social History* 15, 32–53.

Crawford, W.H., 1991 'Women in the domestic linen industry', in Margaret MacCurtain and Mary O'Dowd (eds), *Women in early modern Ireland,* 255–64. Edinburgh. Edinburgh University Press.

Crawford, W.H., 2005 *The impact of the domestic linen industry in Ulster*. Belfast. Ulster Historical Foundation.

Cressy, David, 1997 *Birth, marriage and death: ritual, religion and the life-cycle in Tudor and Stuart England.* Oxford. Oxford University Press.

Crossman, Virginia, 2006 *The poor law in Ireland, 1838–1948.* Dublin. Irish Economic and Social History Society of Ireland.

Curran, Cynthia, 1993 'Private women, public needs: middle-class widows in Victorian England', *Albion: A Quarterly Journal concerned with British Studies* 25(2), 217–36.

Davis, Natalie Zemon, 1987 *Fiction in the archives. Pardon tales and their tellers in sixteenth-century France.* California. Stanford University Press.

Day, Angélique, McWilliams, Patrick, Dobson, Nóirín and English, Lisa (eds), 1990–8 *Ordnance Survey Memoirs of Ireland* (40 vols). Belfast. Institute of Irish Studies in association with the Royal Irish Academy.

Daybell, James, 2001 'Introduction', in James Daybell (ed.), *Early modern women's letter writing, 1450–1700*, 1–15. Basingstoke. Palgrave Macmillan.

Debutts, R.E.L., 2007 'Lee in love: courtship and correspondence in Antebellum Virginia', *Virginia Magazine of History and Biography* 115(4), 486–575.

Delay, Cara, 2015 'Women, childbirth customs and authority in Ireland, 1850–1930', *Lilith: A Feminist History Journal* 21, 6–18.

Delay, Cara, 2019 'Pills, potions, and purgatives: women and abortion methods in Ireland, 1900–1950', *Women's History Review* 28(3), 479–99.

Devlin, Shannon, 2025 *Siblinghood and sociability in nineteenth-century Ulster.* Liverpool. Liverpool University Press.

Dolan, Frances E., 2013 *True relations. Reading, literature, and evidence in seventeenth-century England.* University of Pennsylvania Press. Philadelphia.

Durey, Michael, 2006 'Abduction and rape in Ireland in the era of the 1798 rebellion', *Eighteenth-Century Ireland* 21, 27–47.

Earle, Rebecca, 1999 'Introduction. Letters, writers and the historian', in Rebecca Earle (ed.), *Epistolary selves: letters and letter-writers, 1600–1945*, 1–18. Aldershot. Routledge.

Earner-Byrne, Lindsay and Urquhart, Diane, 2019 *The Irish abortion journey, 1920–2018.* Cham, Switzerland. Palgrave Pivot.

Evans, Jennifer, 2014 *Aphrodisiacs, fertility and medicine in early modern England.* Woodbridge. Boydell Press.

Evans, Jennifer and Read, Sara, 2015 '"Before midnight she had miscarried": women, men and miscarriage in early modern England', *Journal of Family History* 40(1), 3–23.

Eustace, Nicole, 2001 '"The cornerstone of a copious work": love and power in eighteenth-century courtship', *Journal of Social History* 39(3), 517–46.

Farrell, Elaine, 2012 '"The fellow said it was not harm and only tricks": the role of the father in suspected cases of infanticide in Ireland, 1850–1900', *Journal of Social History* 45(4), 990–1004.

Farrell, Elaine, 2013 *'A most diabolical deed': infanticide and Irish society, 1850–1900*. Manchester. Manchester University Press.

Fitzgerald, Patrick, 2005 'Scottish migration to Ireland in the seventeenth century', in Alexia Grosjean and Steve Murdock (eds), *Scottish communities abroad in the early modern period*, 27–52. Leiden and Boston. Brill.

Ffeary-Smyrl, Steven C., 2009 *Dictionary of Dublin dissent: Dublin's protestant dissenting meeting houses, 1660–1920*. Dublin. A. & A. Farmar.

Fleming, Peter, 2001 *Family and household in medieval England*. Basingstoke. Palgrave.

Foley, Ronan 2015 'Indigenous narratives of health: re(placing) folk-medicine with Irish health histories', *Journal of Medical Humanities* 36(1), 5–18.

Freist, Dagmar, 1999 'Religious difference and the experience of widowhood in seventeenth- and eighteenth-century Germany', in Sandra Cavallo and Lyndan Warner (eds), *Widowhood in medieval and early modern Europe,* 164–77. Harlow. Longman.

Gallagher, Fióna, 2023 'Mapping the Miasma; the geographies of a forgotten Irish epidemic', *Irish Geography* 55(2), 69–98.

Geary, Frank, 2005 'The evolution of the linen trade before industrialisation: why did firms not replace the market', in Brenda Collins, Philip Ollerenshaw and Trevor Parkhill (eds), *Industry, trade and people in Ireland, 1650–1950. Essays in honour of W.H. Crawford,* 131–53. Belfast. Ulster Historical Foundation.

Gibson, Kate, 2020 '"I am not on the footing of kept women": extra-marital love in eighteenth-century England', *Cultural and Social History* 17(3), 355–73.

Gilleard, Chris, 2017 *Old age in nineteenth-century Ireland. Ageing under the union.* London. Palgrave Macmillan.

Gillespie, Raymond, 2013 'The early modern economy, 1600–1780', in Liam Kennedy and Philip Ollerenshaw (eds), *Ulster since 1600: politics, economy and society,* 12–26. Oxford. Oxford University Press.

Gilmore, Peter, 2018 *Irish Presbyterians and the shaping of western Pennsylvania, 1770–1830.* Pittsburgh. University of Pittsburgh Press.

Gray, Paul, 2000 'A social history of illegitimacy in Ireland from the late eighteenth to the early twentieth century'. Unpublished PhD thesis. Queen's University Belfast.

Griffin, Patrick, 2001 *The people with no name. Ireland's Ulster Scots, America's Scots Irish, and the creation of a British Atlantic world, 1689–1764.* New Jersey. Princeton University Press.

Griffin, Patrick, 2002 'The people with no name: Ulster's migrants and identity formation in eighteenth-century Pennsylvania', *William and Mary Quarterly* 58(3), 587–614.

Goldsmith, Sarah, Haggerty, Sheryllynne and Harvey, Karen (eds) 2023, *Letters and the body, 1700–1830. Writing and embodiment.* New York. Routledge.

Gowing, Laura, 1997 'Secret births and infanticide in seventeenth-century England', *Past and Present* 156, 87–115.

Hahn, Sylvia, 2002 'Women in older ages–"old" women?', *History of the Family* 7(1), 33–58.

Hanawalt, Barbara, 1998 '"The childe of Bristowe" and the making of middle-class adolescence', in Barbara Hanawalt (ed.), *'Of good and ill repute': gender and social control in medieval England*, 178–202. Oxford. Oxford University Press.

Hardwick, Julie, 2020 *Sex in an old regime city. Young workers and intimacy in France, 1660–1789.* Oxford. Oxford University Press.

Hatfield, Mary, 2019 *Growing up in nineteenth-century Ireland. A cultural history of middle-class childhood and gender.* Oxford. Oxford University Press.

Hayton, David, 1997 'Presbyterians and the confessional state: the sacramental test as an issue in Irish politics, 1704–1780', *Bulletin of the Presbyterian Historical Society* 26, 11–31.

Hempton, David and Hill, Myrtle, 1993 *Evangelical Protestantism in Ulster society, 1740–1890.* London. Routledge.

Hill, Myrtle, 1990 'Ulster reawakened: the '59 Revival reconsidered', *Journal of Ecclesiastical History* 41(3), 443–62.

Hill, Myrtle, 2000 'Expressions of faith: Protestantism in nineteenth century Tyrone', in Charles Dillon and H.A. Jefferies (eds), *Tyrone: history and society*, 637–63. Dublin. Geography Publications.

Hill, Myrtle, 2005 '"Women's work for women": the Irish Presbyterian Zenana Mission, 1874–1914', in Rosemary Raughter (ed.), *Religious women and their history: breaking the silence*, 82–97. Dublin. Irish Academic Press.

Hill, Myrtle, 2024 'Religion, gender, and sexuality in Ireland, 1800–1922', in Gladys Ganiel and Andrew R. Holmes (eds), *Oxford handbook of religion in modern Ireland*, 124–44. Oxford. Oxford University Press.

Holloway, Sally, 2016 '"You know I am all on fire": writing the adulterous affair in England, *c.* 1740–1830', *Historical Research* 89(244), 317–39.

Holloway, Sally, 2018 *The game of love in Georgian England: courtship, emotions and material culture.* Oxford. Oxford University Press.

Holloway, Sally, 2019 'Love, custom & consumption: Valentine's Day in England *c.* 1660–1830', *Cultural and Social History* 17(3), 295–314.

Holmes, Andrew R., 2004 'Community and discipline in Ulster Presbyterianism, *c.* 1770–1840', *Studies in Church History* 40, 266–77.

Holmes, Andrew R., 2006 *The shaping of Ulster Presbyterian belief and practice, 1770–1840.* Oxford. Oxford University Press.

Holmes, Andrew R., 2006 'Ulster Presbyterianism as a popular religious culture, 1750–1860', *Studies in Church History* 42, 315–26.

Holmes, Janice, 1994 'The world "turned upside down": women in the Ulster Revival of 1859', in Janice Holmes and Diane Urquhart (eds), *Coming into the light: the work, politics and religion of women in Ulster, 1840–1940,* 126–53. Belfast. Institute of Irish Studies.

Holmes, R.F.G., 1985 *Our Irish Presbyterian heritage.* Belfast. Publications Committee of the Presbyterian Church in Ireland.

Holmes, R.F.G., 2000 *The Presbyterian church in Ireland: a popular history.* Blackrock. The Columba Press.

Howlin, Niamh, 2017 'Adultery in the courts: damages for criminal conversation in Ireland', in Niamh Howlin and Kevin Costello (eds), *Law and the family in Ireland, 1800–1950,* 87–106. London. Palgrave.

Houlbrooke, Ralph, 2013 *The English family, 1450–1700.* Oxford. Routledge.

Hunt, Margaret, 1996 *The middling sort: commerce, gender and the family in England, 1680–1780.* London. University of California Press.

Johnson, Alice, 2020 *Middle-class life in Victorian Belfast.* Liverpool. Liverpool University Press.

Kelly, James, 1992 'Infanticide in eighteenth-century Ireland', *Irish Economic and Social History* 19(1), 5–26.

Kelly, James, 1994 'The abduction of women of fortune in eighteenth century Ireland', *Eighteenth-Century Ireland* 9, 7–43.

Kelly, James, 2019 '"An unnatural crime": infanticide in early nineteenth-century Ireland', *Irish Economic and Social History* 46(1), 66–110.

Kennedy, Liam, 1985 'The rural economy, 1820–1914', in Liam Kennedy and Philip Ollerenshaw (eds), *An economic history of Ulster, 1820–1940.* Manchester. Manchester University Press.

Kennedy, Liam and Clarkson, L.A., 1993 'Birth, death and exile: Irish population history, 1700–1921', in B.J. Graham and L.J. Proudfoot (eds), *An historical geography of Ireland,* 158–78. London. Academic Press.

Kennedy, Liam, Miller, Kerby A. and Gurrin, Brian, 2013 'People and population change, 1600–1914', in Liam Kennedy and Philip Ollerenshaw (eds), *Ulster since 1600: politics, economy and society,* 58–73. Oxford. Oxford University Press.

Kennedy, Liam and Solar, Peter M., 2013 'The rural economy, 1780–1914', in Liam Kennedy and Philip Ollerenshaw (eds), *Ulster since 1600: politics, economy and society,* 160–76. Oxford. Oxford University Press.

Kenny, J.G. (ed.), 1988 *As the crow flies over rough terrain: incorporating Diary 1827–1828 and More a divine.* Newtownabbey. J.G. Kenny.

Kilroy, Phil, 1994 *Protestant dissent and controversy in Ireland, 1660–1714.* Cork. Cork University Press.

Kinmonth, Claudia, 2006 *Irish rural interiors in art.* London. Yale University Press.

Laqueur, Thomas, 2003 *Solitary sex. A cultural history of masturbation.* New York. Zone Books.

Leneman, Leah and Mitchison, Rosalind, 1998 *Sin the city: sexuality and social control in urban Scotland, 1660–1780.* Edinburgh. Scottish Cultural Press.

Lindsey, Kiera, 2014 '"The absolute distress of females": Irish abduction and British newspapers, 1800–1850', *Journal of Imperial and Commonwealth History* 42(2), 625–44.

Loughridge, Adam, 1984 *The Covenanters in Ireland.* Belfast. Cameron Press.

Luddy, Maria, 2011 *Matters of deceit: breach of promise to marry cases in nineteenth- and twentieth-century Limerick.* Dublin. Four Courts.

Luddy, Maria, 2013 'Abductions in nineteenth-century Ireland', *New Hibernia Review* 17(2), 17–44.

Luddy, Maria, 2017 'Marriage, sexuality and the law in Ireland', in Eugenio F. Biagini and Mary E. Daly (eds), *The Cambridge social history of modern Ireland,* 344–62. Cambridge. Cambridge University Press.

Luddy, Maria and O'Dowd, Mary, 2020 *Marriage in Ireland, 1660–1925.* Cambridge. Cambridge University Press.

Lyons, Martyn, 1999 'Love letters and writing practices: on *écritures intimes* in the nineteenth century', *Journal of Family History* 24, 232–9.

Lystra, Karen, 1989 *Searching the heart: women, men and romantic love in nineteenth-century America.* New York and Oxford. Oxford University Press.

Macafee, William, 2000 'The population of County Tyrone, 1660–1991', in Charles Dillon and H.A. Jefferies (eds), *Tyrone: history and society,* 433–61. Dublin. Geography Publications.

Macafee, William and Morgan, Valerie, 1982 'Mortality in Magherafelt, County Derry, in the early eighteenth century reappraised', *Irish Historical Studies* 23(89), 50–60.

MacFarlane, Alan, 1986 *Marriage and love in England: modes of reproduction, 1300–1840.* Oxford. Basil Blackwell.

McBride, Ian, 2018 'Protestant Dissenters, *c.* 1690–1800', in James Kelly (ed.), *The Cambridge history of Ireland.* Volume 3: *1730–1880.* Cambridge. Cambridge University Press.

McBride, I.R., 1994 'Presbyterians in the Penal era', *Bullan* 1, 73–86.

McBride, I.R., 1998 *Scriptural politics: Ulster Presbyterians and Irish radicalism in the late eighteenth century.* Oxford. Clarendon Press.

McBride, I.R., 2001 'Ulster Presbyterians and the confessional state, *c.* 1688–1733', in D.G. Boyce, Robert Eccleshall and Vince Geoghegan (eds), *Political discourse in seventeenth- and eighteenth-century Ireland*, 169–92. Houndsmills. Palgrave.

McClive, Cathy, 2015 *Menstruation and procreation in early modern France.* Farnham. Ashgate.

McCormick, Leanne, 2015, '"No sense of wrongdoing": abortion in Belfast, 1917–1967', *Journal of Social History* 49(1), 125–48.

McEwen, Joanne, 2015 '"At my mother's house": community and household spaces in early eighteenth century Scottish infanticide narratives', in Susan Broomhall (ed.), *Spaces for feeling: emotions and sociabilities in Britain, 1650–1850*, 12–24. London. Routledge.

McGowan, Deirdre, 2017 'Class, criminality and marriage breakdown in post-independence Ireland', in Niamh Howlin and Kevin Costello (eds), *Law and the family in Ireland, 1800–1950*, 125–41. London. Palgrave.

McGrath, Charles Ivar, 2021 'The Penal laws: origins, purpose, enforcement and impact', in Kevin Costello and Niamh Howlin (eds), *Law and religion in Ireland, 1700–1970,* 13–48. Cham, Switzerland. Springer.

McNeill, Mary, 1962 *Little Tom Drennan. Portrait of a Georgian childhood.* Dublin. Dolmen Press.

Malcomson, A.P.W., 2006 *The pursuit of the heiress. Aristocratic marriage in Ireland, 1740–1840.* Belfast. Ulster Historical Foundation.

Marshall, Emma, 2025 'Absent parents, sick children, and epistolary relationships in England, *c.* 1640–*c.*1750', *History of the Family* 30(1), 44–71.

Masterson, K.W., 1977 'The law of abortion in England and Northern Ireland', *Police Journal* 50(1), 50–61.

Middleton, Kathleen M., 2010 'Religious revolution and social crisis in southwest Scotland and Ulster, 1687–1714'. Unpublished PhD thesis. Trinity College, Dublin.

Mitchison, Rosalind and Leneman, Leah, 1989 *Sexuality and social control: Scotland, 1660–1780.* Oxford. Basil Blackwell.

Morgan, Valerie, 1974 'Mortality in Magherafelt, County Derry, in the early eighteenth century', *Irish Historical Studies* 19(74), 125–35.

Muir, Angela Joy, 2017 'Courtship, sex and poverty: illegitimacy in eighteenth century Wales', in *Social History* 43(1), 56–80.

Murphy, Eileen M., 2021 '"The child that is born of one's far body": maternal and infant death in medieval Ireland', *Childhood in the Past* 14(1), 13–37.

Murphy-Lawless, Jo, 1991 'Images of "poor" women in the writing of Irish men midwives', in Margaret MacCurtain and Mary O'Dowd (eds), *Women in early modern Ireland,* 291–303. Edinburgh. Edinburgh University Press.

Norman, Frances, 2022 '"She comitted that abominable act of uncleanness": locating female sexual agency in Presbyterian Ireland, *c.* 1690–1750', *Women's History Today* 3(3), 4–11.

Nugent, Janay, 2010 '"None must meddle betueene man and wife": assessing family and fluidity of public and private in early modern Scotland', *Journal of Family History* 35(3), 219–31.

O'Dowd, Mary, 2004 *A history of women in Ireland, 1500–1800.* Oxford. Routledge.

O'Dowd, Mary, 2017 'Marriage breakdown in Ireland, *c.* 1660–1857', in Niamh Howlin and Kevin Costello (eds), *Law and the family in Ireland, 1800–1950,* 7–23. London. Palgrave.

O'Dowd, Mary, 2017 'Men, women, children and the family, 1550–1730', in Jane Ohlmeyer (ed.), *The Cambridge History of Ireland,* volume II: *1550–1730,* 298–320. Cambridge. Cambridge University Press.

O'Hara, Diana, 2000 *Courtship and constraint: rethinking the making of marriage in Tudor England.* Manchester and New York. Manchester University Press.

O'Neill, Kevin, 2011 '"Pale & dejected exhausted by the waste of sorrow": courtship and the expression of emotion, Mary Shackleton, 1783-1791', in Willemijn Ruberg and Kristine Steenbergh (eds), *Sexed sentiments: interdisciplinary perspectives on gender and emotion,* 47–70. Amsterdam and New York. Rodopi.

Paperno, Irina, 2004 'What can be done with diaries', *Russian Review* 63(4), 561–73.

Poppel, Frans von, 1995 'Widows, widowers and remarriage in nineteenth-century Netherlands', *Population Studies* 49(3), 421–41.

Porter, Classon Emmet, 1975 *Congregational memoirs: the old presbyterian congregation of Larne and Kilwaughter.* Larne, County Antrim. Non-Subscribing Presbyterian Church.

Porter, Roy and Hall, Lesley, 1995 *The facts of life. The creation of sexual knowledge in Britain, 1650–1950.* New Haven and London. Yale University Press.

Power, Thomas P., 2010 *Forcibly without her consent. Abductions in Ireland, 1700–1850.* Indiana. iUniverse.

Reid, James Seaton, 1867 *History of the Presbyterian church in Ireland* (3 vols), vol. 3. Belfast. W. Mullan.

Ridner, Judith, 2018 *The Scots Irish of early Pennsylvania*. Philadelphia. Temple University Press.

Robertson, Stephen, 2005 'What's law got to do with it? Legal records and sexual histories', *Journal of the History of Sexuality* 14(1/2), 161–236.

Rushton, Peter, 1991 'The matter in variance: adolescents and domestic conflict in the pre-industrial economy of northeast England, 1600–1800', *Journal of Social History* 25(1), 89–107.

Sauer, R., 1978 'Infanticide and abortion in nineteenth-century Britain', *Population Studies* 32(1), 81–93.

Sharpe, Pamela, 1999 'Survival strategies and stories: poor widows and widowers in early industrial England', in Sandra Cavallo and Lyndan Warner (eds), *Widowhood in medieval and early modern Europe*, 220–39. Harlow. Longman.

Smith, J.E., 1984 'Widowhood and ageing in traditional English society', *Ageing and Society* 4(4), 429–49.

Smith, W.S., 1888 *Historical gleanings in Antrim and neighbourhood*. Belfast. Printed by Alex Mayne & Boyd.

Smout, T.C., 1976 'Aspects of sexual behaviour in nineteenth century Scotland', in A.A. MacLaren (ed.), *Social class in Scotland: past and present*, 55–85. Edinburgh. Donald.

Smout, T.C., Landsman, N.C., and Devine, T.M., 1994 'Scottish emigration in the seventeenth and eighteenth centuries', in Nicholas P. Canny (ed.), *Europeans on the move: studies on European migration, 1500–1800*, 76–112. Oxford. Oxford University Press.

Smyth, Lauren, 2022 'Child welfare and education in the industrialising town', in Olwen Purdue (ed.), *The first great charity of this town. The Belfast Charitable Society and its role in the developing city*, 80–91. Dublin. Irish Academic Press.

Sneddon, Andrew, 2015 *Witchcraft and magic in Ireland*. Basingstoke. Palgrave Macmillan.

Sneddon, Andrew and Fulton, John, 2019 'Witchcraft, the press, and crime in Ireland, 1822–1922', *Historical Journal* 62(3), 741–64.

Snell, K.D.M., 1996 'The apprenticeship system in British history: the fragmentation of a cultural institution', *History of Education* 25(4), 303–22.

Spindler, E.D., 2011 'Youth and old age in late medieval London', *London Journal* 36(1), 1–22.

Steiner-Scott, Elizabeth, 1997 '"To bounce a boot off her now and then…": domestic violence in post-Famine Ireland', in Maryann Gialanella Valiulis and Mary O'Dowd (eds), *Women in Irish history: essays in honour of Margaret MacCurtain*, 125–43. Dublin. Wolfhound Press.

Stewart, David, 1950 *The Seceders in Ireland, with annals of their congregations*. Belfast. Presbyterian Historical Society.

Stolberg, Michael, 2000 'An unmanly vice: self-pollution, anxiety, and the body in the eighteenth century', *Society for the Social History of Medicine* 13(1), 1–21.

Stolberg, Michael, 2000 'Self-pollution, moral reform, and the venereal trade: notes on the sources and historical context of *Onania* (1716)', *Journal of the History of Sexuality* 9, 37–61.

Strain, R.M., 1961 *Belfast and its charitable society: a story of urban social development*. London. Oxford University Press.

Stretton, Tim, 2019 'Women, legal records, and the problem of the lawyer's hand', *Journal of British Studies* 58(4), 684–700.

Tait, Clodagh, 2005 'Spiritual bonds, social bonds: baptism and godparenthood in Ireland, 1530–1690', *Cultural and Social History* 2(3), 301–27.

Tait, Clodagh, 2012 'Some sources for the study of infant and maternal mortality in later seventeenth-century Ireland', in Elaine Farrell (ed.), *'She said she was in the family way': pregnancy and infancy in modern Ireland*, 55–74. London. University of London Press.

Todd, Barbara J., 1985 'The remarrying widow: a stereotype reconsidered', in Mary Prior (ed.), *Women in English society, 1500–1800*, 549–71. London. Metheun.

Todd, Margot, 2002 *The culture of Protestantism in early modern Scotland*. New Haven and London. Yale University Press.

Uqruhart, Diane, 2013 'Irish divorce and domestic violence, 1857–1922', *Women's History Review*, 22(5), 820–37.

Urquhart, Diane, 2017 '"Divorce Irish style": marriage dissolution in Ireland, 1850–1950', in Kevin Costello and Niamh Howlin (eds), *Law and the family in Ireland, 1800–1950*, 107–24. London. Palgrave.

Urquhart, Diane, 2020 *Irish divorce. A history*. Cambridge. Cambridge University Press.

Whan, Robert, 2013 *Presbyterians of Ulster, 1680–1730*. Woodbridge. Boydell and Brewer.

Whan, Robert, 2021 'Irish Presbyterians and the quest for toleration, *c.* 1692–1733', in Kevin Costello and Niamh Howling (eds), *Law and religion in Ireland, 1700–1970*, 157–84. Cham, Switzerland. Springer.

Wiesner, M.E., 1993 *Women and gender in early modern Europe*. Cambridge. Cambridge University Press.

Wilson, Lisa, 1992 *Life after death: widows in Pennsylvania, 1750–1850*. Philadelphia. Temple University Press.

Wright, J.J., 2012 *The 'natural leaders' and their world: politics, culture and society in Belfast, c. 1801–1832.* Liverpool. Liverpool University Press.

Wright, J.J., 2015 'Robert Hyndman's toe: romanticism, schoolboy politics and the affective revolution in late Georgian Belfast', in Catherine Cox and Susannah Riordan (eds), *Adolescence in modern Irish history: innocence and experience,* 15–41. Basingstoke, Hampshire. Palgrave Macmillan.

Wright, J.J., 2016 'Love, loss and learning in late Georgian Belfast: the case of Eliza McCracken', in David Hayton and Andrew R. Holmes (eds), *Ourselves alone? Religion, society and politics in eighteenth- and nineteenth-century Ireland,* 169–91. Dublin. Four Courts.

Wright, J.J., 2023 'Frustrated ambition in the eighteenth-century Atlantic: Robert Tennent in Jamaica, *c.* 1784–95', in Toby Barnard and Alison Fitzgerald (eds), *Speculative minds in Georgian Ireland: novelty, experiment and widening horizons,* 229–55. Dublin. Four Courts Press.

Wright, S.J., 1991 'The elderly and the bereaved in eighteenth-century Ludlow', in Margaret Pelling and Richard M. Smith (eds), *Life, death and the elderly: historical perspectives,* 102–33. London. Routledge.

Yarbrough, Anne, 1979 'Apprentices as adolescents in sixteenth-century Bristol', *Journal of Social History* 13(1), 67–81.

Websites

Christine Ryan, 'Breaking, scutching and hackling', https://christineryan.co.uk/2020/06/06/breaking-scutching-and-hackling/ (accessed 30 May 2025).

'Department of Health. Life expectancy in Northern Ireland 2020–22', https://www.health-ni.gov.uk/news/life-expectancy-northern-ireland-2020-22 (accessed 15 July 2025).

'Dictionary of Irish Biography', www.dib.ie/ (accessed 15 July 2025).

'Dictionaries of the Scots Language', https://dsl.ac.uk/ (accessed 15 July 2025).

'National Folklore Collection', https://www.duchas.ie/en (accessed 15 July 2025).

ACKNOWLEDGEMENTS

This book would not have been possible without the support of numerous organisations and individuals. The research in this book finds its roots in my PhD project, which was generously funded by the Arts and Humanities Research Council UK. Its subsequent development into a manuscript owes much to financial support from the R.J. Hunter Bursary. Over the years, further funding has supported its completion. I am very grateful to the Royal Irish Academy (R.J. Hunter Research Bursary Scheme), Women's History Association of Ireland (Anna Parnell Travel Grant), and internal funding from the University of Hertfordshire. The RIA team are superstars. Thank you to Aifric Downey, Fiona Dunne, Gill Fitzgerald Kelly, Ruth Hegarty, Helena King, Trevor Mullins, Eileen O'Neill and Fidelma Slattery for believing in my book. I am also grateful to the two anonymous reviewers, whose detailed feedback helped to better shape not just this manuscript, but my next book too.

The research for this book was kindly assisted by staff at various archives and libraries across Ireland, including the Presbyterian Historical Society of Ireland, Belfast (thank you especially to Valerie Adams); the Public Record Office of Northern Ireland; the Special Collections Library at Queen's University, Belfast; Belfast Charitable Society archives; Clontarf and Scots Presbyterian Church, Dublin (thank you to Hilary Fairman); Union Theological College (thank you to Joy Conkey); and library staff at the University of

Hertfordshire and the University of Limerick. When I was unable to visit archives myself, I was able to avail of the skills of some brilliant researchers; thank you to Eliza McKee, Shannon Devlin and Sorcha Clarke for their assistance in tracking down documents.

I owe this book and my research career to Professor Mary O'Dowd, who has been an unwavering source of support since my days as an undergraduate student at Queen's University, Belfast. It was Mary who first introduced me to women's history, and it was she who first suggested that I look at Presbyterian records. Words really cannot express how grateful I am to Mary for her critical eye, her willingness to read drafts of my work, and her encouragement when I felt things were not working. But most of all, I am grateful for her mentorship. I aspire to do the same for my students and pay her kindness forward.

I want to pay special thanks to Elaine Farrell, who kindly read drafts of chapters and offered much-needed advice on things to leave on the cutting-room floor. I want also to thank Maria Luddy for responding to my lengthy queries about paternity suits and for sharing examples from her own unpublished research.

The research and writing of this book have been enriched by the friendships, collegiate relationships and online interactions that I have developed over the years. Thank you to everyone who showed an interest in my work, including Andrew Sneddon, Aoife Bhreatnach, Clodagh Tait, Coleman Dennehy, Ian Walsh, Jim O'Neill, John Privilege, Katie Barclay, Leanne McCormick, Lindsey Earner-Byrne, Ned (Nerys) Young, Nigel Farrell, Robyn Atcheson, Tara McConnell and Tim Watt. Maeve O'Riordan, my RIFNET research partner, continues to be a source of inspiration, navigating as she does the worlds of academia and mamahood like a pro. Former colleagues at the University of Hertfordshire have lent their advice and support in many ways too. Thank you to Ceri Houlbrook, Daniel Grey, Eureka Henrich, Grace Lees-Maffei, Katrina Navickas, Owen Davies, Rowland Hughes, Serena Dyer, Tony Shaw, William Bainbridge and, especially, Jennifer Evans – who else would hop on Teams at 8.30a.m. to chat with me about eighteenth-century masturbation?! I want to thank my new colleagues in the School of History and Geography at the University of Limerick, who have welcomed me into the department and supported me as I finished this book while navigating a new place and a new job. I also extend my gratitude to every student who enrolled on my research-led modules and who were the first audience of the material in this book. I hope they love Presbyterians by now.

This is a book about family life. The families we belong to and the families we make for ourselves. I want to thank my parents, Debbie and Mark, for encouraging me to do my best and, importantly, for reminding me that my best is good enough. My elder sister, Michelle, for being at the end of the phone and, perhaps most joyfully, for making me an auntie to Zoey and Ethan. My younger sister, Sammi, who despite being on the other side of the world and in a different time zone, has listened to me fret about this book and not complained about the often podcast-worthy length of my voice-notes. To my brother Glenn (otherwise known as number two), with whom I enjoy friendly sibling rivalry, I say: I wrote a book first. Last in my human list of thanks is Patrick O'Brien, also known affectionately as 'Pedantic Pat', who not only read drafts of my work, but has been an important source of emotional support as I spent long days (and nights) cooped up in my office finishing this book.

And finally, special thanks are owed to Frank, my constant companion for over eleven years and without whom this book would never have been finished. I thank him for reminding me to leave my desk, for all the walks we took together while I finished the manuscript, and for making sure I kept putting one foot in front of the other. Love you, son.

INDEX

A

abductions 110–13
abortifacients 2, 9–10, 11, 26
abortion 8–9
Act for the More Effectual Preventing the Taking Away and Marrying Children against the Wills of Their Parents or Guardians (1707) 111
Act to prevent the destroying and murdering of bastard children (1707) 12, 13, 14
Adam, William 134
Adams, J.R.R. 3, 42
Ading, James xxi
adultery xxi, 14, 116, 118, 119, 125–30
Affleck, John 20
Aghadowey Kirk Session, County Londonderry 109
Agnew, Jean 164
agricultural labourers xvii, 59, 159
Allister, Robert 123–4
Amicable Assurance Society 143
Anderson, Doctor 94
Anderson, Robert 100
Anderson, Samuel 100
Anglicans xii, xiii, 97, 101, 104, 107, 158
Anti-Burgher Seceders xiii
Antrim, Presbytery of xiii, 145
apprenticeships 49, 50, 59–69

B

Bailey, Joanne 132
Bailie, Martha (*later* Kennedy) 150, 151
Ballybay, County Monaghan 46, 147
Ballybay Kirk Session, County Monaghan 22
Ballyblack Kirk Session, County Down 124
Ballycarry Kirk Session, County Antrim xx, 1, 14, 15–16, 18, 76, 109, 128
Ballycor, County Antrim 33, 75
Ballykelly, County Londonderry 31
Ballymoney, County Antrim 75
Ballymoney Kirk Session, County Antrim 34
Ballynahinch Kirk Session, County Down 102
Ballynure, County Antrim 68
Ballyrobin, County Antrim 42
Ballyroney, County Down 102
Bangor, Presbytery of xxi–xxii
baptism xiv, xx, xxii, 6, 15, 29–34, 77, 95, 135, 163
Baptists xii
Barbauld, Mrs 42
Barber, Francis 32
Barclay, Katie xxvii
Barker, Hannah xxviii
Barkley, J.M. xvi, 163
Barnard, Toby 44
Barnes, John 112–13
Barnes, Joseph 112–13
Barr, Revd Isaac and Mrs 146
Barry, Paul 55
Bartley, Mrs 66
Baxter, Thomas 54
Bayly, Margaret (*later* Stephenson) 106
Beaty, William 112, 113

Beck, Elinor 103
beds/bedsharing 52–3, 74
Belfast Charitable Society 61–2, 63–4, 67, 68
Belfast Newsletter 61–2, 68, 121, 122
Belfast xvi, xix, 61
Bell, Elizabeth 99
Bell, Walter 133
Benstead, Susan 64
Berry, Hugh 58
Berry, Richard 57–9
bigamy xxi, 117, 120, 123, 155, 160
Billy, County Antrim 42
Black, Thomas 52
Bogs, Andrew xxiii
Bonhote, Elizabeth 51
Botanalogia Universalis Hibernica, The 9–10
Boyd, James 130–1
Boyd, Margaret (*née* Kerr) 130
Branagan, James 67
breastfeeding 35
Broughshane, County Antrim 79
Browne, Roisin 164
Brozyna, Andrea Ebel 164
Bruce, William 143, 144
Bryson, Robert 20
Buchan, William 35
bundling 53–4
Burgher Seceders xiii
Burnett, Anne 64
Burns, John 54
Burt Kirk Session, County Donegal xiv–xv, 4, 55, 98
    abductions 111–13
    breach of promise 101–2
    sexual misbehaviour xxi, xxiii, 12, 57–9
Byers, Archibald 5

C

Cahans Kirk Session, County Monaghan 16, 17, 52, 76
    adultery 126–8, 129–30
    marriages 98, 99, 103, 104, 108
    sexual misbehaviour 54, 74, 79, 105
Cahoon, James 62
Caldwell, Revd James and Mrs 147
Caldwell, John 36, 61, 74–5
Campbel, Isabel 4

Campbell, Agnes 5–6
Campbell, Sarah ix–x, xi
Carland, County Tyrone 44, 150
Carland Kirk Session, County Tyrone 109
Carnmoney Kirk Session, County Antrim x, xv, xvii, 10–11, 36, 97, 108, 135
    bedsharing 7, 53–5
    child maintenance 25–6
    desertion/marital breakdown 115–16
    disorderly marriage 104, 106
    illegitimate children ix, 20, 21
Carrick-on-Suir, County Tipperary 137, 138, 141
Carson, Katherine 18
catechisms 43, 44, 80
Census (1841) 137
certificates (testimonials) 5–6, 31, 131, 141, 145
charity schools 61, 62–4
child maintenance 15, 25–6, 135
childcare
    and widowers 139, 141, 148–9, 151
    see also nursemaids
children 27–8, 38–9
    deaths 45, 46–7
cholera epidemic 45, 136–7
Church of England 39, 107–8
Church of Ireland xii, 97, 98, 101, 107, 158, 159
Church of Scotland xxii, 15, 29, 94–5
Clarkson, Leslie 137, 138, 141
Cloghog, County Antrim 42
Clontibret Kirk Session, County Monaghan 123
Cochran, Mrs 147
Code xxii, xxiii, 15, 95, 97
Colvill, Agnes 1
Colvill, Jane 1, 2, 26
communion xiv, xxii, 15, 77, 163
Connell, K.H. 9
Cooke, Revd Henry 154
Cookstown, County Tyrone 42, 43
Cord, Agnes 121
Cord, Samuel 121
Coronary, County Cavan 155
Coronary Kirk Session, County Cavan 100–1, 105, 155–6
cotton industry xviii, xix
courtship 53–4, 71–3, 74

232

gifts 73, 77, 78–9, 80, 81, 82–4, 154
letters 71–2, 73, 84–7, 89–90
Covenanters xiii, xx
Cowan, Martha 23
Cowper, William 41
Craford, Agnes x, 21–2
Craford, James 105
Craford, Malcome 5
Craig, John 13, 14
Craswell, Elinar xxi
Crawford, Revd Alexander xxvii, 3, 34, 35, 41, 45
Crawford, Anna (*née* Gardner) xxvii, 3–4, 35, 41, 45–6
Crawford, Christina 41
Crawford family xxvi, xxvii, 3
Crawford, M.E. 141
Crawford, Olivia 35
Crawford, W.H. xvi
Crossin, Michael 65
Crosskennan, County Antrim 32
Cry, Widow 139–40
Cudbert, Gavine 5, 6
Cudbert, Jean 13, 14
Cudbert, Margaret 53–4
Cudbert, Widow 54
Cuddy, David 121–2
Cuddy, Jane (*née* Kirk) 121–2
Culpeper, Nicholas 3
Cunningham, Margaret 99
Cunningham, Mary (*later* Hamilton) 115–16, 135
Curran, Cynthia 142
Currie, Matthew 69
Currie, Robert 53
Curry, Frederick 30–1

D

dances xx, 72, 76
Darragh, Anne (*née* Fixter) 132, 133–4
Darragh, Revd Robert 131–2, 133–4
Davis, Revd Jacob and Mrs 147
Davison, Jane 25
Deal, Mary 52
death penalty 9, 111, 123
Defoe, Daniel 39–40
Delay, Cara 9
Derriaghy, County Antrim 62
Dervock, County Antrim 77
Desart, John xxi

desertion 115–16, 119, 120–1, 122–4, 155, 160
Devlin, Arthur 42
Devlin, Shannon xxvii, 164
Directory for the Public Worship of God 29, 94–5
discrimination xii, 97
Dissenters xii, 39
divorce 116–20, 130
 a mensa et thoro 117, 118
 a vinculo matrimonii 117, 118
 court-based system 119
 'crim con' suits 118, 125
 ecclesiastical courts 117, 118, 119
 parliamentary 117–19
 Presbyterian options 119, 155, 156
 social stigma of 119–20
Divorce and Matrimonial Causes Act (1857) 118–19
Doak, Alexander 67
domestic servants xvii–xviii, 7, 12, 17, 23, 54–5, 59, 64, 74, 150
Donegore, County Antrim 32, 33, 104
Douglas (apprentice) 67
Down, Presbytery of 102, 107, 124
Drennan, Ann (*née* Lennox) 28
Drennan family xxvi, 47–8
Drennan, John 47
Drennan, Martha *see* McTier, Martha (*née* Drennan)
Drennan, Mary Anne 47
Drennan, Sarah (*née* Swanwick) 27, 28, 35, 36–7, 39, 41, 85–7
Drennan, Thomas Hamilton (Tom) 28, 39, 41, 47–8
Drennan, William 27–8, 36–7, 38, 41, 42, 71–2, 73, 83–4, 85–7, 89–92
Drumachose, County Londonderry 147
Drumlough, County Down 31
Drummond, Henry 68
drunkenness xiv–xv, xx, xxi, xxii
Dublin, Presbytery of 147
Dublin xi–xii, 32, 37, 66, 71, 85, 86, 89, 114, 143
Dumphy, Widow 141
Dunboe, County Londonderry 97
Dunlap, Janet 112
Dunlap, Widow 112
Dunn, John 127
Dutton, Matthew 64

233

E

Easter 50, 75
ecclesiastical courts 117, 118, 119, 125, 158, 159
education xii, 39–44, 61, 62–3
Elder, John 113
Elder, Margaret 113
Elder, Revd Matthew 77
elders xiv–xv, 5, 106, 126, 127–8, 143
Eliot, Hannah 103
Elliott, Marianne 109
Elliott, William 67
elopement 104, 105–6, 120–3, 155
emigration xviii, xix, 36, 110, 123–4, 147
Erwin, Robert and Margaret 31
Erwin, William 76
Established Church *see* Church of Ireland
Eustace, Nicole 85, 88–9
Ewings, Mary xxiii

F

fair days and festivals 12, 19, 73, 74–6, 77, 101
fama clamosa xxi
farmers/farmer-weavers xvi, xvii, xix, 76, 110–11
Farrell, Elaine 11, 13
Faulkner, John 67
Ferguson, Anne 14
Ferguson, Revd xxi
Fintona, County Tyrone 146
Finvoy Kirk Session, County Antrim 120
First Antrim (Millrow) congregation 32, 79, 139, 154
First Donagheady congregation, County Tyrone 147
First Dromara Kirk Session, County Down 98, 140
First Dromara Presbyterian Church, County Down xxx, 139
First Kilraughts congregation, County Antrim 77
First Monaghan congregation 131
First Randalstown Presbyterian Church, County Antrim 3, 34, 45
Fixter, Anne (*later* Darragh) 132, 133–4
Flood, Patrick 19
Ford, Mr 44
Form of Process xxii, 15

fornication xxi, xxiii, xxx, 6, 16, 31, 99, 103, 104, 125
Fox, John 32

G

Gardner, Anna (*later* Crawford) xxvii, 3–4, 35, 41, 45–6
Gardner family xxvii
Gardner, Helen 35, 41
Gebby, Hugh 124
General Synod of Ulster xiii, xx, 30, 134, 142, 143, 144–7
Gilbreath, John 100, 101
Gilleard, Chris 137
Girvan, Margaret 20
Givin, Samuel xxviii, 49, 61
Glascar Kirk Session, County Down 107
Glencooss, Widow 141
Glendinning, Jean xxiii–xxiv
Gordon, Mrs David 38
Gordon, Henry 45
Gortnaglush, County Tyrone 151
Graham, Elicia 64
Granger, Mary 113
Gray, Elizabeth 129
Gray, Margaret 103
Gray, Paul xxx
Green, Benjamin 99
Grels, Thomas 128
Greyabbey, County Down 74
Gribben, John 68
Gultry, Mary (*later* Wilson) ix, x

H

hair, locks of 77, 81–2, 83
Hamel, John 108
Hamilton, Agnes 115–16, 135
Hamilton (apprentice) 61
Hamilton, Mary (*née* Cunningham) 115–16, 135
Hamilton, Thomas 115–16, 135
'handywomen' 22
Hardwick, Julie xxvi
Hardy, Robert 68
Harper, Mr 94
hedge schools 42
Henderson, John 7
Henderson, William 52
Henry, Anne 114

Henry, Jean 20, 21
Henry, John 54
herbs/plants 9–10, 11
Heron, Jane 53
Hill, Myrtle xxxi, 164
Hincks, William xvii, 59–60, 85
hiring fairs xvii
Hoey, Fanny (*née* Sharp) 155–6
Hoey, James 155–7, 160
Holloway, Sally 78
Holmes, Andrew xiii, xix, xx, xxiv, 29, 32, 110, 157–8, 163, 164
Holmes, Janice 164
Holy Communion xii
Howlin, Niamh 125
Huggins, Aunt 151
Huggins, Nancy (Ann) 151
Hutchenson, Robert 76

I

illegitimacy ix–x, xxix, 12–13, 14, 18, 20, 22, 23, 114
infanticide xxxi, 11, 12–13
Irish parliament 12, 107, 111, 117–18
Irwin, David 100
Irwin, Jean 100
Irwin, Mary 100–1
Islandmagee, County Antrim xxix, 76

J

Jackson, Eleanor (*later* Tennent) 114
Jackson, Revd James and Mrs 147
Jackson, Letitia 148–9
Jackson, Ma 149
Jackson, Robert 99
Jamison, Jean 104
Jeffries, William 100–1
Johnson, Alice xix, 164
Johnson, Sidney 64
Johnston, James 23–4
Johnston, Janet 23
Johnston, Mrs 38
Johnston, William 10–11
Jordan, James 68

K

Kane, Catharine 62
Keefe, George 130
Kelly, James 110, 111
Kennedy, Elizabeth 150, 151
Kennedy family xxvi, 150–1
Kennedy, Jane 44, 150, 151
Kennedy, Martha (*née* Bailie) 150, 151
Kennedy, Robert 44, 151
Kennedy, Revd William 44, 150–1
Kernaghan, John 100
Kerr, Elizabeth 67
Kerr, Margaret 130–1
Kerr, Revd and Mrs 146
Kerr, Thomas 98
Killaloe, County Clare 125
Killead, County Antrim 33
Killfillan, Robert 101–2
Killinchy, County Down 140, 141
Kilmore, County Down 42–3
Kilwaughter, County Antrim 33, 74
Kinmonth, Claudia 39
Kirk, Agnes 74
Kirk, Jane (*later* Cuddy) 121–2
Kirk Sessions xiii–xiv, xviii, xx–xxi
    minute books xx, xxiv–xxvi, 125–6, 159
    poor-money funds 139–40
    punishment, method of xxiii
Kirkdonald (Dundonald), County Down 7
Kirkpatrick, Revd James 25
Kirkwood, James 120
Knox, Martha 76

L

Lacey, William 68–9
Landon, Letitia Elizabeth 88
Larne, County Antrim 33, 74
Latimer, Mary 101–2
Lauchlin, Thomas 78–9
Legion of Honour 70
Leneman, Leah 16, 165
Lenighan, Widow 141
Lennox, Ann 28
Letterkenny, Presbytery of 147
letters xxvii–xviii 71–2, 73, 84–7, 89–90
libel cases 132
life expectancy 137, 138
life insurance 142–7
Liggat, Abraham 154
Liggat, Ellen (*later* Magill) 154
linen industry xvi–xvii, xviii, xix

Lisburn, County Antrim 5, 6, 122
Lister, John 74, 126
literacy 3, 40, 72, 84
Little, Mrs C. 66
Little, Jean 5, 6
Little, John 68
Lock, Jean 18
Lockart, Moses 98
Londonderry congregation 65
Londonderry, Presbytery of xxiii
Long, William 112, 113
Lord Ellenborough's Act (1803) 8–9
Loughaghery, County Down 74, 96
Loughaghery Kirk Session xv, 31, 33, 34, 76
Loughbrickland, County Down 33, 43, 103, 146
Luddy, Maria 73, 110, 119–20, 121, 131, 158, 164
Lurgan, County Antrim 121
Lurganearly, County Monaghan 78
Lyk, Margaret 130

M

McAdam, Doctor 22
Macafee, William 45
McAlexander, Jannet 25–6
McAnnally, Peter 68
McAuley, William 34
McBride, Revd John 125
McByrd, James 20
McCabe, James 129–30
McCabe, Mary 129
McCanles, Ann 53
McCanles, Mary 6
McCarter, Thomas 112
McClaine, Mary 19
McClintock, Samuel 20
McComb, Thomas 23
McConnal, James 55–6
McConnel, Catharin 20
McConnell, Thomas 20
McCormick, Leanne 9
McCracken, Eliza 85
McCracken, Joseph 104
McCraken, William 36, 54–5
McCrakin, William 103
McCreagh, Adam 21, 22, 23–4
McCrim, James 111–12
McCrory, Ann Eliza 33

McCullan, Jean 18–19
McDowell, John 113
McFarland, Patrick 109
McGage, Alexander xvii
McGallard, Kathrine 109
McGaw, Elizabeth xxi–xxii
McGee, Hannah 81–3
McGladrye, Henry 121
McGladrye, Martha 121
McGregor, Martha 17
McIlroy, James 20, 21
McKee, Samuel 11
McKeifer, Jane 123
McKeifer, Margaret 123–4
McKenna, Mary 105
McKeown, Andrew 18–19
McKewn, Mr 42
McKide, Elizabeth 104
McKiernan, Edmund 111
McKimm, Agnes 11
McKinstrey, Margaret 23
Macky, Florence 12
Macky, James 12
McLaughlin, Andrew 65
McLaw, Elizabeth 109
McLery, Robert 1, 26
McMechan, John 14
McMullan, Mr 44
McMurthrie, Mary 23
McPhillipps, Hugh 100–1
Macrea, Margaret (*later* Scot) 126–8
Macrone, Eliza (*later* Tennent) 36, 87–8, 149
McTier, Martha (*née* Drennan) 28, 35, 37–8, 39, 41–2, 83–4, 90, 91–2
McTire, John 18
Magill, Ann Jane (*née* Skelton) 79–81, 88, 96, 136–7, 148, 149–50, 154
Magill, Ellen (*née* Liggat) 154
Magill, James 129
Magill, Jane 129–30
Magill, Revd Robert 136–7, 139, 148–50, 154
  courtship and marriage 79–81, 88, 96
  diary xxvi, 32, 33, 43–4, 45
  poems written by 40–1
Magill, Samuel 54
Magill, Sarah 40–1, 148, 154
Maginnis, Mr 108
Magouran, Mr 42
Maguire, Alice 79

Maguire (apprentice) 67
Main, Mary 16, 24, 25
Makee, John 79
Malcomson, Andrew 19
Malcomson, Margaret 19
Malhallon, Catharine 21
manslaughter cases 131
Manson, David 43
Margress, Margaret 20
marital violence 130–4
marriage xx–xxi, 73–7
   abductions 110–13
   banns 95, 96–7, 100
   breach of promise 99–102
   disorderly 104, 107–8
   economic and social implications of 89–91
   irregular 98, 104, 106, 109, 120
   mixed marriages 107–10, 159
   parental consent 95, 98, 103–6
   power to dissolve 117–20
   Presbyterian guidelines 94–8
   private ceremonies 96
   private promises of 99–103
   remarriage 116, 117, 118, 120, 123–4
   runaway matches 104–5
   verba de futuro 99
   see also bigamy; courtship; desertion; divorce
Marriages (Ireland) Act (1844) 97
Marshal, Jane 122–3
Marshal, John 122–3
Marshal, Widow 141
Martin, Elizabeth 33
Mason, James 112–13
masturbation 56–9
maternal medicine 22
   see also midwives
Mathison, Grizell 20, 78–9
Maxwell, James 132, 134
medical pamphlets 2–3, 9–10
Methodists xii
midwives 3, 7, 17, 20–2, 28, 29–30, 37, 89
migration xi, 147
   see also emigration
Millar, Revd Thomas 42
Millar, William 69
Miller, Helen 54
Minning, John 104

Minterburn, County Tyrone 146
Miscambell, Elizabeth (Betty) 37–8, 39
Mitchison, Rosalind 16, 165
Moany, Edward 62
Monaghan, Presbytery of 123–4, 131–2, 133–4, 155–6, 160
Moor, John 16
Moore, Mr 93–4
Moorhead, Revd 146
moral pamphlets 56–7, 58, 125
Moravian preacher xxii
Morell, Revd James xxvi, 46, 142
Morell, Letitia 47
Morgan, Revd James xxvi, 42, 142–3
Morgan, Manns 100
Morgan, Valerie 45
Morton, Elizabeth 10–11
Morton, Isobel 128
Morton, Robert 23
Moywater (Killala), County Mayo 146
Mulholland, John 69
Mullaghmossagh, County Tyrone 122
murder cases 131
Murray, Jane 7
Murryfield (apprentice) 67

N

Napoleonic wars xviii, xix
National Schools System (1831) 42
Neil, James 7
Neilson, Elizabeth 128
Nesbit, Elizabeth 22
Nesbitt, Robert 17
Netherlands 138
Neuse, Walter 103
'New Light' Presbyterians xiii
New Sugar House, Belfast 70
Nisbet, Revd Hugh and Mrs 144–5
Nivan, Samuel 11
Nugent, Janay 132–3
nursemaids ix, 34–9

O

Oath of Purgation 24, 25, 127
O'Dowd, Mary xviii, 73, 119–20, 121, 131, 158, 164
Offences Against the Person Act (1861) 9
Offences Against the Person (Ireland) Act (1829) 9

'Old Light' Presbyterians xiii
Onania, or the Heinous Sin of Self-Pollution 56, 57, 58
O'Neill, Kevin 85
O'Quigg, Donald 109
ordinations 76–7
Ordnance Survey Memoirs xxix, xxx, 33, 75, 76
O'Riordan, Maeve 159–60
Orr, Ann 36
Orr, Patrick 4
Osburn, Mary 4
Ossory, diocese of 73
Owens, William 105

P

parlour games 77–8
paternity disputes xviii, 2, 15–26
    maintenance payments 25–6
Patton, Ann (*later* Tennent) 60, 94, 105–6, 114, 152
Paul, Michael 13, 14, 16, 24–5
Pearley, William 121
Pollock, John 76
Pollock, Sarah 76
Pomfret, Samuel 51
poor relief xiii, xx, 15, 139–41
Popery Act (1704) xii
Porter, Adam 57–8
Power, Thomas 110
pregnancy 2–7
    bridal xxix, xxx
    extra-marital ix–xi, 2
    miscarriage 8–9, 14
    unmarried women and 4–5, 10, 12, 15
    see also abortifacients; abortion; paternity disputes
Presbyterian archive xix–xxviii, 119, 157, 158–61
    diaries xxviii, 32, 33, 44, 45, 46–7, 49–50
    family records/personal papers xx, xxvi–xxviii
    minute books xv, xx, xxiv–xxv
Presbyterian Church
    discipline xiii–xvi
    General Synod (or Assembly) xiii, 110
    non-established status in Ireland xv–xvi

quarters (geographical districts) xiv
sacramental expressions xiv
Presbyterian ministers 98, 107, 142–3
    orphaned children of 143, 144, 147
    regium donum 143, 144
    widows of 142–8
Presbyterian Missionary Society 80
'Presbyterian paradox' xxx
Presbyterian Widows' Fund 144–7
Presbyterians 157–8
    origins in Ireland xi–xiii
    perception of xxix, 157, 158
    population (1835) xi
    role of the laity xiii
    Sacramental Test xii
    social status xiii, xxvi
    theological belief xiii
Presbytery xiii, xx, xxiii, 119
profane swearing xx, xxii
Protestants xii, 107, 109–10
Public Record Office, Dublin 158
punishments xxiii–xxiv, 14, 15, 19
Purdie, Jean 15–16

Q

Quakers xii, 85

R

Rademon, County Down 33
Rainey, Mr and Mrs 38
Randell, John 134
rape 12, 16–17, 111
Rashee, County Antrim xxx
Rathfriland, County Down 67, 97
Rea, Daniel 25–6
Rebellion (1798) 36
Reed, Janet 108
regium donum 143, 144
Reid, James Seaton 144
Remonstrants xiii
reputations, discrediting 22–4, 127
Richard, Mr 42
Riddel, Jean 16
Ring, John 150
Robison, Agnes 5, 6
Robison, John 53
Roman Catholics xi, xii, xiii, 30, 42, 109–10, 158

mixed marriages 107, 108, 109
   priests 97, 98, 104, 107, 159
Roseyards, County Antrim 44, 93, 149
Route, Presbytery of 120, 130–1
Rowan, Cornelius 134
Rowland, William 129
Royal Exchange Office 142
Russell, Agnas (*later* Johnston) 11
Russell, George 36, 54–5

S

Sabbath
   breaches of xx, xxi, xxii, 31, 52, 76
   role in social life 77
Sacramental Test xii
St Catherine's Parish, Dublin 32
'scandalous carriage' xxi
Scarva Kirk Session, County Down 103
Scathern, Bernard 67
Scot, Margaret (*née* Macrea) 126–8
Scot, William 126
Scotland xi, xxv, 16, 132–3
Scott, Sally 83
Seaton, Thomas 25
Seceders xiii, xx
Seceding Kirk Sessions xx
sectarian tensions 109–10
sexual misbehaviour xv, xxi, xxx, 6, 7,
      13, 15, 105, 109, 127
   pre-marital sex xxi, xxx, xxxi
   see also adultery; fornication; rape
Shackleton, Mary 85
Sharp, Fanny (*later* Hoey) 155
Shaw, John 105
Simrall, Joseph 76
Skelton, Ann Jane (*later* Magill) 79–80,
      81, 88, 96
Skelton, Eliza 81, 150
Skelton, Ellen 81, 96
Skelton, John 96
Skelton, Mrs 81
Skelton, Samuel 79, 80, 81, 137
Skelton, William 79, 137
slander xxi, xxiii, 31
Sloan, Thomas 103
Smith, John 134
Smith, William 12
Smyth, Revd Hugh xxi, xxii
Smyth, Revd John 146

Smyth, Lauren 63
Smythson, Hugh 35
social life xiv, 32, 33, 75–7
social status xiii, 44, 110, 132–3
Southwell Charity School, County Down
      63, 64
Sproat, Eliza 31
Steel, Widow 19
Steenson, Thomas 104
Stephenson, James 106
Stephenson, Margaret (*née* Bayly) 106
Sterrat, Rebekah (*later* Lockart) 98
Stewart, Alexander 67
Stewart, Samuel 69
Story, Doctor 67
Strabane, County Tyrone 147
Strabridge, James 55
Strabridge, Janet 55–6
Stuart, Ann Jane 66
Stuart, George 68
Stuart, Jean 102
Stuart, John 66, 105, 152–3
Stuart, Margaret (*née* Tennent) 42, 44,
      60–1, 105–6, 152–3
Stuart, Margaretta 66
Sunday Schools xx, 42–3, 79–80
Swanwick, John 91
Swanwick, Sarah (*later* Drennan) 36,
      71–2, 83, 85–7, 88, 89–92
Sweetman, Michael 128
Synod of Ulster *see* General Synod of
      Ulster

T

Tait, Clodagh 32
Taylor, George 22
Templepatrick, County Antrim 154
Templepatrick Kirk Session 4–7, 16, 104
   paternity cases 18–21, 25–6
   sexual misbehaviour xxx, 13–14,
      53, 78
Templeton, Katherine 82
Tennent, Ann (*née* Patton) 60, 94,
      105–6, 114, 152
Tennent, Eleanor (*née* Jackson) 114,
      148–9, 152
Tennent, Eliza (*née* Macrone) 36, 87–8,
      149
Tennent family xxvi

Tennent, Isabella (*later* Shaw) 105
Tennent, John xxviii, 42, 44, 49–50, 61, 69–70, 75, 77
Tennent, Revd John 60, 61, 93–4, 105, 114, 149, 152–4
Tennent, Letitia 148–9
Tennent, Margaret (Peggy) (*later* Stuart) 42, 44, 60–1, 105–6, 152–3
Tennent, Nancy 61
Tennent, Robert 44, 60, 87–8, 105–6, 149, 151, 153
Tennent, Robert James 36, 81–3, 85, 149
Tennent, Samuel 61
Tennent, William 61, 66, 70, 81, 93–4, 114, 148–9, 151–2, 153
Third Cookstown Sunday School 43
Thoburn, Samuel 11
Thompson, Eupham 35–6, 54
Thomson, Esther 62
Thomson, Martha 53
Three Mile House, County Monaghan 108
Tissot, Samuel Auguste 56
Todd, Margo xxv
Townsley, John 31
Tubman, Jane 111
Turbitt, Revd James and Mrs 147
Tyrone, Presbytery of 146

U

United Irishmen 70, 89, 114
unmarried mothers ix, xxx, 12–13, 15
Urquhart, Diane 117–18, 125
Usher's Quay, Dublin xii, 147

V

Vaughan Charity School, County Fermanagh 62–3, 64, 67

W

Wales, John 126–7
Walker, Thomas xxiii–xxiv
Wallace, Margaret 112
Wallace, Robert 55
Wallace, Thomas 112, 113
Wark, William 68
Wat, Mary 129
weavers xiii, xvi, xvii, xviii, xix, 61, 159
Weir, David 128
Weir, Margaret 7
Westminster Confession of Faith 29, 94, 108, 119
Whitecastle, County Donegal 78
widowhood 28, 137–54
　gendered conception of 138–9
　widowers 148–54
　widows of ministers 142–8
Willison, John 43, 51–2
Wilson, John ix–x
Wilson, Mary 21–2, 23
Wilson, Mary (*née* Gultry) ix, x
Wolveridge, James 2–3, 4, 8
Wood Street congregation, Dublin 143
Work, Henry xxi
Work, Samuel 55
Wray, Revd William 96
Wright, Jonathan Jeffrey 60, 85, 164

Y

Young, Revd David 65
Young family xxvi
Young, Hugh 23
Young, James 130
Young, Jane 23
youth, perception of 50–2, 65